ALEXANDER
THEROUX

ALEXANDER THEROUX

A Fan's Notes

Steven Moore

ZEROGRAM
PRESS

Los Angeles, 2021

ZEROGRAM PRESS
1147 El Medio Ave.
Pacific Palisades, CA 90272
EMAIL: info@zerogrampress.com
WEBSITE: www.zerogrampress.com

Distributed by Small Press United / Independent Publishers Group
(800) 888-4741 / www.ipgbook.com

Second Edition 2021

Book design: Pablo Capra
Cover image: Robert Fields

LIBRARY OF CONGRESS CATALOGING-IN-PUBLICATION DATA

Names: Moore, Steven, 1951- author.
Title: Alexander Theroux : a fan's notes / Steven Moore.
Description: First edition. | Los Angeles : Zerogram Press, 2020.
    | Includes bibliographical references and index.
Identifiers: LCCN 2019046709 | ISBN 9781953409058 (paperback)
Subjects: LCSH: Theroux, Alexander--Criticism and interpretation.
Classification: LCC PS3570.H38 Z76 2020 | DDC 813/.54--dc23
LC record available at https://lccn.loc.gov/2019046709

Printed in the United States of America on acid-free paper.

Contents

Preface 7
Chronology 11
1. Introduction 13
2. *Darconville's Cat* and the Tradition of Learned Wit 38
3. On *An Adultery* 52
4. *Darconville's Cat* Redux 57
5. The Original of Laura: The Making and Unmaking of
   Laura Warholic 59
6. *Collected Stories*: A Note on the Text 92
7. Poems on Sundry Occasions 103
8. The Novelist as Critic 132
9. Books of Curious Facts 169
10. The Brothers Theroux 178

APPENDIX

An Interview with Alexander Theroux 217
Herbert Head: The Unfinished Novel 225

Checklist of Publications 231
Index 253

Alexander Theroux and Steven Moore, Cambridge, Mass., 23 August 1985. Theroux is wearing a "REVENGE" button an admirer had sent him but which Theroux deemed "unholy." (Photograph by Richard Scaramelli)

Preface

It was my fate, my destiny, my end, to be a fan.
— Frederick Exley, *A Fan's Notes*

AS THE SUBTITLE might suggest, this isn't so much a book as a compilation of things I've written on Alexander Theroux over the years, with the early ones retained in their original form rather than reworked into a harmonious whole with the much later ones in order to record my changing opinions of his work. It's an assortment of literary essays, textual studies, biographical anecdotes, book review summaries, and bibliographic research—a little eccentric, as is its subject. It attempts to be both a personal and impersonal evaluation of Theroux's multifarious oeuvre, and if nothing else provides a treasure trove of Therouviana to aid others in making their own evaluations of this most singular writer.

I've known Theroux since 1981, when I wrote him a fan letter expressing my swooning admiration for *Darconville's Cat* and asking him to sign it and his earlier books. We began corresponding after that, which has continued on and off ever since. I met him only once, in Cambridge in August 1985, accompanied by my friends Cliff Mead and Richard Scaramelli (who took a few photos of him). After I joined Dalkey Archive Press/*Review of Contemporary Fiction* in 1988, I was able to devote a special issue of our journal on him and to publish his book of poetry, *The Lollipop Trollops and Other Poems*. Plans to publish a book of his fables fell through, leading to the first of a few rough spots in our relationship. I wrote a few essays on his work back in the 1980s and '90s, but I never intended to write a book on him. However, after I wrote an essay on Theroux's novel *Laura Warholic* in September 2018, prompted by some archival material I purchased on its origins, I realized that I had written about seventy pages of material on him over the years (chapters 1 through 4, plus the interview and bibliographic checklist), and that if I wrote a few more chapters I would have enough for a short book. So between October 2018 and March 2019 I wrote chapters 6 through 10 (though not in that order). I concluded in mid-June with a visit to my Theroux archive at the Harry Ransom Center (University of Texas at Austin), which yielded many valuable nuggets of information.[1]

Although this book covers most of his work, it doesn't cover everything. To get a sense of the enormity of Theroux's output, one need only glance at the checklist of writings at the end of this book, which I first published in 1991 and then posted online and occasionally updated: twenty-one books and pamphlets of his own, almost thirty contributions to edited books, and nearly 300 publications in magazines and newspapers on an astonishing range of topics—not to mention a half-dozen unpublished book-length manuscripts. The handful of books for which he is generally known (the novels and his two books on colors) are just the tip of a gigantic iceberg of writing. Some of these works are covered in depth, some briefly, and much of the journalism—along with the booklets on Al Capp and Edward Gorey—not at all.

The title of the first essay is misleading: it's an introduction only to the first half of Theroux's career—the better half, I think most readers would agree. Wearing my heart upon my sleeve, I wrote this in 1990 as the introduction to a special issue on Theroux that I edited for the *Review of Contemporary Fiction*, which came out in the spring of 1991. It covers his work up through his third novel, 1987's *An Adultery*, and I've retained the few references to the special issue to underline its original purpose. One unintended but felicitous outcome was that it attracted the attention of the Lannan Foundation: the second half of the issue was devoted to novelist Paul West (my idea, but guest-edited by David W. Madden), and in the summer of 1991 someone from the foundation called me to request copies of the issue because they were considering awarding West a Lannan Fellowship (worth about $35,000 then). I told the caller I was happy to oblige—the nonprofit book publishing arm of RCF, Dalkey Archive Press, had been trying to attract Lannan's attention for a few years—but told them they should really check out the Theroux half of the issue. They did, and a few weeks later they called back requesting out-of-print copies of *Darconville's Cat* for their board members. Luckily I had purchased a half-dozen at New York City's Strand bookstore when it was remaindered in the late 1980s, mostly first editions. I reluctantly sent them along—I knew they'd be valuable some day—and a few months later Theroux was awarded the fellowship in-

---

1 I want to thank Austin resident and David Foster Wallace expert Matt Bucher for assisting me, and Megan Barnard, Associate Director for Acquisitions and Administration, for other kindnesses.

tended for West. The transplanted Englishman got one in 1993, the same year Dalkey reprinted West's *Words for a Deaf Daughter and Gala*, so it all worked out.[2]

"Alexander Theroux and the Tradition of Learned Wit" was written in 1983, just before I returned to grad school to pursue a PhD at Denver University. I talked with the *Denver Quarterly*'s editor Eric Gould about publishing it there, but I left after a year to go to Rutgers, and it was published instead by *Contemporary Literature* in summer 1986. Two years later I reviewed *An Adultery* for *Conjunctions*, back when they still ran book reviews. After the 1991 introduction for *RCF* I didn't write anything further on Theroux (except for a brief review of the limited edition *Watergraphs* in the summer 1995 issue of *RCF*) until 2015, when I was invited to contribute a short piece on *Darconville's Cat* to a festschrift called *The Syllabus*, which consisted of the editors' choices for the best 100 books of the last 100 years, heavily weighted toward the unusual.

I sort of gave up writing at that point and limited myself to tying up loose ends: all of the above pieces were reprinted in my retrospective collection *My Back Pages: Reviews and Essays* (2017). But in August 2018 I received an email from poet/editor Alexander Laurence, whom I had known slightly since the mid-1990s. He had been aware for years that he was the model for a major character in *Laura Warholic*, but hadn't bothered to read the entire novel until that summer. He informed me of the originals of some of the other characters, including Laura herself (and emailed me photos of them), and agreed to sell me a cache of materials from 1998 that related to the novel. Originally I planned only to compile some notes for the benefit of future scholars, but then decided I may as well write an essay myself, especially since I was the copyeditor for the novel and still had a great deal of material relating to that infuriating project. You can read all about it in "The Original of Laura." It was then that I decided to write some further essays for a book, throwing into the pot an interview with Theroux I did for that special *RCF* issue, which also contained the first version of the checklist of writings.

So: a mulligan stew of essays written over thirty-five years tracking the waxing and waning of my enthusiasm for Theroux's works—my original subtitle was the Yellow Nineties-ish "Essays in Appreciation and Depreciation"—the waning largely due, I now realize, to my original miscategorization of him. When I discovered him in 1981, I assumed he was

2 In the small world of book reviewing, West favorably reviewed *Darconville's Cat* in the 19 April 1981 issue of the *Washington Post*, and Theroux favorably reviewed West's *A Stroke of Genius* in the 19 February 1995 issue of the *Chicago Tribune*.

a recruit to the U.S. fiction vanguard of the time—Barth, Barthelme, Coover, Davenport, Elkin, Gaddis, Gass, Mathews, McElroy, Pynchon, Sorrentino—whereas he turned out to be more of a mainstream literary all-rounder like Norman Mailer (they both wrote on Marilyn Monroe, for example) or, better yet, Theroux's acquaintance John Updike, who alternated between literary fiction, commercial stories, essays and journalism, popular culture (both wrote about cartoonist Al Capp and baseball player Ted Williams), book reviews, art criticism, and light verse. Better still, he was a throwback to early 20th-century outsiders like D. H. Lawrence, Djuna Barnes, Ronald Firbank, Edgar Saltus, and especially Frederick Rolfe—eccentric, intransigent artists who produced a singular but uneven body of work. In one of his essays Theroux speaks admiringly of "such iconoclasts, madmen and unbudging literary originals as, say, Laurence Sterne, James Joyce, Vladimir Nabokov and Nicholson Baker."[3] He's closer to them than to anyone else, and I shouldn't blame him for not being the kind of writer I thought he was, or wanted him to be. He followed his own path, as does every great writer.

3 "Tolstoy Need Not Apply," *Wall Street Journal*, 22 October 1999, W15.

Chronology

1939	Born 17 August 1939 in Medford, MA
1954–58	Attends Medford High School
1958	Joins Trappist Monastery at St. Joseph's Abbey in Spencer, MA
1960	Joins Franciscan Seminary at Callicoon, NY
1961–64	St. Francis College, Biddeford, ME, B.A. Contributes fiction, poetry, and essays to the school magazine, the *Canticle*
1964–65	University of Virginia, M.A. Thesis: "Samuel Beckett: The Emunction of Language (an Approach to the Epistemology of Words)"
1965	Visits France and Italy
1965–68	University of Virginia, PhD. Thesis: "The Language of Samuel Beckett." Contributes fiction, plays, and poetry to the school literary magazines, *Rapier* and the *Plume & Sword*
1968–69	Fulbright Grant in England. Travels to Berlin and Moscow in March–April 1969
1969–73	Teaches at Longwood College, VA
1972	*Three Wogs* published in January
1973	Begins publishing stories and essays in major magazines while writing *Darconville's Cat*
1973–78	Teaches at Harvard as Briggs-Copeland Lecturer, at invitation of Monroe Engel
1975	*The Schinocephalic Waif* and *The Great Wheadle Tragedy* published
1976	Guggenheim Fellowship awarded
1978–82	Teaches at Phillips Andover Academy
1979	*Master Snickup's Cloak* published in April
1981	*Darconville's Cat* published in May
1982–86	Teaches at MIT

1986–91	Teaches at Yale University; becomes regular contributor to *Art & Antiques* (until 1992)
1987	*An Adultery* published in October
1991	*Review of Contemporary Fiction* devotes half-issue on Theroux
1991	Lannan Literary Award for Fiction
1992	*History Is Made at Night* (March) and *The Lollipop Trollops and Other Poems* (August) published
1994	*The Primary Colors* published in April
1995	Lives in San Diego on-and-off researching and writing essays for the *San Diego Reader*
1996	*The Secondary Colors* published in April
1999	*The Enigma of Al Capp* published by Fantagraphics Books, which becomes his regular publisher
2000	*The Strange Case of Edward Gorey* published in August; revised editions follow in 2002 and 2011
2000	Completes draft of *Laura Warholic*, expands it over the next seven years
2002	Clifton Fadiman Medal from the Mercantile Library
2005	Marries artist Sarah Son (b. 1966) on 16 July
2007	*Laura Warholic* published in November
2008	Joins his wife in Estonia, the subject of his next book
2011	*Estonia: A Ramble Through the Periphery* published in November
2013	*The Grammar of Rock* published in February
2014	Twin daughters Shiloh and Shenandoah born on 30 March
2015	*Collected Poems* published in May
2017	*Einstein's Beets* published in May
2017–19	Prepares *Collected Stories*, revising older stories and writing several new ones
2019–20	Revives a decades-old biography of Amelia Earhart and continues to write poetry

Introduction

I MUST CONFESS at the outset that I love Alexander Theroux's work as I love no other. I had never heard of him prior to seeing an ad for *Darconville's Cat* in *Publishers Weekly*, but during that intriguing series of ads—three corner ads on succeeding pages culminating in a full-page one, reproduced at the end of this essay—I experienced something akin to love at first sight. That ad appeared in January of 1981, and since the novel was not scheduled to appear until May, I beguiled the time by searching out and reading the two other books of his that were still in print, *Three Wogs* and the children's fable *Master Snickup's Cloak*. These I enjoyed, confirming my instinct that I had found an author after my own heart. Then *Darconville's Cat* arrived, dark and elegant, and swept me off my feet. This is the novel I had been waiting for all my life, I realized, nor has the succeeding decade dimmed my ardor. I want to be buried with this novel clasped to my heart.[1]

With that same heart throbbing on my sleeve, let me introduce this brilliant writer; that he still needs to be introduced to most readers at this late date, nearly 20 years after the publication of his first book, is of course an outrage, but we burn daylight to grumble at the neglect. Born in 1939, Alexander Theroux is a member of a prolific family of writers stretching back to the 18th century and including in the present generation best-selling writer Paul, Joseph (with one novel to his credit), and Arabic translator and commentator Peter. Alexander's younger years are recounted in Martin Battestin's essay later in this issue,[2] and in re-

---

1 [David Markson was so bemused by this declaration that he quoted it, without attribution, in his novel *Reader's Block* (Normal, IL: Dalkey Archive Press, 1996, 106), which I consider an honor, however he intended it. NB: Bracketed footnotes like this contain material added to previously published essays.]

2 ["Alexander Theroux in Virginia and London, 1964–1973," *Review of Contem-*

cent years Theroux has made a modest living by teaching (Harvard, Yale, MIT) and from journalism on a wide variety of subjects. His creative writing ranges across most genres—poetry, short stories, fables, plays— but most masterfully in three remarkable novels: *Three Wogs* (1972), a triptych of comic novellas; *Darconville's Cat* (1981), a 700-page anatomy of love and hate; and *An Adultery* (1987), a Jamesian analysis of betrayal. They bear little resemblance to anything else in current fiction: because of his ornate style and manipulation of literary forms, Theroux has been grouped with postmodernists like Barth and Sorrentino, but the under-lying conservatism in his work and his preference for linear storytelling make this an awkward grouping. But that same style, formalist concerns, and general excessiveness disqualify him from the ranks of more tradi-tional novelists like Bellow and Updike (both of whom have expressed admiration for his work). Instead, Theroux belongs to the line of literary outsiders, writers like Frederick Rolfe ("Baron Corvo"), Ronald Firbank, and Djuna Barnes, whose work has little in common with that of their contemporaries and which instead amalgamate curious byways of liter-ary tradition and eccentric genius into something unique.

Both Rolfe and Firbank, in fact, come to mind during the three novellas that comprise *Three Wogs*, which offers three views of British racism. The first, "Mrs. Proby Gets Hers," opens with a rhymed pair of hexam-eters (after the manner of Rolfe's *The Desire and Pursuit of the Whole*, where each chapter ends with one or more hexameters[3]) and introduces the fountainhead of much British Sinophobia in the nefarious person of Fu Manchu, "the Yellow Peril incarnate in one man," as Rohmer's heroic but fanatically bigoted Nayland Smith solemnly insists. A particularly menacing scene in one of the many B-movie adaptations of "Sax Rohm-

---

porary Fiction 11.1 (Spring 1991): 50–83. This special issue on Theroux will be alluded to a few more times. As stated in the preface, this introduction covers only the first half of Theroux's career.]

3 Theroux's familiarity with Rolfe's Venetian romance is also evident from a quotation that appears in "The Wife of God": the reference on p. 147 of *Three Wogs* (Boston: Gambit, 1972) to "St. Theodylus, patron saint of those who suffer from cruel apprehension," is taken verbatim from p. 153 of *The Desire and Pursuit of the Whole* (Norfolk, CT: New Directions, 1953). As his letters to Battestin printed elsewhere in this issue attest, Theroux discovered Rolfe in London and immediately began quoting him: the quotation above is used in letter #7, and his quotation from Martial in #8 is actually from Rolfe's *Nicholas Crabbe* (London: Chatto and Windus, 1958), 29.

er's great Manichean saga" (as Pynchon calls it in *Gravity's Rainbow*) elicits from Mrs. Proby a scream, which she later ascribes to her distrust of her Chinese neighbor Yunnum Fun, proprietor of a small Chinese market in *her* neighborhood (which is also, as the last line of the story remarks, *his* neighborhood). She imagines him to a friend in the same jingoistic terms popularized by Rohmer's Nayland Smith:

> "He lights incense sticks at night, worships the devil, I think. I don't know if he's grinding tea or muttering A-rab chants, I don't, but I turn my wireless up so as not to hear, you see. What I'm driving at, Mrs. Cullinane, is this: some morning, Mrs. Proby's going to turn back the covers, take off her hairnet, and find she's shoulder-to-shin with the Yellow Peril, she is."[4]

But beneath these ridiculous notions is a stronger, if not the true, motive for British prejudice, the main theme on which the three stories in the novel are variations: England's loss of prestige as a world power and the concomitant loss of the Edenic purity of English life before the influx of "wogs" (Westernized [or Worthy] Oriental Gentlemen). "In those days," the first of many nostalgic reveries in the novel, "England had a voice in the world, people could understand the lyrics of songs, and there were no Chinese" (10). The complicated political and economic changes that have reduced England's status are, of course, above the heads of Theroux's Britons, and so Mrs. Proby (and Roland and Lady Therefore in the succeeding stories) fixes the blame on the most visible targets available, and in no uncertain terms:

> "You see," she fumed [at Yunnum Fun], "we were always taught that if people go mucking about and foraging around with yellows, blacks, or any other cribbage-faced nit who steps here and about as free as Dick's hatband *in a country not his*, well then, the country won't be worth tuppence." Her full face was wide, flapping, incarnadine. "And don't you think for one iota we're going to become another Shanghai with all its cheap cloth and jerry-made cameras, because you've got another thing coming, dearie. We've had the war. Once burned, twice shy, they say. Mark me well, we know what you're about, too, and you are not, you heard me just say *not*, pulling the wool over anybody's sheep's clothing. Certainly not mine, least of all." Her womb

4 *Three Wogs* (Boston: Godine, 1975), 12. This paperback reprints the essay "Theroux Metaphrastes" as an appendix and hereafter will be cited parenthetically.

was smoking with wrath. And then the exit line came. "Rice or no
rice," she said, "if I was a Chinaman I'd flap right back where I flew
from." (32–33)

But she decidedly does not know what he's about; like the "fat white
woman whom nobody loves" in the epigraph, Mrs. Proby misses so
much.[5] Her denunciation follows a brief biographical sketch of Yunnum
Fun's 40 years of hardship and abuse leading to his present position,
and by the time Mrs. Proby delivers this declaration, "onto her he had
telescoped a revenge informed by years and years of scorn and obloquy"
(27); thus, "It was then that Yunnum Fun decided to kill her." Mrs. Proby
gets hers, as both the title and Mrs. Cullinane predicted (13), and the
story ends with a deliberate echo of the closing sentences from the first
paragraph: "'Simple,' said Yunnum Fun as he sat on the No. 22 bus which
took him back to the Brompton Road roundabout, where he lived. It was
his neighborhood" (52).

In his otherwise enthusiastic review of *Three Wogs*, novelist D. Keith
Mano felt the first 20 pages of the book were the weakest and consequently advised readers to put the second or third story first.[6] But "Mrs.
Proby Gets Hers" establishes the general dynamics of racial prejudice
(the other two stories are more specialized applications), and for that
reason it is a more suitable introduction than the others. An important
refrain (adapted from Isaiah 55:8–9) is repeated three times in the story:
"Their how is not necessarily our how," Mrs. Proby gravely warns Mrs.
Cullinane, "nor is yours theirs" (8), a statement akin to that Yunnum Fun
heard from his father many years earlier: "Your how is not necessarily my
how, nor is ours theirs" (22); a final variation occurs to Yunnum Fun on
the last page of the story: "my how is not necessarily their how, nor is
theirs mine" (52). Theroux will continue ringing changes on this theme
through his later short stories (often concerning American travelers at
odds with foreigners) up to *Darconville's Cat* (where Darconville's how
is not necessarily Isabel's how, nor is hers his) and *An Adultery* (ditto Kit
Ford and Farol Colorado). The insistence on this theme may or may not
argue the inevitable conflict that will exist between people of different
cultures or backgrounds, but it is central enough to Theroux's fiction to
be sounded at the beginning of his first book. Mrs. Proby's prejudice is
not confined to the Chinese; Americans and Irish also come in for verbal abuse, as would anyone of the wrong color, culture, or religion. The

5 The epigraph is from Frances Crofts Cornford's once-popular poem "To a Fat
   Lady Seen from the Train" (1910).
6 *New York Times Book Review*, 16 April 1972, 4.

establishment of this middle-class theme will allow Theroux to move on surer footing down to the lower classes (Roland) and up to the upper classes (Lady Therefore) and provides more than a hint that bigots, despite their wide class differences, are all sisters and brothers beneath the skin.

"Childe Roland," the longest and most virtuosic of the three stories, opens not with hexameters but with a "Once upon a time" and ends with a predictable (but ambiguous) "live happily ever after." The fairytale conventions are seconded by the title itself, taken from Browning's enigmatic poem "'Childe Roland to the Dark Tower Came.'" Browning's knight is consumed by doubts: of himself, of his fellow questers, even of the nature and validity of his quest, to the point where—"After a life spent training for the sight!" (l. 180)—he does not recognize his Dark Tower. Similarly, Theroux's Roland, a young loner who has lost both parents,[7] conceals beneath his breezy cockiness a maelstrom of doubts and uncertainties, brought to the surface in his dramatic confrontation with a gentle Indian electrical student.

The most obvious parallel between Browning's poem and Theroux's story is the "starved ignoble nature" (l. 56) common to both. Nothing thrives in Childe Roland's "grey plain":

> No! penury, inertness, and grimace,
> In some strange sort, were the land's portion. "See
> Or shut your eyes," said Nature peevishly,
> "It nothing skills: I cannot help my case:
> 'Tis the Last Judgment's fire must cure this place,
> Calcine its clods and set my prisoners free." (ll. 61–66)

Penury, inertness, and grimace likewise characterize Roland McGuffey's Houndsditch:

> Sunday—how say it?—dawned, the only invincibility it seemed to possess. From its broken tenements, lonely streets, and empty squares had all emotions ebbed, and Houndsditch seemed a limit gone beyond, a kind of stone leprosarium of gutted doors through which the metaphorical inmates, as if suppurating with the afflictive screwworm

---

7 Theroux relates the manner of Roland's father's death in a succinct parenthesis: "(picnic, kipper bone)" (58) à la Nabokov's Humbert Humbert, "whose very photogenic mother died in a freak accident (picnic, lightning)." Theroux uses this device again in *Darconville's Cat* to account for the death of Mrs. McAwaddle's husband: "(tainted knockwurst, Jaycee picnic)."

of helminthiasis, willingly decamped in crawls, belled, as it were, to the nether of their dungeons where, in a sickly and zombie-like *lacher prise* from the weekly obligations that beat them down, they could spoon away their Sunday dinners, suck their dirty pipes, doze half-naked slumped into the sofa, or, without the slightest expectation, stare down silently through old thread-bare curtains with tired gull-like eyes to the streets below which sheered off abruptly at corners and in turn closed off pretty much of their world. Everyone had withdrawn, it seemed, so as not to be intimidated by the intimidating click that snapped them away like the catch of a cheap lock,[8] shut fast and buried hopelessly within those monstrous building projects, tall as the Cities of the Plain, being everywhere winched toward the sky, where each building, disfigured, hulks higher and higher, its shit-coloured self rising into space like a cement Kraken out of the inattentive and varicose earth. It was like a surrealistic dream, as if all the buildings were actually cardboard and, if but tapped, would hurtle down in a spray of dust and scaffolding, revealing a vast desert of grey which reached to the fag-end of infinity. (64–65)

After a brief encounter with a Pakistani that foreshadows the later one with Dilip, Roland sets off on his usual Sunday quest, his path indicated by the same "hoary cripple" (68) who maliciously points Childe Roland's way (l. 2).[9] As he makes his way toward Hyde Park he plays an imaginary game of soccer, with rocks and rolled bread for balls and trash barrels for opponents ("huge monocular Welsh cretins, he decided, running around with the stupidity ascribed to giants and salivating in leek-coloured uniforms" [68])—the Tottenham Hotspurs standing in, apparently, as the nearest 20th-century equivalent to a band of knights. Throughout the story Theroux thus undercuts the paradigmatic noble quest (as Browning did before him) with Roland's restless wanderings, sometimes with deflated comparisons (the girl he soon meets is, Roland admits to himself, "not really Snow White" [73]), but more often with the clanging juxtaposition of rich, orotund descriptions against Roland's saucy slang and sordid activities. The effect is deliberately comic—in-

---

8 Cf. stanza 29: "Yet half I seemed to recognize some trick / Of mischief happened to me, God knows when— / In a bad dream perhaps. Here ended then, / Progress this way. When, in the very nick / Of giving up, one time more, came a click / As when a trap shuts—you're inside the den!"

9 [In the interview that followed the original appearance of this essay, Theroux remembered "effortfully working to make the perambulations in London of Roland McGuffey recapitulate the lines of the Union Jack" (30).]

deed P. G. Wodehouse made a career from the same technique—as when Theroux follows Roland's trashy song with the remark, "His was the lyrical mode" (67). Thus the Horatian admonition (from *Ars Poetica*) that stands as epigraph to the story: "Mountains will be in labor, the birth will be a single laughable little mouse."

Roland's bigotry is as widespread as Mrs. Proby's, but with a crucial added dimension: sexual competition. This theme comes to the forefront after his unsuccessful attempt to pick up a girl named Rose ("Rosamund, actually"), whom he meets lounging in Hyde Park. His bigotry reaches a vicious pitch as he imagines Rose joining two Sikhs who had previously passed by their bench:

> All bloody flap that was, and Roland knew that within a brace of shakes she'd be all hands to the pump in some cul-de-sac in the Edgeware Road, with those two drum-eared jungle bunnies who walked by, just begging for it. That, for Roland, was the *osculum infame*, roughly, "kissing the devil's fundament." The brain-racking insouciance with which he generally met the world here stung Roland into a cold fury, a splenetic grudge which ripened into a bouncing loath specifically for those smut-crazed piratical Asians, roasting with satyriasis and ready with their poison juices to roger anything warm and horizontal, only to send pullulating over the indiscriminate bedsteads of Christendom a witless, sponge-headed progeny of biological variants, all with three breasts and minds like silly putty, conceived to a one in a perfect *Walpurgisnacht* of pithecanthropic howls, reechy innuendo, and drools. (79).

The paragraph that follows cleverly translates Roland's sexual envy into the flag-waving nationalism that often masks such uneasiness:

> His resentment burrowed in bitterness the geometrical, if underground, trenches of philosophical Patriotism from which, when the whistle blew its warning, he would burst, plumed and armiferous,[10] into the irrepressible English ozone, splintering the air with war cries like sprays of dynamite to call to the barricades, into the fight, all who would outface, and must, this Zulu, this Asian, with his endless streaming hordes, those dark plumed beings of the Middle Air, and

10 This word apparently comes, as many of Theroux's outlandish words both here and especially in *Darconville's Cat* must, from Thomas Blount's *Glossographia* (1656), a lexicon (the subtitle informs us) "interpreting the hard words of whatsoever language, now used in our refined English tongue."

buttress all his wrath against that flood which was spilling over the
tidemark of the world like an endless tidal wave of paint and staining
all an excremental brown. Love Thou Thy Land! *Dieu et Mon Droit!*
Into the Valley of Death Rode the Six Hundred! (79–80)

Just as Roland's fury reaches this patriotic pitch, the flames are further
fanned by the windy bombast from the "Speaker's Corner" in Hyde Park,
"a side show of hammering hands and spitting rhetoric" (80), and he
follows with relish an outrageous diatribe against "wogs," excerpted over
the next eight pages—probably the funniest pages in the book. Roland
eventually makes his way to Victoria Station, where he hears the sound
of water "from some sourceless spot" (89)—like the "sudden little river"
that crosses Childe Roland's path, "As unexpected as a serpent comes"
(ll. 109–10)—and finally confronts his own "wog": not an overpaid, lazy,
communist emigrant "putting the boots to your women," as the speaker
had warned Roland against; instead, in a passage as quiet and gentle as
the speaker's tirade was loud and violent, "alone on a bench and huddled
into a tiny embryonic position like a small, brown croissant, a little Indian" (90).

Dilip, the same Indian that Roland spotted earlier and dismissed
as a member of "The Pansy Patrol" (76–77), speaks with the same inflated phraseology, misapplied slang, and nonidiomatic formality as the
protagonists of F. Anstey's *Baboo Jaberjee* (1897) and G. V. Desani's *All
about H. Hatterr* (1948), Theroux's probable models. Anxious to culti-
vate Roland's friendship, Dilip politely ignores his innuendos and subtle
bullying during the first round of their confrontation, which ends with
Roland "contented in the knowledge" that "the Indian, among others,
remained, ineluctably, that shuttlecock which must drop to the ground
if its elevation is not secured, and constantly maintained, by frequent
blows" (98–99). And blows, indeed, seem imminent.

But here Theroux interrupts his narrative as he did in "Mrs. Proby
Gets Hers" for a biographical digression: a marvelously realized excur-
sion into Dilip's early days in India (99–106, 112–14).[11] As was Yunnum
Fun's, Dilip's life has been one of hardship and tribulation, but one in
which he has attained a degree of dignity unobtainable by guttersnipes
like Roland. Again, Roland's self-defense against such unobtainable dignity is more flag-waving patriotism and darker suspicions of miscegena-
tion. When Dilip excuses himself to make a phone call, Roland jumps to
the inevitable (for him) conclusion:

11 Theroux has traveled widely, but never to India, which makes these sections
   of "Childe Roland" all the more remarkable.

It's the girl, Roland thought, it's the girl! The telephone call was obviously urgent, and even now the line would be jumping with his wheedling artifices, or, worse—like that movie of The Incredible Hulk— filled with evil commands whispered huskily in likerish and diabolical croaks, the brain-trepanning spells that those bottle-nosed nigs, Congoids, and Hottentots cast at midnight in pointed hats and trick coats, using corpsedust, newtliver, and toads filled with mercury as magic barometers to swallow children, blow up churches, and work love potions on those harmless but not terribly percipient English salesgirls, who were later posted off in lumpy parcels to Port Saïd or Bombay, too ashamed, of course, to go back to Chepstow or Boodle and the happy life they had known there selling lollies over the toy counter in Woolworth's or shining the torch down the stalls at the Roxy. It was clear. It was horrible even to think of someone exposed to the fleers of this lustmonger, ready to wipe his smears of shoe-polishy discharge on some poor Trilby with skin like goldenrod and hair like down, probably now bound hand and foot and stuffed like a Norfolk pheasant into some dirty old wardrobe in a Brighton hotel, where her mother didn't even know where she was, never mind her father. It was a dead giveaway. But he had to have proof. (116–17)

Actually, Dilip has been invited for an innocent weekend of tennis at the seaside cottage of his 63-year-old tutor, Miss Lorna Bunn, "who looked like she lived in a cottage of gingerbread and brewed toads" (119). But Roland gets his proof, misinterpreted of course, and from this point on the tension builds dramatically:[12] at any moment, it seems, Roland's bigotry, wounded patriotism (his country comes off the worse in what Dilip assumes is merely a game comparing England to India), and his fears of sexual inadequacy (Roland pitifully boasts that Rose is actually his sweetheart) will explode into violence. But just as Roland backed down from the Pakistani ice-cream vendor at the beginning of the story, his anger suddenly fizzles out, and Dilip, drawing strength from a Buddhist parable, just as suddenly disappears.

Roland turns and descends back down to the station cellar; images of death surround him as they do Childe Roland toward the end of Brown-

---

12 I deliberately refer to the dramatic qualities of "Childe Roland," for the story is an outgrowth of a play Theroux wrote as a graduate student at the University of Virginia entitled *The Sweethearts and Chagrin of Roland Maguffey* and published in *Rapier: The University of Virginia Magazine of Satire and Broad Discussion* 1.3 (April 1967): 29–31, 37–38.

ing's poem, and he finally comes upon his Dark Tower:

> Roland heard his own whickering footsteps echo to the end of a long
> tunnel where, in these catacombs, one bus sat alone in a kind of
> Scotch mist, the glassed-in sign, top front, having been rolled to show
> its destination: Houndsditch. Roland boarded it and sat down in the
> shadows, a sort of violet deathlight round his jaw. (141)

In the bus he notices a dark blot on a panel. He tries to wipe away the
blot with the handkerchief the Hyde Park speaker had given him as a
souvenir, but to no avail. Exhausting every means to expunge it, he finally decides, "why not simply pretend the blot was part of the bus?" (142).
Roland takes small comfort in this parable of racial integration, but realizes "it was *only* that single frail resolve, made there in the shadows, that
alone could make the busride back to Houndsditch less painful, and,
if to speak of perpetuity, the only possible way one might ever possibly
believe he could live happily ever after" (143). And on that inverted note
Theroux's modern fairy tale ends.

The final story in the book, "The Wife of God," is a high camp romp
written with such exquisite style that it is necessary to remind oneself
that beneath the frivolity is yet another example of simple bigotry: this
time not from ill-educated members of "the non-propertied classes" (147)
as in the first two stories, but from cultured, propertied members of the
Anglican *bon ton.* Lady Fanny Therefore, determined to keep intact the
"brushed and curried elegance of the lyric past" (147), is as convinced
as Mrs. Proby and Roland that "wogs" are lowering the tone of civilized
life, if not ruining England altogether. Specifically, she is concerned for
her son, who is introduced in the first sentence engaged in a suggestive
act that reveals his sexual orientation as well as the color of the object of
his affections: "The Reverend Which Therefore sucked, then swallowed
a black jujube, one on which he could just as easily have bitten down, he
was that agitated" (147). A kissing cousin to Firbank's eccentric Cardinal
Pirelli, Reverend Therefore is enamored of a black African named Cyril,
his current choirmaster. But Lady Therefore, "a repository of racial dec-
lamation" (169), feels nothing but disgust for her son's companion:

> She pictured Cyril mythopoeically: a Dark Morlock, sloppy, smokeyed,
> limping through her dreams with his socks down, a salivating anthro-
> pophagus chewing khat, punching mandrils and hartebeest, and, with
> his thousand tribal members sitting on their haunches in the clear-
> ings, drinking strip-me-naked from wooden bowls, polishing their

teeth with pieces of soft stick, and farting into the grass. (154)

(It will be noticed that all three protagonists of *Three Wogs* picture foreigners "mythopoeically" in terms that bear no resemblance to reality
but reveal much concerning their psychological fears.) Consequently,
when she hears of Cyril's plans to marry an African girl—a ballerina also
in London—she eagerly supplies the necessary financial backing, unbe-
knownst to the Reverend Which Therefore, who does everything he can
to dissuade Cyril from his plan, inviting him to join him instead in holy
matrimony with God. The Edenic England of Lady Therefore's girlhood,
evoked in a series of beautiful reveries throughout the story, included no
blacks; she feels no compunction, then, in sacrificing her son's future
happiness that she may preserve her dream of England: "The Lion and
the Unicorn would always boldly guard the door that led to that paradise, the land of sweetness, light, and transforming prevenient grace,
and yet, asked Lady Therefore, could she at last unto that sacred portal,
into that sacred land, one day bring her son to spend their final days
together, only themselves, alone?" (216). This rhetorical question concludes a two-page reverie of great beauty, similar to the famous paragraph that concludes Lytton Strachey's *Queen Victoria* (1921), but much
finer. The question is followed by the concluding paragraph of the story,
in which Rev. Therefore is left drowning in a black pool of despair. Despite its frivolity, learned wit, catty misogyny, and Catholic camp, then,
"The Wife of God" ends on a tragic, somber note, in much the same way
as Firbank's frivolous *Flower beneath the Foot* does. (Firbank comes to
mind more often than any other author during this story.) The tragedy is
inevitable: even without his mother's intervention the Reverend Therefore would have lost his "Dark Angel" (175),[13] who does not share his
patron's sexual tastes. Nor is Lady Therefore's Edwardian England ever
to be recaptured. It is a measure of the power of Theroux's style that he
can evoke such tragic sympathy for such characters, for such concerns.
Even the bigotry that is the subject of the novel gives way at the end to
the greater themes of love, loss, and sorrow: the very thematic seeds that
would grow through the decade and bloom in Theroux's great anatomy,
Darconville's Cat.

---

13 The Catholic convert Lionel Johnson personified his homosexuality as "The
   Dark Angel" in an excellent poem of that name (1893). Theroux quotes from
   this poem on several occasions in *Darconville's Cat*, where the alluring (and
   insistently heterosexual) Hypsipyle Poore functions as the schoolmaster's
   dark angel.

※

During the decade between the publication of his first two novels, Theroux published a large body of short fiction, fables, and journalism. The style and content of Theroux's dozen or so short stories are decidedly lighter than the novels. Most feature travelers at the hands of crafty natives: "satiric fiction which showed the ironic contradictions between the characters' confidence in themselves and what the reader knew about them."[14] They range over a variety of locales (England, Virginia, Russia, Italy, Poland) and, more impressively, display Theroux's technical knowledge in a variety of fields (trains, folk-motif scholarship, gastronomy, Latin literature and archaeology, Copernican astronomy). But beneath the light, satirical surfaces a somber theme recurs, one that would play a major role in the long novel he had already begun writing. The key is provided in a quotation from William H. Gass that Theroux glosses in a 1975 essay:

> "You have fallen into art—return to life," warns a coffee stain at the end of William Gass's *Willie Masters' Lonesome Wife* (1968). That old problem, isn't it?—the opposite of Adam's problem, perhaps, who fell from art into life. To fall from art into life! What a pain in the ass it has been for us all ever since. And where have we fallen? We've fallen, bump, crash, splat, into that vast neutral forest, empty of druid and shadow, where the faint voice of Quarles sounds lamenting reedily through the darkness, muttering:
>
> > "Queens drop away, while blue-legg'd Maukin thrives;
> > And courtly Mildred dies while country Madge survives."[15]

Most of Theroux's stories concern just such a fall from art into life, a confrontation in which a character's insulated, private world (usually one of culture if not art) is punctured by a representative from "that vast neutral forest" of real life: a Protestant minister's Bible-belted security is disrupted by a Russian bellhop eager to supply him with pornography

---

14 *Darconville's Cat* (Garden City: Doubleday, 1981), 408—a kind of writing at which Darconville becomes adept.
15 "Theroux Metaphrastes," 26. [In turn, Gass admiringly quotes from both "Theroux Metaphrastes" and *Three Wogs* in his essay "The Sentence Seeks Its Form," in *A Temple of Texts* (NY: Knopf, 2006), 281–82. I've corrected Theroux's "dries" to "dies"; the couplet is best known from an 1810 letter by Charles Lamb, often reprinted.]

("Fark Pooks"); a fussy folklorist has a harrowing encounter with an alleged witch of Somersetshire ("Mrs. Marwood's Spunkies"); a fastidious lady novelist's world comes undone when her tightly bunned hair is knocked undone by an obnoxious child of tourists ("A Wordstress in Williamsburg"); a feminist magazine editor is almost seduced by a lascivious Italian ("Scugnizzo's Pasta Co."); a Californian classicist is almost seduced by his Roman guide ("Finocchio"); and so on. This recurring theme is merely satiric here in the stories; in his second novel, Theroux elevates this theme to great tragedy and high art.

Darconville's Cat (or "The Jilt's Companion," as Theroux once referred to it in conversation) is a monumental novel in several senses of the word: it is a lasting reminder of a love affair, erected in memory of the great love of Darconville's life, and a record of the tragic course of their affair; it is a monument to the English language, a vast burial ground of archaic words and sentiments, intellectual traditions, literary forms and rhetorical devices rarely used anymore; and it is monumental in the more idiomatic sense of *massive*: over 700 pages long, an encyclopedic range of references to literature, art, history, religion, and philosophy from every era of human history, thick with learning and lore, aflame with excoriating satire, alight with love, choked with hate, and waterlogged with grief. Simply thinking of the novel can bring tears to my eyes, yet it is also laugh-out-loud funny. It exhausts my superlatives.

The storyline is fairly straightforward. Alaric Darconville, a learned and rather aloof ex-novice, comes to Quinsy College in Virginia to teach and write. There he falls in love with one of his students, Isabel Rawsthorne, who seems to return his love. But soon feeling out of her league with Darconville, she admits to herself that she would feel "safer" with a neighborhood boy, Gilbert van der Slang. She strings Darconville along until she is sure of Gilbert's reciprocal feelings, and then tells Darconville she no longer loves him. Darconville, who is teaching at Harvard at this point and finalizing arrangements for their marriage, is destroyed by the news, and as he realizes the extent of her betrayal, contemplates revenge with the encouragement of Dr. Abel Crucifer, a strange ex-professor he meets at Harvard. Darconville returns to Virginia and waits outside Isabel's house with a gun, but seeing the tree upon which he had carved the word *Remember* in happier days, he abandons his plans for revenge and instead travels to Venice to stay in his grandmother's palazzo and write a novel about the affair. Racing against a fatal illness, he manages to finish and dies.

Summarized this baldly, *Darconville's Cat* sounds conventional and melodramatic, more like a 19th-century opera than a 20th-century novel.

What is unconventional about the work, however, is Theroux's extraordinary language, his rhetorical power to transform a commonplace boy-loses-girl story into a profound meditation on love, hate, and the tie that binds them. Hawthorne remarks in the concluding chapter of *The Scarlet Letter*, "It is a curious subject of observation and inquiry, whether hatred and love be not the same thing at bottom," and Theroux brings unmatched "observation and inquiry" to this subject. To find a parallel, one would have to go back to Burton inquiring into the causes of melancholy, or Rabelais on whether Panurge should take a wife: ordinary questions, extraordinary responses.

In a recent essay on Proust and Vermeer, Theroux cites Bergotte's late realization (upon seeing Vermeer's *View of Delft*), "My last books are too dry, I ought to have gone over them with several coats of paint, made my language exquisite in itself, like this little patch of yellow wall"; Theroux goes on to explain that "It was Proust, after all, who taught us that art by no means represents a copy of reality, rather it creates a truer, a nobler, more poetic reality."[16] Theroux transfigured his simple story by similar means: he chose a genre—the anatomy—that would be flexible enough to accommodate a wide variety of materials, but he encased this loosely structured genre in a design as balanced as a Greek temple. His novel consists of exactly 100 chapters; chapter 50 recounts the day on which Isabel decides to betray Darconville, thus acting as a hinge for the two halves of the novel. An essay on love in the first half is balanced by one on hate in the second;[17] a benevolent elder advisor in Virginia, Miss Thelma Trappe, has her counterpart in Massachusetts in the malevolent Dr. Crucifer; the southern setting contrasts with the northern one, angelic imagery changes to demonic, and so on. At the physical center of the book is the short chapter entitled "Odi et Amo"; this is the Catullan text for Theroux's sermon, with the emphasis on that paradoxical *et*.

Unlike Bergotte, Theroux went over his book with layer after layer of verbal paint, resuscitating hundreds of obsolete words that stand out on the page like blobs of bright paint, and adding layers of literary allusions and quotations. At times this reaches a density where an entire paragraph might consist of buried quotations. Take this paragraph from chapter LXXIX, where Crucifer is taunting Darconville about Isabel's deceptive love:

"Stories to delight your ears, favors to allure your eyes? She touched

---

16 "The Sphinx of Delft," *Art & Antiques*, December 1988, 85, 124.
17 [Theroux later informed me those two essay-chapters were the first sections he wrote for the novel.]

you here and there? Oh yes. The adverse party, with a suitable amount of proleptic irony, was your advocate. But the time that went by! Is it any wonder that Vulcan fashioned creaking shoes for Venus that he might hear her when she stirred?" Crucifer swept his arm from him. "She loved you—pish! She was loyal—bubble! Fair proportioned—mew! gentle of heart—wind!" (535)

This sounds like Cruficer's usual conversation, and yet hardly a word is his own. The first two sentences are from Shakespeare's "Passionate Pilgrim," the third from Shakespeare's sonnet 35; the Vulcan reference from an unidentified source, probably also Elizabethan;[18] and the final four exclamatory sentences adapted from John Marston's play *The Malcontent* (1604). In one sense, *Darconville's Cat* is a collage of texts, hundreds of quotations and allusions strung together as a narrative, a necklace of literary pearls. Even the final sentence of the novel, "Sorrow is the cause of immortal conceptions," is an unacknowledged quotation (from *The Confessions of Edward Dahlberg*), maintaining to the end the essential literariness of the novel.[19]

Actually, Theroux is extending here the practice he followed in *Three Wogs*, especially in "Mrs. Proby Gets Hers," which is a kind of linguistic mosaic of Britishisms: English slang, idioms, holidays, quaint-sounding city names, culinary items, habits, herbs, as well as prejudices. The characters are as much creations of language as users of it. But in *Darconville* Theroux moves further away from representation and exposition to create what Roland Barthes called the "paradise of words," where "every kind of linguistic pleasure" exists. Even more than Severo Sarduy's *Cobra* (Barthes's exemplar), *Darconville's Cat*

> is in fact a paradisiac text, utopian (without site), a heterology by plenitude: all the signifiers are here and each scores a bull's-eye; the author (the reader) seems to say to them: *I love you all* (words, phrases, sentences, adjectives, discontinuities: pell-mell: signs and mirages of objects which they represent); a kind of Franciscanism invites all

18 [Turns out this is from the section on jealousy in Burton's *Anatomy of Melancholy* (part 3, sec. 3, member 1, subsection 2), as I learned from Sam Endrigkeit (see n22 below).]

19 [Dahlberg wouldn't have minded, Theroux implied in a later essay: "Edward Dahlberg calls originality the act of a cutpurse Autolycus who makes his thefts as invisible as possible" ("Hateful, Hurtful and Hellish," *San Diego Reader*, 1 June 1995). Autolycus is a comic thief—"a snapper-up of unconsidered trifles"—in Shakespeare's *The Winter's Tale*.]

words to perch, to flock, to fly off again: a marbled, iridescent text; we are gorged with language, like children who are never refused anything or scolded for anything or, even worse, "permitted" anything.[20]

"How I adore the language that can tell you this," Crucifer interrupts himself at one point (544), and how Theroux adores the language that let him compose *Darconville's Cat*. But this very verbal exuberance is thematically functional as well, not merely self-indulgent. In *Darconville*, Isabel is first invested with the entire literary heritage of romantic love, then stripped and reviled with the English language's disturbingly large vocabulary of misogyny. Isabel is by turns ennobled and disfigured by this language, which points to Darconville's tragic flaw: his tendency to see people as literary stereotypes rather than as people. He treats Isabel as the heroine of his romantic reveries, and the reason he doesn't write much while involved with her is because she's the literary work he's creating. A simple girl, Isabel doesn't deserve (nor desires) these literary trappings, however ennobling they may be. During the second half of the novel, Darconville moves in the opposite direction, painting her (with Crucifer's assistance) as a new Messalina, again allowing artistic preconceptions to cloud his vision. Only at the end of the novel does his vision clear with the realization that art and life are two different (usually incompatible) realms and that his literary creation more properly belongs between the covers of a book than beneath the covers of his marriage bed.

Despite a number of good reviews, a National Book Award nomination, and inclusion in Anthony Burgess's *99 Novels: The Best in English since 1939* (1984), *Darconville's Cat* failed to make much of a mark. (True to form, the *New York Times Book Review* didn't even list *Darconville* in its year-end roundup of the hundred or so best novels of the year.) Some of the reasons for this criminal neglect are mundane: no paperback edition was issued,[21] and a year after Burgess honored it, *Darconville* went out of print. A few academic articles have been written on it and *Darconville* is discussed briefly in a recent survey of postwar American fiction,[22] but otherwise few readers seem to know of the work,

---

20 *The Pleasure of the Text*, translated by Richard Howard (New York: Farrar, Straus and Giroux, 1975), 8.
21 [It was eventually published in paperback in 1996 by Henry Holt; Theroux took the occasion to revise a few passages, identifiable by their lighter type (e.g., pp. 643–44).]
22 The essays are Jo Allen Bradham, "The American Scholar: From Emerson to Alexander Theroux's *Darconville's Cat*," *Critique* 24.4 (Summer 1983): 215–

even among specialists in contemporary fiction. Granted, the novel is long and difficult, but not nearly as long or difficult as Gaddis's *Recognitions* or Pynchon's *Gravity's Rainbow*. It may be that *Darconville's* chief virtue, its style, is for many its chief fault. It is a mode no one uses these days and that fewer and fewer readers seem capable of appreciating. Just as sparse Atticism ousted spacious Asianism in classical Rome 20 centuries ago, minimalism is preferred over maximalism by a majority of this century's readers and writers. Theroux's style, which has affinities with Greek Alexandrianism (a happy coincidence), medieval scholasticism, the learned wit of the 17th and 18th centuries, French decadence, and Corvine invective, is a style that demands of its readers an almost antiquarian devotion to English language and literature. Consider this paragraph, again from the grandiloquent Dr. Crucifer:

> "The state, it could be argued, must be called to account as to one of its highest functions, that of law—the hubris of human ingenuity—and even possibly condemned by the standards implied in the utopian idea of Primal innocence, for hasn't it taken upon itself one form of dominion after another," asked Crucifer, crossing the room with his forefinger in the air, "and lorded it over all the others, pretending, as though it were the daughter of the gods, to a privilege beyond all other disciplines? Primal innocence?" He winked. "Dwale and delusion! So laws were grafted. Lawcraft? Sheepcraft! I won't bore you with a history of all its agathokakological claptrap, Darconville, but simply point out that, at bottom, it owes its essential existence to the depraved and fallen nature of mankind—which it can never riddle, which it can never rectify—and in my considered opinion is styled, when at its most efficient, only to jingle at justice and to twill at truth, especially in matters touching on that curious but primal antagonism:

17; Larry McCaffery, "And Still They Smooch: Erotic Visions and Re-Visions in Postmodern American Fiction," *Revue Française d'Etudes Américaines* 9.20 (May 1984): 275–87; Steven Moore, "Alexander Theroux's *Darconville's Cat* and the Tradition of Learned Wit," *Contemporary Literature* 27.2 (Summer 1986): 233–45; and Michael Pinker, "Cupid and Vindice: The Novels of Alexander Theroux," *Denver Quarterly* 24.3 (Winter 1990): 101–24. The survey is John Kuehl, *Alternate Worlds: A Study of Postmodern Antirealistic Fiction* (New York: New York University Press, 1989), 94–96, 106–8, and passim. [Nor has there been much since, aside from a few appreciative online blogs—most notably Colin Marshall's "Linguistic Revenge: An Alexander Theroux Primer," posted on *The Millions* in 2010—and an excellent thesis by Sam Endrigkeit entitled "'Do Your Worst': Maximalism and Intertextuality in Alexander Theroux's *Darconville's Cat*" (Universität Duisburg-Essen, 2015).]

the just thing versus the legal thing. The law and the gospel," he glubbed with obvious delight, "are hereby made liable to more than one contradiction, and if a mooching and piety-faced forgiveness is all you know of either, where punishment you take to be a crime, I must then reinstruct you that all law has its beginning in that first crime of our first mother and her low tongue—Johannes Goropius Becanus (1519–1572) in his *Origines Antuerpianae*, Antwerp, 1569, maintained that the original language of Adam and Eve, and so the tongue of primal betrayal, was Dutch!—and thereby cry out that you might let your severe and impartial doom imitate divine vengeance and rain down your punishing force upon this temerarious strumpet, this mistress of the adroit lie, until like that fen-born serpent she resembles at the root of all our woe she eat the dust of her penalty for the rest of her life!" (542–43)

What a treasure chest of language is opened here! A geological survey of words ranging from Anglo-Saxon monosyllables ("dwale," "twill") and monstrous inkhorn words ("agathokakological")[23] to words apparently of Theroux's own invention ("Sheepcraft"); ornate adjectival phrases ("a mooching and piety-faced forgiveness") and epigrammatic asides ("which it can never riddle, which it can never rectify"); cranky scholarship (Becanus's *Origenes Antuerpianae*)[24] and obscure literary allusions ("fen-born serpent"—from Milton's *The Reason of Church Government Urged against Prelatry*); and an arsenal of rhetorical devices to move the paragraph from its calm, forensic opening to its wrathful, Old Testament conclusion. But this tour de force of Quintilian rhetoric also functions at the levels of plot development (Crucifer is persuading Darconville to take the law into his own hands), iterative patterns of reference (Dutch as "the tongue of primal betrayal" recalls his rival Gilbert van der Slang's ancestry), and at the thematic level, where Darconville, having fallen like Adam from art into life, is trying to reverse the fall and regain Barthes's paradise of words and (eventually) his Catholic paradise. In other words, this paragraph isn't just a patch of purple prose but a highly efficient (and entertaining) paragraph that fulfills several narrative functions. And there are a thousand more as richly textured as this one.

23 The *OED* cites only one appearance of this word (which means "composed of good and evil"): Robert Southey's *The Doctor* (1834–47), a *Tristram Shandy*-like novel in seven volumes.
24 I'm guessing Theroux found this among the annotations in John Wilder's edition of Samuel Butler's *Hudibras* (New York: Oxford University Press, 1967), 326.

But the American reading public wasn't interested. (Nor the British, apparently; 1500 copies were exported to Britain, but a good number of these were returned to the United States a few years later, with the British publisher's sticker still on them, to ornament remainder tables.) From 1981 until the appearance of his third novel in 1987 Theroux continued to teach and to write magazine articles, most notably a series of increasingly sophisticated essays in art criticism for *Art & Antiques*. (The protagonist of his next novel would be a painter.) Only two short stories were published during this period: "Watergraphs" (1983) and "A Woman with Sauce" (1985), both for the *Boston Globe Magazine*. The latter is interesting for the similarities between the narrator's relationship with a young girl of Italian descent named Angela Capitalupo and Christian Ford's relationship with angelic Marina Falieri in *An Adultery*.[25]

※

Theroux's third novel, with its stark, Deuteronomic title, marks a departure from his previous flamboyant style. Gone are the obsolete words, the parodies, and most of the exotic references (though one obscure reference to Rolfe remains).[26] Instead, *An Adultery* is written in a neo-Jamesian style that recalls the Master's inexhaustible fascination with the subtleties of manners and morals, as well as Proust's exhaustive analyses of character and culture. The result is a novel that some readers and reviewers found too obsessive and exasperating, especially with regard to the adulteress of the novel, a thoroughly detestable woman with none of the appeal of an Emma Bovary or Anna Karenina. Near the end, the narrator realizes "she wasn't worthy of the energy required to form the words that sentenced her" (372), but the fact he found the energy to form the 145,000 or so words that precede that sentence is the paradox readers must unriddle.[27] (The words *paradox* and *paradoxically*, in fact,

---

25 [I later learned they were based on the same woman: see p. 96 below.]

26 The couplet Christian Ford recites on p. 174 of *An Adultery* (New York: Simon & Schuster, 1987) is the opening of Rolfe's poem "Dux Amor" (1889). Discovered after the publication of Cecil Woolf's edition of Rolfe's *Collected Poems* (1974), it was reprinted in the introduction to Donald Weeks's pamphlet *Frederick William Rolfe, Christchurch, and "The Artist"* (Edinburgh: Tragara, 1980), 9.

27 [I now wonder if Theroux isn't echoing the end of the "Swann in Love" section of Proust's *Swann's Way*, when the art critic exclaims to himself: "To think that I wasted years of my life, that I wanted to die, that I felt my deepest love, for a woman who did not appeal to me, who was not my type" (trans. Lydia Davis [New York: Viking, 2003], 296).]

appear conspicuously throughout the novel.)

An Adultery is the first-person account by a painter, Christian ("Kit")
Ford, of his messy affair with a twice-married woman named Farol Colorado (which, traced to Greek and Spanish roots, means "red light"). At
first the attraction is merely physical, but as Kit learns more about this
troubled woman, his pity and sensitivity to her vulnerability cause him to
fall in love with her, despite his better judgment, and despite an on-again,
off-again girlfriend named Marina Falieri. (Marino Faliero [1285–1355]
was a Venetian doge and the subject of a tragedy by Byron and a novel
by Hoffmann.) Kit's neglect of the impossibly sweet Marina in favor of
the offensively neurotic Farol is perplexing, even to Kit, who, like a dog
returning to its vomit, keeps returning to Farol despite their many fights
and his numerous complaints about her. Or perhaps *because* of these
fights and complaints; at one point Kit writes: "I had heard of a thing
called obstacle love and how certain people needed complexity, barriers
in fact, to assure the love that one demanded be proven by it and for
the reassurance all was worth it in the many things to be overcome. Or
not worth it. I'm sure it explained both of us" (189). Marina presents no
obstacles; her love is open and unconditional. Farol, on the other hand,
is more than a challenge: "trying to fathom Farol Colorado has become
part of my own personal exorcism" (223). Kit is enchanted with angelic
Marina, but is possessed by the demonic Farol, and *An Adultery* charts a
Faustian battle for Christian Ford's soul.

As with the two earlier novels, *An Adultery* has a clear formal structure. It is divided into three parts, the first sentence of each forming a
syllogism:

> All women are mortal. (11)
> Farol Colorado was a woman. (139)
> Farol Colorado was mortal. (259).[28]

At the very center of the novel is an essay on adultery (196–200), reminiscent of the essays on love and hate in *Darconville's Cat*. This appeal
to formal logic and exposition is characteristic of Kit; his muddled mistress, on the other hand, "hadn't the art or ability to reach conclusions
by means of the usual premises which involved steps of thought and
demanded language, whether interior or interchanged. The cliché here
applied: she *leapt* to conclusions. She reached conclusions by determi-
nation alone, excluding middles and hopfrogging the logic of thought"

---

28 Of the numerous reviews I've seen, only Richard Scaramelli's in the *Review
of Contemporary Fiction* (8.1 [Spring 1988]: 190–91) noted the syllogism.

(233). Throughout the novel Farol displays much discomfort with language, distrusting its capacity for precision and clarity, and fearful of its ability to expose deception. Kit's commitment to language as a means for analysis clashes with Farol's use of it for obfuscation, and at this level *An Adultery* is a heroic attempt to prove that it is still possible for rigorous thought and incisive language to fight and triumph over the foggy, imprecise language, generalities, and clichés that both Farol and much of our society employ as its lingua franca. "Love is not only a talkative passion," Kit argues. "Language itself can lose chastity and in its ambiguity become also depraved, as when on the adulterous tongue two meanings that should remain separate become suddenly coupled. A parody of communication begins to take place. And soon all distinctions are lost" (113).

Loss is, in fact, the principal theme of *An Adultery* and the impetus of its form and content. The loss of distinctions in language is only one of many forms of loss with which Kit is concerned: loss of clear thinking, of manners, of judgment in art—his scathing critiques of Farol's artsy-craftsy world are the funniest bits in the novel—and, perhaps most importantly, emotional loss. His childhood fear of desertion (26)—Kit lost his parents at an early age—has caused him to become obsessed with avoiding loss: "I suppose the sad truth was," he writes to justify clinging to Farol, "I could be satisfied with very little if I was only delivered from the dread of losing it" (239). Initially, Kit found Farol "a symbol of all sorts of beautiful lost things" (15), two pages after stating "I've always found something terrible in what we have that can also be lost" (13). Eventually he loses both Farol and Marina; like Darconville, all he is left with are memories, and determined not to lose *them* as well, Kit writes the novel we have been reading.

"I can't forget anything," he notes early in the novel (27), and a little later admits "I love details. Details are never small" (47). The struggle against loss and the recovery of memories generate the novel's verbal energy, the very urgency of Kit's project justifying his obsessive recording of detail. What saves the novel from becoming wearisome is the language, of course; the endless examples of Farol's shortcomings may not always be interesting in themselves, but Kit's manner of relating them always is. Elegant, aphoristic, metaphoric, ranging in tone from sweetly sentimental to fiercely satiric, showing great psychological acumen, Kit is a consistently entertaining narrator. Consider this account of Farol's distaste for Kit's Cape Cod house:

> I hated her fastidious pessimism and found it uncomfortably disingenuous of her, under the circumstances, to be so queenly. The whole

day passed that way, with her remarks as she drifted from room to room confined to exiguous and monosyllabic quacks of disapproval, devoid of variety, wit, and compass. One had to go far, believe me, to find a more exemplary fusion of insecurity and snobbery or dependence and resentment. And it was very easy, I remember, to criticize her on the way home for accepting under false pretenses the bicycle her husband gave her. But who trades in contradiction will not be contradicted. "I took the bicycle," she replied—her eyes cold as highshoe buttons—"because it was incumbent on me to take it," she said, "because I'd have seemed guiltier," she snapped, "*not* to take it, do you *understand?*"

   Incumbent. (241)

Every sentence is a complaint, yet here, as throughout the novel, Kit has the "variety, wit, and compass" to keep the reader engaged, even when (elsewhere) the reader suspects Kit's lucidity has something in common with the deceptive lucidity of Poe's deranged narrators. (The occasional references to Poe—Marina recites his poetry, one of Farol's sisters is named Lenore—suggest Theroux encourages this particular suspicion, especially toward the end of the novel when Kit writes "Madness, do I say? It wasn't madness. I was completely rational, as calm as I was cold and as cold as camphor" [383].) As a first-person narrator Kit may be (by definition) unreliable to some extent, but like Marcel in Proust's great novel he earns this reader's confidence and even admiration, despite his faults. (Other readers find Kit as reprehensible as Farol—see Michael Pinker's essay later in this issue.[29])

   It is in this regard that *An Adultery* differs from most of the classics of the genre; in them, the adulteress claims our attention and often our sympathy. In Theroux's novel, even though Kit spends most of his 400 pages talking about Farol, it is he that holds our attention and wins our sympathy. Nor does Theroux give adultery any of the dangerous glamour it has in the classics, or even the civilized charm it possesses in W. M. Spackman's novels. Working against reader expectations, Theroux takes a number of risks, as if he too believes in an "obstacle love" relationship with the reader, needing "complexity, barriers in fact" to force the reader to abandon any notions of the illicit allure of adultery and to see it for the psychologically complex and morally destructive activity it is. The depth of Theroux's psychological penetration and the brilliance of his language assure *An Adultery* a place among the classics in this genre,

29 ["The Rhetoric of Disintegration: Alexander Theroux's *An Adultery,*" *Review of Contemporary Fiction* 11.1 (Spring 1991): 117–26.]

which in turn encourages us to reevaluate them in the powerful light he shines on this perennial theme.

As Thomas Filbin shows elsewhere in this issue,[30] *An Adultery* received mixed reviews, and even some of Theroux's fans (myself included) were reluctant to trade the exuberance of *Darconville's Cat* for the inquisitorial grimness of *An Adultery*. But repeated readings bring out the third novel's many strengths and it could be that, for many readers, it will represent the fullest maturation of Theroux's art. A fourth novel is in progress [*Herbert Head*, eventually abandoned], reportedly a comically pedantic novel in the form of a biography, but unfortunately bread-and-butter journalism, by necessity, claims most of his time.

※

Writing of the Theroux family in 1978, James Atlas said of *Darconville's Cat*, then nearing completion:

> I would not care to predict the fate of Alexander's novel. It is a brilliant, idiosyncratic work, graced with the quaint vocabulary that abounds in "Three Wogs," and I hope it becomes one of those books kept alive by a few loyal readers in each generation, like Edmund Gosse's "Father and Son" or Corvo's novels. But perhaps it is too literary; perhaps Alexander would do better to put more of Medford [his Massachusetts hometown] in his work. If this cumbersome novel remains unread, Alexander's character will continue to be talked of and appreciated, like Oscar Wilde's, as if it were itself a work of art.[31]

Alexander Theroux is indeed a colorful character, as several of the contributors to this issue agree. But it is the work, not the man, that should command our attention and respect. The depressing fact that, as of this writing, all of his books are out of print suggests that he may have to wait as long as Corvo, Firbank, and Barnes to win an audience.

30 ["The Duelist's Second," ibid., 127–30.]
31 "The Theroux Family Arsenal," *New York Times Magazine*, 20 April 1978, 64.

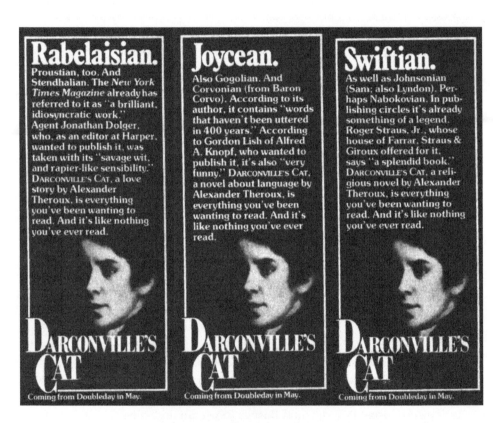

Ad sequence in *Publishers Weekly*, 23 January 1981, pp. 115, 117, 119, 121.

Darconville's Cat and the Tradition of Learned Wit

IN HIS ESSAY "*Tristram Shandy* and the Tradition of Learned Wit," D. W. Jefferson identifies Sterne as perhaps the last great writer in a tradition that goes back through the Augustan satirists to Burton, Cervantes, Erasmus, and Rabelais, and ultimately back to classical satirists such as Lucian and Petronius. Although it is possible to find scattered examples in subsequent British literature of the witty manipulation of the materials of erudition—*Sartor Resartus*, the Alice books, Rolfe, Joyce, Beckett, and a few contemporary writers such as Durrell and Burgess—Jefferson is justified in considering *Tristram Shandy* the last major work in British literature whose theme "may be seen in terms of a comic clash between the world of learning and that of human affairs."[1] But just as this genre crossed over from the continent to England in the 17th century, a case can be made for a second crossing in the 18th from England to America where, after a long and sporadic period of growth, it has bloomed in post-World War II fiction. Most of the components and techniques of learned wit identified by Jefferson and other commentators on the genre can be found in a series of American works that begins with Brackenridge's *Modern Chivalry*, with its pseudo-philosophical digressions in the Swiftian manner, and continues with the whimsical erudition of Irving's *A History of New York* (especially in the first, unexpurgated edition of 1809) and the more sophisticated use of erudition in *Moby-Dick*, and develops through the somewhat idiosyncratic works of various writers at the beginning of the 20th century, such as Edgar Saltus, James Branch Cabell, and Djuna Barnes. With William Gaddis's 1955 novel *The Rec-*

1 D. W. Jefferson, "*Tristram Shandy* and the Tradition of Learned Wit," *Essays in Criticism* 1.3 (July 1951), rpt. in *Tristram Shandy*, ed. Howard Anderson, A Norton Critical Edition (New York: W. W. Norton, 1980), 516.

ognitions, the tradition reached full strength, and since then a number of writers have availed themselves of the techniques of this genre, including Nabokov, Barth, Pynchon, Mathews, Markson, Davenport, and Sorrentino. But without a doubt, the fullest flowering of the tradition of learned wit—and the "purest" example of the genre established and perfected by Rabelais, Swift, and Sterne—is Alexander Theroux's 1981 novel *Darconville's Cat*, a dazzling 700-page satire that attracted little attention when published (although it was nominated for the National Book Award) but that surely will soon come to be celebrated as the finest example of learned wit ever produced in American literature.

As this novel is not yet widely known, some background might be in order. Alexander Theroux, older brother of the best-selling author Paul,[2] has published two novels—*Darconville's Cat* is his second; the first, *Three Wogs* (1972), was also nominated for the National Book Award and won the *Encyclopaedia Britannica*'s "Book of the Year" award; a third novel will appear shortly—and has published a large number of stories, fables, and essays. Nearly everything he has written is characterized by far-ranging erudition and a high style whose elitism has troubled not a few reviewers too lazy to use their dictionaries. In a brilliant essay written between the two novels to defend his amplified style, Theroux declared:

> I pay taxes to nowts, listen to nowts daily, watch nowts perform on television. But I don't write for nowts. I don't speak to everyone; why should I write for everyone, speak, say, through the pneumatically controlled head of some shovelmouthed dummy whose libretto of operative words, because of those impossible to ventriloquate, reaches to the number of no more than fifteen or twenty? The glory that was the ancient hero—Odysseus, Achilles, Aeneas, Beowulf, even Hamlet and Milton's Satan—was, in fact, often bound up with the glory of his speech; his gift that way seemed to be the linchpin of that very hero-

2 Both brothers make guest appearances in each other's novels. The prolific Paul appears in *Three Wogs* as "bespectacled Paul the Pseudo-plutarch, American oligosyllabicist," author of *Velocity: The Key to Writing*. (Paul has published almost a book a year since 1967.) And Dr. Crucifer's misogynist library (in *Darconville's Cat*) includes a copy of Paul's novel *Girls at Play* (1969). Alexander was the model, to a certain extent, for the flamboyant Orlando in Paul's *Picture Palace* (1978) and, to a lesser extent, for Allie Fox in *The Mosquito Coast* (1982). Paul's high opinion of Alexander's work is recorded in the *New York Times Book Review*, 4 December 1977, 70. [See "The Brothers Theroux" later in this volume.]

ism, the logical extension of his grandeur.[3]

And what of the man who has inherited this mantle of eloquence? Like Stephen Dedalus,

> I am a fearful Jesuit, I don't doubt. I am an antiquary, a pedant, a metaphysical deacon and special student on lease from the University of Padua with a swag-bag filled with ciphers, bolts, and refutations. I am a Roman Catholic, born to its jewels and bulls, and constantly aware of its byzantine smoke, wrought chasubles, traditional liturgies, and litanies infinite. You can find me, you're thinking to yourselves— and O, I suppose you're right—hunched over Albert Pigghe's *Hierarchiae Ecclesiasticae Assertio*, Demosthenes' *Exordia*, or Ebo's "Life of the Apostle of Pomerania" or, beclosetted, pushing notions around on foolscap with a goblet of mulled wine at my elbow and finding everything after Joyce an impertinence. Well, that may be so.[4]

One might expect elaborate historical novels from such a Mitty-like medievalist, reactionary moonpenny, and Tory Catholic (as he once obliquely described himself),[5] erudite reconstructions in the manner of Flaubert's *Salammbô* or, better yet, of Frederick Rolfe's historical romances.[6] But only his fables have historical settings; all the fiction— short stories as well as novels—is contemporary, but features the same cross-fertilization of past and present as in Joyce's later works and those

3 "Theroux Metaphrastes: An Essay on Literature," appended to the 1975 paper reprint of *Three Wogs* (Boston: David R. Godine), 5. This essay, occasioned by Diane Johnson's review of *Three Wogs* in *Book World* (*Chicago Tribune/ Washington Post*, 13 February 1972, 8), is the best introduction to Theroux's work and cannot be recommended too highly.

4 "Theroux Metaphrastes," 9. A more factual account of his life can be found in James Atlas's group profile "The Theroux Family Arsenal" (*New York Times Magazine*, 30 April 1978, 22–24, 49, 52, 54, 58, 60, 62, 64). Dr. Theroux has informed me, however, that the article is misleading and inaccurate in several instances; for example, he does not own "an assortment of esoteric sex books" as reported on p. 62: in fact, this is a collection of books on eunuchry—in Latin, no less—that Theroux used in working up Dr. Crucifer's background for *Darconville's Cat*.

5 "Silent Nights, Holy Daze: A Seasonal Meditation," *Boston Phoenix*, 9 December 1975, 22.

6 Theroux is a collector of Rolfe's works—as rare as they are eccentric—and has been influenced by them to an extent I hope to delineate in a future paper [never written, but see pp. 146–48 below and the numerous other page references in the index].

of his contemporaries Gaddis and Pynchon. (He also shares with these contemporaries a deep interest in religion—not surprising from one who spent two years in a Trappist monastery and dedicated his first book to the Holy Ghost—as well as in religion's shadow, the occult.) A historical resonance is maintained throughout his work not so much by historical allusions and set pieces—as in Gaddis and Pynchon—as by his astonishing vocabulary: no word is too arcane, too obsolete for his use. Though Theroux chooses these words for their precision and color rather than from a perverse desire to force his readers to memorize the *OED* (as some resentful reviewers have hinted), the historicity of these words maintains a continuous and highly ironic tension between the colorful past and "this sad, psychiatric century" of ours (as Theroux describes it in his preface to *Darconville's Cat*), a century as colorless as it is vulgar. On the other hand, such diction confers an Elizabethan splendor on the few aspects of modern life of which Theroux can approve.

The grandiloquent "Theroux Metaphrastes" had been written in defense of the high style of *Three Wogs*, but it can now be seen also as prolegomenon to the novel that was already in progress by that time. *Darconville's Cat* is largely autobiographical, and its genesis is recounted in Atlas's profile of the talented Theroux family:

> Eight years ago [i.e., 1970], he was engaged to one of his students from Longwood College ("an unremarkable Southern girl," as [younger brother] Peter describes her; "a common piece of licitation," in Alexander's blunt formulation), who used to complain to her fiancé, "You talk like a book." Still, Alexander was in love with her and busied himself with lavish plans for a wedding ceremony in Westminster Cathedral. But this young woman was obviously bewildered by the grandiose, unkempt, loquacious novelist nine years her senior, and "no more prepared to marry Alex," [older brother] Eugene asserted, pointing across a restaurant, "than [to marry] that man over there."
>
> When she left him, Alexander vowed to avenge himself in a novel. "Do your worst," she taunted. . . .[7]

Darconville's Cat was his answer. But what began as a shorter, personal novel of revenge[8] grew over the years into a huge, universal meditation

---

7 Atlas, 62. Both quotations ascribed to the girl appear in the novel (Garden City, NY: Doubleday, 1981), 274, 611. Subsequent references to *Darconville's Cat* will be placed parenthetically in the text.

8 The headnote that introduced two excerpts from the novel in the Fall 1974 issue of the *Harvard Advocate* announced that they were from a novel entitled

on love and hate,

> with thoughts, unsummoned and unannounced, pensioned out of the
> blandishments of common reality, constantly stealing upon him for
> inclusion, transmitted down through the memory of those who lived
> in ancient times, races illimitable, to be resumed across the years in
> all the emotions, passions, experiences of the millions and millions
> of men and women whose lives of love and the loss of it insensibly
> passed into his own and so composed it. (697)

With a universality thus approaching that of *Finnegans Wake*, Theroux
borrowed his theme and structure from the closing pages of *À la recherche du temps perdu*: on the night Darconville plans to consummate his
revenge by murdering the girl who left him, he unexpectedly beholds the
tree on which, in happier days, he had carved the word *Remember*:

> He stood before it in the pouring rain.
>   What hand made it? Whose carved? The very hand, he saw with-
> out elaborate calculation, that would now mock memory by murder.
> It was quietly, an overpowering accumulation, in the midst of that
> storm—with the feeling of what was impending swiftly opening to
> him in violent contrast the intensity of past consciousness and the
> idea that it might cease forever—that Darconville suddenly realized
> that the source of all error in life was failure of memory! A recept,
> made of many precepts, exploded into concept—and the past, for-
> merly thought adversary to the future, spoke to him. Remember! Re-
> member! Remember the king's words in the old story: which arrow
> flies forever? The arrow that has found its mark! All forgetfulness, he
> understood, almost on the edge of exultation, was in itself immoral,
> for the permanence with which experiences stay with a man is pro-
> portional to the significance which they had for him: memory must
> be preserved *from* time! A thing has the more value, it came to him,
> the less it is a function of time, and the effort of men to probe the
> past? Why, it was nothing less than an exertion toward immortality, for
> the consciousness and vision of the past but pointed to a desire to be
> conscious in the future, didn't it? And if, he suddenly reasoned, we do
> not free what we have known from time by memory, can we have any
> knowledge of remembrance any more than we can have one jot more
> of time? Memory was eclogue! "What have I got left?" asked Time.
> "Your genius," answered Eternity. (677–78)

Linda van der Lubbe, to be published in September of that year.

Like Marcel at the end of Proust's novel, Darconville decides to rescue memory from time by means of art: dying in Venice,[9] he writes the novel that we have been reading for nearly seven hundred pages. Once it is completed, he dies; but his creator, happily, survived to tell the tale.

This is one of the few instances in which Theroux differs from Darconville, for in almost every other respect the novel is very much a portrait of the artist as a young man. Like Theroux—and like Rolfe and Joyce, two major influences—Darconville studies for the priesthood before deciding to become a writer. He wastes four years teaching at a Southern college similar to the one at which Theroux taught from 1969 to 1973, and there falls in love with a student named Isabel Rawsthorne.[10] The affair proceeds as outlined in Atlas's profile quoted earlier, with Isabel withholding her misgivings about marrying Darconville. (There is, however, a good deal of foreshadowing of Isabel's eventual betrayal by way of literary allusions linking her with such figures as Keats's La Belle Dame [52], Milton's Delila in "Samson Agonistes" [96], and Irving's Katrina Van Tassel [168, 241].) On the strength of Darconville's book on angelology— more or less equivalent to Gustav Davidson's *A Dictionary of Angels* (1967), from which Theroux quotes extensively—he is invited to teach at Harvard (as was Theroux for *Three Wogs*). It is there he receives word that Isabel will not marry him, preferring to give herself to a childhood sweetheart instead.

But at this point, three-fifths through the autobiographical novel, fact and fiction part ways. Upon learning of the girl's desertion of him for another, Theroux threw himself into a whirl of literary activity. But Darconville is paralyzed by the news, and in this condition is taken under the wing of one of the most bizarre characters in modern fiction, Dr. Abel Crucifer, a retired Harvard professor. The initial motive for Crucifer's interest in Darconville ties together a curious thread that has been running through the novel in the form of abusive references to Queen Eliza-

---

9 Though Mann comes first to mind, it is more likely that Theroux invokes Baron Corvo, who also died in Venice. Or perhaps both are recalled: Donald Weeks finds several parallels between Gustave von Aschenbach and Frederick Rolfe in his *Corvo: Saint or Madman?* (New York: McGraw-Hill, 1971), 430–31.

10 Darconville's beloved takes her name from the subject of a dozen or so paintings by British artist Francis Bacon (1909–1992): her face in each is distorted and grotesque, and can be viewed in any of the half-dozen books devoted to Bacon's work. The name of Isabel's real-life counterpart appears throughout the novel in various disguised forms, though perhaps most plainly in the acrostic poem on pp. 122–23.

beth I, "she of the judas wig: bastard, usurper, excommunicate, baldpate, heretic, murderess, schismatic, and willing copulatrix" (13; cf. 235–37, 313–14, 529–30, 578). Crucifer recognizes Darconville as a descendant of "Pierre Christophe Cardinal Théroux-d'Arconville (1532–1601)" (234),[11] which leads the bedridden Darconville to realize:

> some perverse fealty owed to an ancient in his family was being paid to him in some kind of insane transferral or reciprocity centuries old.
>
> "A Prince of the Church, murdered in the red of his robes," said Crucifer, adding a reverence intercalated with an Italian phrase while in the same breath sniping at the woman who in killing that old man could kill again—such was the madness up there—in the proxy of Darconville's bride-to-be. (436)

Elizabeth was not only responsible for the fictitious execution of Cardinal Théroux-d'Arconville in 1601, but in the same year ordered the very real execution of her favorite, the Earl of Essex. The fatal relationship between them is described in Lytton Strachey's *Elizabeth and Essex*—Atlas reports that Theroux owns a signed copy of this book—and an identification of Darconville with Essex (and thus Isabel with Elizabeth) is made by way of numerous historical and literary allusions throughout the novel. "In the history of Essex," Strachey writes, "so perplexed in its issues, so desperate in its perturbations, so dreadful in its conclusion, the spectral agony of an abolished world is discernible through the tragic lineaments of a personal disaster."[12] Theroux surely intends the reader to discern a similar agony in the tragic lineaments of Darconville's personal disaster. Crucifer does, at any rate, and just as Essex embodies for Strachey "the colours of antique knighthood and the flashing gallantries of the past" at the very point in England's history when such qualities were giving way to a grayer, if more democratic social order, Crucifer regards Darconville as a final descendant of a better, more cultured world: a world of learning, refinement, aristocratic Catholicism—Crucifer has sold his soul to the devil, an option open only to a true believer—and a world free from the perfidious influence of women. "Your style is like mine," he confides. "We are co-supremes" (434).

---

11 The cardinal and his monograph *The Shakeing of the Sheetes*—a remarkable parody of Elizabethan style—are Theroux's own invention, but all the other "writing d'Arconvilles" in the long footnote on page 234 of the novel are quite historical.

12 *Elizabeth and Essex* (New York: Harcourt, Brace, 1928), 2. The quotation that follows is from the same page.

Darconville's initial reaction to Crucifer is one of undisguised contempt, which deepens when he learns of Crucifer's consuming misogyny. But slowly, under the repeated onslaughts of Crucifer's fantastic rhetoric, Darconville's resistance is worn away and he agrees that revenge against Isabel is imperative if he is to recover the world of art from which, like Adam, he has fallen.[13] Their calculating collaboration results in the terrible chapters that darken the last third of the novel, during which the hapless reader is subjected to a library of misogynistic book titles, a formal oration against women (which compares favorably with Juvenal's famous sixth satire), an unholy litany of female malefactors (each with her own exotic epithet), a diabolical pact in reversed Latin and a satanic invocation, essays on hate and revenge, and, finally, a gruesome catalogue of hypothetical tortures (the horror of which is relieved only by what one reviewer called their giddy surrealism). Even a reader inured to the writings of Sade, the Jacobean dramatists, and the so-called Catholic Diabolists (Barbey d'Aurevilly, Baudelaire, Villiers de l'Isle-Adam, Huysmans—all of whom are quoted or mentioned in the novel) must be overwhelmed by the dazzling rhetoric and dark extravagance of these chapters. The baroque eloquence of *Nightwood*'s Dr. Matthew O'Connor—the nearest parallel in modern fiction—is laconic by comparison. Like a bird before a serpent, the reader is hypnotized.

Though converted reluctantly to Crucifer's philosophy, Darconville never loses his repugnance for the repellent eunuch and realizes—if only subconsciously—that he risks becoming another Crucifer himself, "a puzzle-headed caricature of spite with a large share of scholarship but with little geometry or logic in his head and yet a figure of method and merciless egotism, possessing a sinister genius" (463).[14] Darconville was

13 There is a series of references to Adam's fall that begins on the first page of the novel and continues up to Darconville's Proustian revelation (678). In "Theroux Metaphrastes" the author argues that Adam "fell from art into life" and speculates on this point: "To fall from art into life! What a pain in the ass it has been for us all ever since. And where have we fallen? We've fallen, bump, crash, splat, into that vast neutral forest, empty of druid and shadow, where the faint voice of Quarles sounds lamenting reedily through the darkness, muttering, 'Queens drop away, while blue-legg'd Maukin thrives; / And courtly Mildred dies while country Madge survives'" (26, correcting Theroux's "dries" to "dies").

14 Adapted from Dr. Johnson's description of the French scholar Michel Mattaire: "He seems to have been a puzzle-headed man, with a large share of scholarship, but with little geometry or logick in his head, without method, and possessed of little genius" (Boswell's *Life of Samuel Johnson* [New York: Modern Library, 1931], 909).

earlier described as "tall and white as a paschal candle" (156),[15] and Crucifer is similarly described as "tall and cold and white" (438)—a paschal
candle without its flame. Both share a limitless vocabulary with a special
preference for Elizabethan diction: Crucifer's "cheekfuls of words" include dozens of quotations from Shakespeare, mostly from the sonnets
and narrative poems, and Darconville seems to have by heart the complete works of the Elizabethan love poets. All of Darconville's best qualities are exaggerated and perverted in Crucifer, to the point where he
begins to doubt his separate existence: "There was no real person named
Dr. Crucifer, thought Darconville, I have created him!" (489). To murder
Isabel at this point would be to give birth to the Crucifer within him.

This subconscious realization, coupled with the Proustian revelation
of the immortality of memory, rescues Darconville at the eleventh hour
and allows him to throw off Crucifer's evil influence. His return to the
world of art is a triumphant one—celebrated in the short, Whitman-
esque chapter XCVI—but the contamination contracted from his fall
into life, so to speak, proves lethal. Moribund, he has time only to complete his manuscript, to give artistic form to memory, before he quits this
world for that of his angels. Darconville dies a martyr to love and art, yet
the novel ends on a note of somber victory:

> But the survival is in the art—for *there* the heart begins to measure
> itself, not by its constraints but by its fullness, its poor baffled hopes
> dim now in the light of those infinite longings which spread over it,
> soft and holy as day-dawn. Thus it must be while the world lasts, the
> very misprisions against the spirit coming only to test and reveal the
> power of exaltation. Sorrow is the cause of immortal conceptions.
> (704)

That, in a roundabout fashion, is the plot. But as a character in Buckingham's *The Rehearsal* complains, "What the devil does the plot signify,
except to bring in fine things?" There is no end of fine things in *Darconville's Cat*: a love story that must be ranked with the most charming ever
written; Swiftian swipes at Southern life and manners; erudite flights
into angelology; hilarious speeches and sermons; the catty conversations

---

15 Theroux borrowed this image from Villiers's *Axel*, where the strange heroine
    Sara de Maupers is described as a "young girl, tall and white as a paschal can-
    dle" (trans. June Guicharnaud [Englewood Cliffs, NJ: Prentice-Hall, 1970],
    10). Sara's exotic travelogue in act 4 provided the inspiration for Theroux's
    even more exotic one in chapter LVIII, where a few of Sara's locales appear
    by way of tribute.

of college girls; an anthology of arcane epigraphs, literary allusions, and parodies; "books . . . that haven't been mentioned in 400 years," as Theroux boasted to Atlas, "words that haven't been uttered in five centuries"; meditations on the act of writing; poems, fables, nightmares, a diary, an abecedarium, a blank-verse playlet; the black page of grief from *Tristram Shandy* and a digression on ears reminiscent of Sterne's on noses; a chapter consisting of one word, and another with the title "What Is One Picture Worth?" that consists of—you guessed it—exactly one thousand words; revisionist lectures on Keats and Socrates; and, in perhaps the most ravishing chapter of the entire novel (and John Barth rightly insists ravishment is an essential quality of great fiction), a whimsical travelogue of fanciful places Darconville plans to take Isabel, which ends with a rapturous passage unequalled in modern literature since Molly Bloom said yes:

> Welcome, fate! The future shall be greater than all the past! It shines with prophecies, unborn deeds, liberty and love! Come, finally, with me to the Land of Cinnamon, the olive yards by the river Alpheus, the Isles of Orcades and the promontory of the Cimbri, Aneroid and Gravelburg, the medieval castle of Broglio, the empire of Lugalzaggisi and the masses of Negropont, Maleventum, and Orinoco! Come away with me and wander through the Upper Valley of Greater Zap, eat the ten-pound peaches of Chinaland, climb the spires of the foursquare city of Golgonooza, wave to the gold-guarding griffins in the Deserts of Gobi, pray with the holy apocalypts in the ancient monasteries of St. Neot, Pill, Axholme, Stixwould, Drax, Tiptree, and Burnham-on-Crouch, then watch the Plow of Jehovah and the Harrow of Shaddai pass over the dead, and then maybe sit on a dune in the month of June by the amber waters of the Syllabub Sea where the tide comes in in an opal mist, splashing in sweetly like the sound of a kiss, and we'll trip upon trenches and dance upon dishes and see whither the hither of yon, but if without reason you should find me gone, I won't be buried among the dead—no, go instead and look for me where eternity goes, in another world where the rain makes bows, for there'll be restored by the hand of art whatever's lost in the human heart, for something of us will always be, and forevermore I'll live for you if forevermore you'll live for me. (386–87)

But such fine things are not pointless pomposities as in *The Rehearsal*. The rhyming conclusion of this passage, for example, loosely adapted from Edward Lear's "The Jumblies," recapitulates the entire movement of the novel—life moving toward art—as does the subject of the poem in chapter XXIII, a sonnet written by Darconville, who thinks at the time life is more important than art. The novel is likewise encapsulated in the fable that constitutes chapter XXVII, "Master Snickup's Cloak."[16] Under the guise of a bedtime story Darconville narrates to Isabel, it too predicts in fairytale terms the fate of their love. (Isabel's counterpart in the fable, Superfecta van Cats, ends up as the madam of a brothel called De Zwarte Hertogin—the Dutch form of *The Black Duchess*, the ship on which Gilbert and Isabel marry [701].) Torn between "the world of learning and that of human affairs" (to quote Jefferson again), Darconville betrays his allegiance to the former by translating every emotion into its literary equivalent. As a perceptive British reviewer points out,

> Darconville believes, in fact, that experience has to be *avoided* in order for him to be able to write, but the richness of his imaginative life can't insulate him from suffering. His imagination is even the source of his pain because, as he comes to see, his love for Isabel has been an imaginative invention, the transmuting into a goddess of a commonplace, silly, snobbish girl.[17]

This process of transmutation is responsible for the highly allusive nature of the novel. When Isabel sends him a note reassuring him of her love after their first break-up, Darconville responds: "O angels, clap your wings upon the skies, and give this virgin crystal plaudities!" (333)—the exact words with which Vindice celebrates his sister's chastity in Tourneur's *The Revenger's Tragedy* (2.1.243–44).[18] The unattributed quotation is not only appropriate both in its particular setting and as another feather in the angelology motif, but also warns that Darconville will come dangerously close to becoming a Vindice himself. Most of Theroux's hundreds of quotations, allusions, and parodies function likewise on several different levels. The novel's title, for example, refers to (a) Spellvexit, Darconville's actual cat; (b) Isabel, often compared to the cat, both of whom he loses at about the same time; (c) his Catholicism

---

16 The fable appeared in an earlier form first as "Lynda van Cats" in *Antæus* 19 (Autumn 1975), 47–51, which was reprinted in the first *Pushcart Prize* annual the following year, and appeared in its final form as a book published in 1979, under its present title, by Paper Tiger in England and Harper & Row in America.

17 Tom Treadwell, "From Rage to Redemption," *Times Literary Supplement*, 3 February 1984, 116—the most insightful review the novel received.

18 [Formerly attributed to Cyril Tourneur, this play is now thought to be by his contemporary Thomas Middleton.]

("Cat" is British slang for Catholic), which he is also in danger of losing; (d) the flagellatory cat-o'-nine-tails, his satiric bent as well as his pain-inflicting imagination; and (e) God, Whom the six-year-old Darconville had drawn with the face of a cat (7).

Throughout the novel there is a lively intelligence that finds metaphors everywhere—his female students "had hearts like chocolate bars, scored to break easily"—and that constantly harmonizes the abstract with the concrete in the best manner of the metaphysical poets:

> It is an emotion, love, the moral implications of which quicken out of time, passing the clouds, to touch the instant of Creation. Love murders the actual. (Reverse the sentence, it's still true, but terrifying.) You must be what you are, always, however, in the hope that what you can be is exactly what you pursue in love; and ideally, of course, you shouldn't be anything but what you should be, a difficulty which the thought itself raises. Loved, nevertheless, you find yourself favored with the greatest of all possibilities for transfiguration, assisted, paradoxically, by what you would attain, but failing that, a kind of devastation few can know. *Cave amantem!* It carries the full weight of your soul with it. Our ideals are our perils. The heart of the loved one is an autoclave in which you have placed your own. Ravens bleed from their eyes during coition. (225–26)[19]

As in earlier examples of learned wit there is also the comical citation of erudite authorities on a variety of subjects, no end of rhetorical wit, scholastic logic-chopping with evidence taken from every field of human endeavor, and lists with the "rhetorical value" of those in Burton's *Anatomy of Melancholy*, where "it is a thing of glory, the inventory of a treasure-house."[20] The treasure-house here is "The Royal Library of Nineveh" Darconville calls his head (335–36), yielding such outlandish inventories as Crucifer's misogynistic library—ten pages of titles such as Tertullian's *De cultu feminarum*, Pierre du Moulin's *Anatomie de la messe* (1624), the 14th-century "Pucelle Venimeuse," *Talmudic She-*

---

19 [The final sentence is another unacknowledged quotation from Dahlberg— from *The Sorrows of Priapus* (1957)—as I discovered shortly after publishing this essay.]

20 Jefferson, 509. He believes "The attempt to exploit the list for rhetorical or comic purposes is not, as a rule, successful in modern writers" (510); that may have been true at Jefferson's time of writing, but postmodern writers such as Gilbert Sorrentino, Stanley Elkin, and Theroux have restored the rhetorical glory of the list.

Things, and *How to Tell Your Mother from a Wolf* by Roland X. True-
heaxe (an anagram for Alexander Theroux)—and his litany of female
seductresses.

"Only in an age which believed in the nobility of learning could the
materials of erudition be raised to such rhetorical heights," Jefferson
argues (510), and it is to that pre-Enlightenment age Theroux really belongs. The novel is piously Roman Catholic, unapologetically elitist, un-
fashionably misogynistic (though sex in this genre of learned wit is almost always at once romantic and bawdy), and unmercifully satiric. The
novel makes no concessions to modern tastes or standards—in life or
literature—and for that reason may appear anachronistically out of place
in contemporary fiction; yet it boasts a pedigree that goes back through
some of the most brilliant writers in Western literature. In a recent essay
Jo Allen Bradham places *Darconville's Cat* in the genre of the academic
novel, but Theroux's novel clearly subsumes that essentially American
tradition into the older tradition of learned wit.[21] It is at once a culmina-
tion of, and a tribute to, a genre whose demands, on writer and reader
alike, are heavy, yet whose rewards often outweigh those from more realistic works. Apropos of which, it might be best to close with Theroux's
own words:

> The "realistic" novel and the way one reports to it is to me a *locus
> molesti*. The threats of the realistic novel, for which I believe I have a
> constitutional disinclination, force me into an anti-world with a fan-
> tasy and bedevilment all its own which refuses (ready?) to "hold a mir-
> ror up to nature." Make nature grovel! Transubstantiate it! Shake your
> multi-colored dreams out of your black disappointing sleep! Will you
> shrink from diversion, whimsy, entertainment, wit? Can you ignore
> the concept of fiction, always erudite, as game, pleasure, hobby, and
> puzzle—a mottage of rich and well-born nouns that can roister with

21 "The American Scholar: From Emerson to Alexander Theroux's *Darconville's
    Cat*," *Critique* 24.4 (Summer 1983): 215–27. Ms. Bradham's conclusion is
    worth quoting: "In any number of ways, Theroux's book concludes a long
    line of academic novels, each of which has diluted the positive image of
    Man Thinking. Since Emerson spent an evening defining and pleading the
    American scholar, hundreds of books have interpreted and reinterpreted that
    scholar. Now the investigation is complete as Theroux, in this archly schol-
    arly book from a decidedly anti-scholarly age, caps a group of works on a
    single subject with such searing finality that nothing more may be said" (226).
    [Theroux later published an essay on the genre: "The Novel of Learning:
    Endangered Species," *Review of Contemporary Fiction* 14.2 (Summer 1994):
    192–98.]

sluttish verbs and prinked-out allusions, snoozy bedfellows all, content and uncomplained of? That's a prose: uncommon quiet dashed with common thunder. We father out our tikes, now coddled with the words of apropositional lullabies, then awakened to the dangers, combustions, and cymbal crashes of Shandean pyrotechnics and goofy but literate words. It is a fool who thinks a smitten adjective or a concerned adverb or an instructive parenthesis impedes the velocity of a sentence. A period does that. Your page is not a linen closet in Miss Pokeberry's Seminary. A great book is no Shaker bedroom. ("Theroux Metaphrastes," 27–28)

Neither, needless to say, is *Darconville's Cat.*

On *An Adultery*

WITH HIS THIRD NOVEL, Alexander Theroux has pulled in the reins a bit on the witty, outlandishly erudite style he employed in *Three Wogs* and the brilliant *Darconville's Cat* to write a more conventional work, yet one that retains the finest features of his earlier style: an unerring instinct for language and a keenly satiric eye for all forms of pretense and folly. *An Adultery* is the confession of a character with just those stylistic qualities who falls in love with a woman who epitomizes pretense and folly; his love for her struggles against his greater love for language, loyalty, and honesty, and the result is one of the most puzzling relationships in recent American fiction.

In the first seven pages Christian Ford, artist-in-residence at a prep school in St. Ives, New Hampshire, meets and begins an affair with a married woman named Farol Colorado. After seven more pages he has seen through most of her pretenses and recognizes her for the ridiculous woman she is, and yet the affair drags on for three years. Throughout the rest of the book Ford catalogues and analyzes her faults with a thoroughness not seen since Marcel trained his sights on Albertine. While Farol betrays her husband, Ford betrays his young girlfriend Marina Falieri, an angel too transcendentally pure for this world. Yet every time he breaks away from Farol he accomplishes work of a much higher caliber than the saccharine portraits he does of Marina.

Chief among his complaints is Farol's language: throughout *An Adultery* she displays a discomfort with language, distrusting its capacity for precision and clarity, and fearful of its ability to expose deception. Ford's commitment to language as a means for analysis clashes with Farol's use of it for obfuscation, and at this level *An Adultery* is a heroic attempt to prove that it is still possible for rigorous thought and incisive language to fight and triumph over the foggy, imprecise language, generalities, and clichés that both Farol and much of the present culture employ as its lingua franca. "Love is not only a talkative passion," he argues. "Language itself can lose chastity and its ambiguity become also depraved, as when on the adulterous tongue two meanings that should remain separate suddenly become coupled. A parody of communication begins to take place."

Theroux's language swells and recedes accordingly. The beginning of the novel is suspiciously flat; the language catches fire only when Ford starts learning of Farol's insincerity, bad manners, and weak-mindedness, provoking sentences of a kind rarely seen in current fiction: aphoristic, colorful with metaphor and allusion, fugally unwinding with a vocabulary rich and strange, yet equally precise. Although the prose is less eccentric, learned, and excessive than in *Darconville's Cat*, Theroux must be ranked with the finest stylists of our day. He is not without humor: Ford's fury with his mistress and her artsy-craftsy world inspires caustic satirical set pieces, burning with Augustan rage at modern manners and nostrums.

An update on earlier classics of adultery, Theroux's novel impugns adulteration of every kind—in love, language, morals, art—and Ford's long and exasperating duet with Farol becomes an attempt to wrestle the numerous adulterations that have debased the quality of modern life. The fight takes its toll: Ford is driven to psychotic extremes in his drive to fathom Farol's equally psychotic iniquities, and Marina is their sacrificial victim. But Ford escapes to tell the tale.

A TEXTUAL NOTE[1]

In the summer of 1987 Theroux kindly sent me bound galleys of *An Adultery* but asked that I read only the final version, "some six or seven crucial pages longer & with some important additions" (letter dated 3 July 1987). For future studies of *An Adultery*, I thought it might be worthwhile to list these additions, for while some are minor, others are indeed crucial and deserve the reader's close attention

Listed below are all substantive additions to the galleys, with longer additions abridged via bracketed ellipses. I have not listed deletions (very few) or corrections of typos and accidentals (unless part of an addition). Page and line numbers refer to the first edition of *An Adultery*, published in October 1987 by the Linden Press, a division of Simon & Schuster.

---

1 This originally followed "Alexander Theroux: An Introduction" but is more appropriate here.

18.18] a case of

20.5] I didn't care. I wanted it that way myself.

21.38] of person who'd bother to find out

22.3] unavoidable

42.27] All the camping, hiking, and outdoor gear didn't suggest adventure to me so much as flight, and I suddenly thought: *travelers have bad marriages.*

51.34] He picks up groceries in the order that they're written on the list [. . .] when he reaches it on his list.

51.39] He goes into a wicked snit.

57.24] What was even more shameless was that the teachers allowed themselves to be co-opted by the school. [. . .] and turned educated people into pensioners and pets.

59.1] There was a mellow beauty about her in which her radiance had the quality of an emotion.

61.20] Marina in a black schoolgirl jumper.

62.28] Love *makes* people profound.

63.4] What about feet? And hands? [. . .] How tall is a person when he sits down?

67.32] in texture lawn furniture webbing

71.29] comparatively

74.20] Was he a king or a cup of custard? [. . .] quite unattractive and even possibly neurotic.

75.13] I felt, while being with both of them, [. . .] while its shadow condensed into mass.

77.17] It's a state that ranks forty-fourth in the nation for punishing drunk drivers.

78.13] elegant Towne Lyne House on beautiful Lake Suntaug [*replaces:* Town Line house

79.20] I kept wondering why [. . .] as less attractive.

84.36] mystery arbors and personalized mugs [. . .] and dried-flower arrangements and

85.21] a dean at St. Ives and

88.13] The construction of it was amazing. [. . .] But I felt uneasy and was anxious only to leave

89.32] two Quelvée landscapes,

95.27] I have a genius for friendship and also a genius for the reverse.

127.12] the happiness of the very person [*replaces:* her happiness]

148.14] Each person in a couple [. . .] I began to feel that way. I thought

163.26] We spent whole afternoons together [. . .] a few blocks from the studio.

163.35] —we came within a biscuit-toss of her—

164.30] "I don't want to leave you anymore." [*replaces:* "I want to be with you."]

166.3] "What do you mean"? [¶] She paused a long time.

167.17] once

167.28] If people with money [. . .] give it a power all its own.

168.3] She expected salvation [. . .] inadequacy or self-defection.

170.4] in her life

173.30] the folds revealing [. . .] Jacques Tissot.

174.23] again one of them—Snow White or Rose Red, I'm not sure— [*replaces:* Lucy]

181.32] —she had a tendency to talk loud when she was either wrong or lying—

182.1] "I loathed the jealousy [. . .] lifting a finger." [*note:* the quotation marks were added by the typesetter in error]

187.9] and *Celine's Dark Cat*

196.20] There is a law that proves it.

201.13] horrible

209.18] actually

211.4] the dwarfed and drunken Monskys, and [*replaces:* the Boustrophedons]

215.25] It wasn't so much a matter of choice.

216.20] to you

223.13] trying to fathom Farol Colorado [*replaces:* fathoming her]

227.1] I was convinced [. . .] the agent of her deliverance.

227.13] I wanted our love to be unconditional [. . .] I asked her if she loved me.

239.34] to

240.15] once

244.28] He was neither king nor custard. [Cf. 74.20 above]

246.39] even

247.14] Sometimes I thought [. . .] between us look ridiculous.

250.5] She knocked on the door, looking bereft and windily indignant, her breast heaving.

252.4] much of

260.29] I was tired of her false promises [. . .] that I *didn't* want.

265.2] Mozart's longest chamber work [. . .] doing a painting in one fast take.

266.14] I've often wished I'd known

267.30] gone [*replaces:* come]

268.5] almost by definition

273.36] any possible infringement by the growing contingent all over the
world, no doubt, desperate to have them [*replaces:* infringement]

279.31] to me our very [*replaces:* our own]

286.10] place

317.19] for the life of me

320.1] The house became the focus [. . .] locked into that house.

330.6] When

338.20] Still I deluded myself. [. . .] very suspicions you fear.

350.24] I wanted to believe [. . .] spirit was still possible.

354.1] I asked her to repeat that. [¶] "Where the rewards are enchanting,"
she said, "the dangers are real."

381.14] Play the "Largo" to *Xerxes* [. . .] softening her words

384.7] I decided to become [*replaces:* I became]

385.34] graduation photo from Harvard Medical School [*replaces:* photo
from medical school]

388.36] It was even more horrible to realize

390.11] I only kept remembering [. . .] strangely pure in feeling.

Finally, it might be worth recording the quotations Theroux inscribed
in the copies he sent me. That for the galleys is a quotation from the
novel itself: "Tomorrow the sun would be lovely with the beauty of day,
& under one aspect or another I knew I'd always had it before me . . ."
(395). The first edition contains a quotation from Wallace Stevens's "The
Common Life": "And a woman without rose and without violet, / The
shadows that are absent from Euclid, / Is not a woman for a man." And
in the copy of the British edition he sent me, Theroux used this quotation from *Faust* (in Kaufmann's translation): "The devils and the demons
have a law; / Where they slipped in, they always must withdraw."

Darconville's Cat Redux

THOUGH OFTEN GROUPED with maximalist, encyclopedic novels because of its elaborate style and range of references, Theroux's novel differs from others of that species (Gaddis's *Recognitions*, Pynchon's *Gravity's Rainbow*) in being the easiest to read. The story is simple, the plot unfolds in linear fashion, and the moral is clear. It's a rare, perhaps unique example of a novel that reads like a best-seller while deploying the kind of literary pyrotechnics associated with rarified postmodern fiction.

Boy meets girl, boy loses girl and vows revenge, then comes to his senses and erects this literary cathedral to unrequited love before romantically dying in Venice. Betrayed by Isabel Rawsthorne, Alaric Darconville devotes himself to the true love of his life, the English language. The language is unusually rich, employs an arsenal of rhetorical devices, and revives words that haven't been used in hundreds of years. And as the dust-jacket boasts, "Its chapters embody a multiplicity of narrative forms, including a diary, a formal oration, an abecedarium, a sermon, a litany, a blank-verse play, poems, essays, parodies, and fables." Playing on a popular phrase, the chapter entitled "What Is One Picture Worth?" contains exactly one thousand words. The black page of grief from *Tristram Shandy* is here, and enough literary allusions to keep an annotator occupied for years tracking them down. It's by turns funny and sad, satiric and mournful.

It's a performance piece, to be sure, taking full advantage of "the opportunity for display that [novels] offered a good mind," as the Canon in *Don Quixote* says, "providing a broad and spacious field where one's pen could write unhindered. . . ." But Theroux's lavish style and far-flung allusions are functional as well: Darconville is well-read, richly imaginative, and individualistic, whereas the girl he falls for . . . isn't. A simple soul who wants to play it safe and consequently dumps Darconville for a local boy, Isabel's plain language and lack of imagination is stylistically at odds with the magniloquent language that surrounds her. Theroux shows that style is substance; he's got it, she doesn't, and 100 pages into this 700-page novel, the reader knows they have no future, though Darconville won't admit it for hundreds of pages, hoping his powerful imagination can trump unimaginative reality. Darconville's language swells and his rhetorical feats grow more outlandish as he resists that conclusion, resulting in some stunning set-pieces, such as a travelogue of imaginary places and an unholy litany of malevolent women. When he realizes all his imagination and rhetoric still can't change the world, he sickens and dies, right after he finishes penning this work.

It's a pattern Theroux would follow in his two subsequent novels, *An Adultery* (1987) and *Laura Warholic* (2007): a sensitive, overeducated man falls for an insensitive, undereducated woman and suffers as a result. But neither reaches the linguistic heights of *Darconville's Cat*, or matches its range of registers, from whimsy to intellection, from broad satire to targeted social criticism. Out of print for years, it deserves to be tracked down by any reader interested in love, language, and the complex relationship between the two.

The Original of Laura

The Making and Unmaking of *Laura Warholic*

> You have to know when to stop, understand
> when the delivery has been made.
> — Alexander Theroux[1]

ALEXANDER THEROUX reviewed Vladimir Nabokov's posthumous novel *The Original of Laura* in the *Wall Street Journal* in November 2009, two years after publishing a novel about a different Laura. Nabokov never finished his, but Theroux managed to complete his long novel over a ten-year period. Nabokov's Laura was fictitious, while Theroux's was inspired by a very real woman named Laura.

Laura Warholic; or, The Sexual Intellectual (2007) was provoked— "inspired" is too benign—by a relationship Theroux had between 1995 and 1997 with a young woman named Laura Markley. It follows the same pattern as his two previous novels, in which an intellectual is mismatched with a dullard: *Darconville's Cat* (1981) was instigated by his breakup with a young woman named Linda Ann Burton, and *An Adultery* (1987) by his affair with a woman closer to his own age named Dale Atkins. Each began as an act of revenge—a topic on which Theroux has often written (see his essay of that title and the poem "The Revenge of Art")[2]—first against a particular woman, then against her gender as a whole, and ultimately against the culture she epitomizes. They are

---

1 "*Peanuts*: The Sagacity of Common Sense," in Charles Schultz, *Peanuts Every Sunday*, vol. 5: 1971–1975 (Seattle: Fantagraphics Books, 2017), 6.

2 "Revenge" appeared in *Harper's*, October 1982, 26–31, and the poem on p. 313 of Theroux's *Collected Poems* (Seattle: Fantagraphics Books, 2015), hereafter abbreviated *CP*. "Prospero is Hamlet who gets his revenge through art," avers protagonist Eugene Eyestones on p. 199 of *Laura Warholic* (Seattle: Fantagraphics Books, 2007), abbreviated *LW* henceforth.

satiric works of cultural criticism, with their faulty female antagonists acting as lightning rods for Theroux's thundering grievances.

Theroux hadn't written much fiction after the publication of *An Adultery*. He began but abandoned a book about Amelia Earhart, and instead spent most of his time from 1987 onward writing nonfiction: several essays on painters for *Art & Antiques*, numerous poems and book reviews, nearly a dozen essays for the *San Diego Reader*, and two books on color: *The Primary Colors* (1994) and *The Secondary Colors* (1996).[3] The latter was completed in 1995 during his time with Laura Markley, an artist/writer who furnishes one of the book's two epigraphs ("Aren't orange, purple, and green like costumes made of felt, *Munchkin* colors?"). Their relationship was apparently in trouble by the time *The Secondary Colors* appeared the following spring, and by 1997 it was over.[4] Thereabouts Theroux began writing *Laura Warholic*, completing a 916-page draft near the end of 2000.[5]

Needing a few details in March 1998 for his growing novel, Theroux contacted Laura's former boyfriend, writer/journalist Alexander Laurence, a contributing editor at *Cups: A Café Journal* (later subtitled *The Café Culture Magazine*).[6] A fan of his, Laurence had published Theroux's poem "The Many and the One" (CP 13) in the September 1994 issue of *Cups*, as well as an interview with him in the February 1995 issue, just about the time Theroux began his relationship with Laura. Laurence had met Laura Markley in San Francisco in 1991 and lived with her from 1992 until January 1995, when she moved back to the Boston area where her family lived.

Thirty-one when she met Theroux (but 35/36 in the novel, where Eu-

---

3 He went on to compile two similar books on black and white, which remain unpublished.

4 Theroux's 1998 poem "The Gospel According to Laura Sparkley" (see note 10) indicates the relationship lasted three years.

5 If set in the same format as the 878-page book published seven years later, the first draft version would be around 700 pages. (Except for the bound galleys and published book, all such page-counts are ballpark approximations.)

6 The contact is fictionalized on *LW* 291–92. In August 2018 Laurence contacted me—I had known him slightly since the 1990s—to give me his reaction to *Laura Warholic*, which he had finally read, though he had known about it for years. Shortly after I purchased a cache of Theroux-related materials from him, on which this essay draws, as well as on some phone conversations and two earlier email exchanges between us from 2005 and 2008. For more on Laurence, see his Wikipedia page as well as his website, The Portable Infinite, at http://portable-infinite.blogspot.com/, especially the page on *Cups* at http://portable-infinite.blogspot.com/2011/08/cups-magazine-1991-1999.html.

gene is 40-something),[7] Markley was a competent writer and Parsons-educated artist—I've seen some of her writings and a sketchbook of hers—and in photographs doesn't at all resemble the slatternly beanpole Laura Warholic. She had learned of Theroux from reading Laurence's interview with him and reading *An Adultery* at his suggestion. Jealous of all the women writers he knew (cf. bottom of *LW* 44), she stole Theroux's address from Laurence and decided to write him to make Laurence jealous. She enclosed a photograph, which he found "winsome" when he wrote back (a word never used of her in the novel). Laurence understands that Theroux became her boyfriend, not her Platonic caretaker (as in the novel), and that *she* ended the relationship, not he. (If so, *LW* 289–91 may be a veiled account of how the Theroux/Markley relationship really ended, and of Theroux's motive for writing the novel.) When Laurence visited Laura in Boston in March 1997, she told him "she was afraid of him and wanted to get a restraining order."[8]

From Laura Theroux had learned some unflattering things about Laurence—which first took the form of two nasty poems, "Alexander Cups" and "Larry Tucker" (both *CP* 110)—and which he later used in his portrayal of Minot ("Mickey") Warholic, Laura's ex-husband and the editor of what was originally called *Bowls* (changed to *Quink* for the published book).[9] In 1998 Laurence was living in Brooklyn, where Theroux sent him eight venomous, hate-spewing poems about Laura.[10] He fol-

---

7 Eugene's age is deliberately vague in the published version, reflecting Theroux's indecision: the first draft gives his age as 41 (p. 109a), but the four-page précis that accompanied it states he's 50.

8 Email to me dated 26 August 2018. In a follow-up email later the same day, he added: "I don't think they were ever on good terms. She didn't want me talking to him, and I don't think either of us have spoken to him for 20 years. The last time I spoke with Laura, she had no interest in reading the book."

9 "Alexander Cups" was entitled "Alexander Laurence" in manuscript, and Lawrence Tucker is Laurence's real name; he adopted the pseudonym in 1987 when he began publishing. *Bowls* is an obvious play on *Cups*, but *Quink* is a less obvious variety of fountain pen ink, mentioned near the top of *LW* 413. Though named after *Cups*, the magazine in *LW* more closely resembles the *San Diego Reader*; Theroux lived in San Diego for a while in 1995 and published nearly a dozen essays in the magazine between 1995 and 1997.

10 They were all eventually published in Theroux's *Collected Poems*: "Scarecrow" (182–83), "Webs" (189–90), "Ratios" (190–91), "Laura Sparkley Takes Her Sketchpad to a Café" (191–94), "Laura" (194), "What Rhymes with Horror" (194–98), "Nutcracker" (1999), and "The Gospel According to Laura Sparkley" (199–201). A ninth, "Anthropophobe Beach," appears on pp. 201–2. In original versions, "Sparkley" read "Markley." Eugene unaccountably calls Laura "Sparkley" on page 423 of the novel, but the only appearance of her

lowed those with a few letters and postcards asking Laurence for details
on the Boston rock scene, specifically about Laura's obsession with Jeff
"Monoman" Conolly, the organist-singer of a garage-rock band called
the Lyres.[11] Since Laurence had resumed contact with Laura by that
time, Theroux asked him to probe her on the matter. (It's clear from the
letter that Theroux was unfamiliar with the band, though he later famil-
iarized himself with the Lyres' oeuvre.) Conolly retained his own name
in the novel—he's called Jeff throughout, "Stereoman" in a few places,
and even Scooter Conolly on p. 291–92, though Jeff Bummely (originally
Croakley) on p. 720—but his band was ignominiously renamed the Craven Slucks.[12] There is however, a hand-tipping reference on p. 726 to
"the Liars" (Lyres in manuscript), "a local rock group still around from
the Eighties, long past it, whose reputation never quite reached beyond
the boundaries of Route 128." They perform in the raucous chapter that
follows, "The Sewing Circle."

A month later, on 21 April 1998, Theroux sent Laurence a postcard
saying he now had all the information he needed and to watch for *Laura
Warholic* around "Xmas or early 1999—thunder and lightning!"[13] In July
1998 there was an ugly letter exchange between the two regarding some
emails of Laura's that ended their relationship, resulting in Theroux's
relentlessly insulting characterization of Minot Warholic.

When Laurence finally read the novel in 2018, he recognized some of
the others caricatured in the novel: Warholic's mistresses Muskrat and
Squishy are modeled on Laurence's friends Otter (Laura Campbell) and
Squishy (Sarah Davison), San Francisco performance artists who did
indeed "wear vampire teeth and dance in black gauze masks and hiss like

---

real name is a ludicrous reference to the 1960s singing group the Markleys
(408)—probably one of Bob Markley's projects—though he gets close when
Eugene calls her "Laura Malarkey" (591). Also note Eugene and Laura's brief
stopover in Markleeville, California (437), a real town, and the reference to
Dean Markley guitar strings (772). Theroux plants these sorts of clues in
many of his writings. Markley is also mentioned in Theroux's *Strange Case
of Edward Gorey*: he took her once to meet the artist/author, who rudely
ignored her (Seattle: Fantagraphics, 2011, 136).

11 Founded in 1979, the Lyres were active until the early 1990s, when Laura
Markley became enamored of Conolly. They went through a dormant period
until 1999, and have played sporadically ever since.

12 Apparently named after Mike Kuchar's short underground film *The Craven
Sluck* (1967). Theroux alludes to Kuchar's camp *chef-d'œuvre Sins of the
Fleshapoids* (1965) in his early story "Herbert Head, Gent."

13 The contributor's note Theroux furnished to the fall 1999 issue of *The Recorder* reads: "His new novel, *Laura Warholic*, will be published in 2000."

indigo snakes" (33);[14] Laura's frenemy Gayle Bagle (279, 367, 433) takes her name from Gail Eigl, a high-school teacher Laurence also knew in San Francisco. (Theroux learned of these three women from Markley; he never met them.) Laura's black friend Lamont was named Andrew Waterman; and Little Bob Merkle reminded him of boxer/writer Robert Anasi. Laurence suspected that the baker/stripper Rapunzel Wisht was inspired by Jeff Conolly's wife Joan (named in full on 300), and that Jim and Judith San Diego were based on Larry and Sinda McCaffery, whom Theroux had met when he was writing for the *San Diego Reader*, which I find unlikely.[15]

Though Theroux's characters in this and his other novels are based on real people, they are closer to caricatures rather than faithful portraits. Theroux uses real people as tailors' dummies on which to drape his unfashionable views and lavish rhetorical accessories; they are barely recognizable after he's through with them, which is as it should be: his novels are fiction, not autobiography, and he uses poetic license as a license to kill. The longer he worked on *Laura Warholic*, the less it became a roman à clef about his relationship with a real person and more an encyclopedic novel about an idealistic but flawed eccentric trying to help an unidealistic, even more flawed Gen Xer, both "continuously pissed off at the world" (368), with tragic results.

His mannequins in place, Theroux began dressing them, beginning with himself. Eugene Eyestones physically resembles his maker (6) and certainly shares most of his opinions and attitudes, his likes and dislikes, but otherwise is an idealized self-portrait displaying his finest as well as "fuddy-duddyish" (402) qualities in their best light. He allows Laura to enumerate his eccentricities during a three-page tirade (697–99),[16] but he siphoned off his darker qualities into the bitter, blasphemous Paul Ratnaster and the fastidious, anti-Semitic Discknickers, ventriloquist's dummies through whom Theroux could vent his most extreme views. Eyestones differs in superficial ways from his author: he is a dozen or more years younger than Theroux was at the time—he turned 56 in August of 1995—an excellent violinist, and fought in Vietnam, which Ther-

---

14 Otter stars in Chris Fiore's documentary *Trip and Go Naked* (1994). See https://vimeo.com/136777006.

15 McCaffery was an early admirer of *Darconville's Cat* and ranked it #84 on his list of "The 20th Century's Greatest Hits: 100 English-Language Books of Fiction" (*American Book* Review, 1999), writing, "Theroux uses love the way Melville used his white whale—a metaphor to be exhausted, improvised, played with, and otherwise endlessly explored until it eventually reveals the utter inexhaustibility and mystery of life itself."

16 Theroux admitted in an email that these are *his* faults (4 April 2019).

oux was smart enough to avoid. It's worth noting that the author's photo the 68-year-old Theroux supplied for the dust-jacket was taken when he was in his early thirties: Eugene Eyestones is his younger, saintly alter ego, scrubbed of all the sins alleged against him by people over the years.

Theroux focused on his good qualities in his characterization of Eyestones, but he focused solely on the bad qualities of the other real people who populate his novel, in the spirit of Laura justifying the notebook she keeps: "I write down people's worst faults so I'll never forget their cruelty" (110). The fictional Laura resembles her original in some particulars: her art-school training, her 244 River Street address in Cambridge, her magenta-dyed hair, an abortion in the past ("several" in the novel [47]), a mentally ill sister ("three" in the novel [95]), her foreign travels and musical tastes, but not much otherwise. In a January 2008 email to me, Laurence said Theroux's version of her is "sort of a cartoon. Laura would say and do some of those things, but half of it doesn't seem like her at all. The real Laura was not that promiscuous. She usually went out with one guy at a time. . . . She would make a bunch of things up [which Theroux apparently took literally]. . . . It's sad that he bought into the whole story, because it's not worth telling. It's like many young girls today who are vain enough to be a groupie with a writer or novelist, because they think that the writer will write something about them."[17] This is verified on p. 343 of the novel: "Popping her eyes, Laura smiled her gummy smile. 'Maybe you'll write a book about me, E^2, and I'll be memorialized for life.'" (Ladies, be careful what you wish for.) Theroux gave the original Laura such a grotesque makeover that Eugene comes to regard her as "Lilith and all prehensile night-flying demons who coursed through the world seeking to enter the souls of men . . ." (88). Her transmogrification is pushed to outlandish, mythic, admittedly comic extremes: "She was in her comic extreme as a single object of invincible but insistent shadeless refusal almost a parody of weird Kundry, that tempting sextress referred to by Klingsor as the Nameless, the Primeval Demon, Rose of Hell, Herodias, his anima, his dark and lunar side, an endless and relentless shadow, crossbraced and inevitable and unquiet" (90).[18] Theroux

17 He had read the short selection from the novel that appeared in *Conjunctions* in 2000 (see note 21), but not the entire novel until 2018.

18 This is adapted from the beginning of act 2 of Wagner's *Parsifal*, when the magician Klingsor "*seats himself again before his magic mirror and calls with mysterious gestures into the depths:* "Come up! Come up! To me! / Your master calls you, nameless one, / primeval witch, rose of hell! / You were Herodias, and what else?" Laura is also compared to Kundry on p. 116, with Eugene in the role of the pure Christian knight: "her seduction strategy [was] specifically calibrated more to Parsifal's innocence than to his stubborn altru-

used Laura Markley the same way that Eugene Eyestones used Laura Warholic for his magazine columns, as he realizes near the end of the novel: "'I remade her on the page, tooled her for my own use, tailored her, cut wafers out of the killed steel of her being as if segments of her heart.' . . . If I used Laura, he thought, I abused her" (838).

Nor does Alexander Laurence much resemble Minot Warholic.[19] The character is a Yiddish-spouting Jewish stereotype in "his late forties" (10), while Laurence was not Jewish and only 31 in 1995 (six months older than Laura; both were born in 1964). Not only did Theroux ludicrously exaggerate Laurence's physical appearance, but he added three more characters—Larry Clucker, Lumpkin (spelled Larry Tucker and Laurence, respectively, in the first draft), and a huge gay man named Larry—in order to fling further insults at him. While Theroux does repeat some of the unflattering things about Laurence that Laura told him, the result is a gross exaggeration rather than a faithful portrait. In fact, Minot Warholic owes as much to Theroux's novelist brother Paul, represented in *Laura Warholic* by Eugene's brother Marysas (sic).[20] "In his awfulness, to Eugene, he was Marsyas Eyestones come alive—Eugene often confused his boss with his own brother" (477). Minot's practice of immediately reimbursing people (35) and the excuse he offers married women for a tryst (43, with further examples in the draft version) are repeated in Alexander's short story about Paul entitled "Envenoming Junior."[21]

Again, to state the obvious, Theroux was writing a novel, not a tell-all memoir, and like most authors he adapted certain aspects of real people to his aesthetic needs. He doesn't hold up a mirror to society, as Stendhal suggests, but instead turns a funhouse mirror on his originals and describes the comically distorted results.[22] It's similar to the approach

---

ism." There are further references to Kundry and Parsifal on pp. 269, 339, 552, and 751, all added later to the first draft version.

19 My old copy of *Webster's Biographical Dictionary* (1980) says this uncommon prename is pronounced MY-nut; I don't know why Theroux chose it. Warholic of course evokes Andy Warhol (born Warhola), the subject of a dismissive sonnet of Theroux's (*CP* 550). Warholic is a Polish version of Warhol, and refers to Markley's Polish heritage on her mother's side (per Laurence).

20 A typo for Marsyas, a Greek mythological figure reviled for his hubris, and once bested in a music competition by Apollo. The name is spelled correctly only twice.

21 Written in 2001, just as Theroux began expanding his first draft of *Laura Warholic*.

22 Theroux told interviewer Sean P. Carroll of *Bookslut* that "*Laura Warholic* is meant to be comic," and complained that some reviewers didn't grasp that. He is not to be confused with the Sean Carroll of Theroux's comic poem

taken by certain modern artists Theroux admires, such as Francis Bacon—whose grotesque *Isabel Rawsthorne* (which furnished the name of the female lead in *Darconville's Cat*) barely resembles his real-life model—or William Allik and Rodion Tikhomirov, "young brilliant painters in their thirties who painted faces like sinister viruses, grotesque, tormented, and desperate" (*LW* 64–65). His novels are very autobiographical, but not in the manner of Jack Kerouac, whose characters are indistinguishable from their real-life counterparts.

Outside the Laurence/Markley circle and his brother Paul, there are other characters in *Laura Warholic* whose originals can be detected, especially by way of the first draft. There are demeaning, score-settling references to Theroux's family and nephews, to ex-girlfriends, to agents who failed him, and to what sounds like a number of local enemies. A lesbian journalist at *Quink* nicknamed The Krauthammer obviously takes her name from the late conservative pundit Charles Krauthammer. Another staffer at *Quink*, the gay movie critic R. Bangs Chasuble, who walks "like a lame duck" (608), was originally called Wronarski, a swipe at straight John Wronoski, owner of Lame Duck Books/Base Canard Press, who published a limited edition of Theroux's story *Watergraphs* in 1994, which Theroux felt he mishandled.[23] But Chasuble is a witty, sympathetic character, another example of how Theroux initially based a character on someone real, with malice aforethought, but then fictionalized the original beyond recognition. In some cases, however, a character was not fictionalized at all and was easily, even libelously identifiable—though sometimes Theroux uses a real name in a first draft with the intention of changing it later. For example, the character named Levinger on page 55 was based on a supportive critic whom Theroux took a dislike to, for some reason. I urged him not to use the critic's real name, and suggested one that was similar to it. Theroux instead changed it to Radziewicz for the bound galleys, then to Levinger for the published book.[24] I also encouraged him to change the real names of some of his ex-girlfriends, which he did in a hit-and-miss fashion.

Like "some malevolent Rumpelstiltskin spinning straw into gold"

"Lit'ry Boston" (*CP* 75–78).

23 Lame Duck was located in the Jamaica Plain neighborhood of Boston, which explains the reference to the rare-book dealer on pp. 199–200 who wants to publish Eugene's controversial essay as a book. There's another insulting reference to Lame Duck on p. 559. Theroux first changed Wronarski to Paul Puck before settling on R. Bangs Chasuble.

24 Theroux used the name Radziewicz instead for one of Laura's mother's husbands (108).

(848), Theroux turned real-life people and situations into art—a long but taut novel that, had it been published by a New York house in 2001 as he had hoped, would have been much better received than the longer, bloated one a Seattle publisher brought out six years later.

❋

In 2001, Theroux began seeking a publisher for his new novel. After placing two selections from it in Bradford Morrow's *Conjunctions*,[25] he sent the manuscript to agent Melanie Jackson (aka Mrs. Thomas Pynchon), but she didn't think much of the novel: "Her singular and idle response to the book was that the matters of love and sex in the book were 'ordinary,'" he later told an interviewer; "she mailed it back to me without so much as a by-your-leave."[26] In one of the many additions to the novel Theroux would make over the next six years, he writes that one of the songs Laura particularly liked was "Mrs. Pynchon and the Black Agents with their big hit, 'I Don't Lift a Fucking Finger'" (560).[27] Theroux tried and failed to find other agents, and I submitted the manuscript on his behalf to a few publishing professionals in the summer of 2002—Gerald Howard at Broadway Books (part of Bantam Doubleday Dell) and Michael Pietsch at Little, Brown—but neither wanted it. His postcard to me of 28 November 2003 was typical of the responses he got elsewhere: "Not a *word* from Overlook . . ." He published a third selection from the novel in Richard Peabody's *Gargoyle* in September 2003 (chap. XX), the last excerpt to appear until the book's publication.

During this period Theroux continued to revise and expand his novel, as he would until the time it went to the printers. One of his additions expresses his frustration at these early rejections; describing the hate-filled Ratnaster, Theroux writes:

25 "Laura Warholic" (the original version of chapter 36) in *Conjunctions* 34 (June 2000): 107–19, and "Queen Gloriana's Revenge" (chapter 26) in *Conjunctions* 36 (June 2001): 221–25.

26 Paul Maliszewski, "The Back of Beyond: An Interview with Alexander Theroux," *Rain Taxi* Online Edition, Winter 2012/2013.

27 She is the subject of his poem "Melanie *et Cie*" (*Collected Poems*, 395–96). Theroux's anger extended to Mr. Pynchon, for among the trashy novels in Laura's mother's bookcase is *Gravity's Rainbow* (106), which Theroux elsewhere has called needlessly difficult. When I copyedited the novel in 2005, I pointed out how unrealistic it was to include that novel there—a woman like Mrs. Shqumb would never own such a book—but he kept it in, one of many instances where he allowed animosity to override aesthetics (consistent characterization, in this instance).

Much of his anarchy paraphrased a deep anger long burning in him for having once written a masterpiece of [a] novel, later published to high acclaim, that had been notoriously mishandled for years by two perfectly stupid literary agents, trollops of Gothic ignorance, and then a series of bird-witted editors at Farrar Straus & Giroux, Little, Brown, Doubleday, and especially at Perseus, where he dealt with one trumpeting drudge wasting his time who actually belonged to sub-zoology.

That's from the 2005 version of the manuscript (cf. *LW* 25–26; see also p. 311 for more on "his brilliant novel"), by which time he had finally found a publisher.

Gary Groth, founder and editor of Fantagraphics Books, met Theroux in the 1990s and then published two slim books by him: one on Al Capp in 1999, and another on Theroux's neighbor Edward Gorey in 2000 (with a revised version following in May 2002).[28] Conveying his problems with finding a mainstream publisher, Theroux asked him if he knew a publisher who would consider it. In an email to me dated 2 October 2018, Groth explained what happened next:

> I told him we were distributed by W.W. Norton and that I could inquire there and perhaps find any editor willing to read it. I went too some trouble to find an editor who was indeed willing to read it; excited by this, I called Alex and told him, and his reaction was this: "Is he serious? Is he a serious reader? I don't want someone who isn't serious reading my manuscript." What kind of question was that? How the fuck would I know if he was "serious" by Alex's standards? He was one editor at a major publisher willing to consider his manuscript. Naturally, that went nowhere and I thought, what the hell, I love his writing, and I've always wanted to publish lit fiction, so I offered to publish it.

To sweeten the deal and save several thousand dollars, Theroux told him he knew someone willing to copyedit the long novel gratis. Theroux had

---

28 See Theroux's untitled statement in the Fantagraphics retrospective *We Told You So: Comics as Art*, ed. Tom Spurgeon with Michael Dean (Seattle: Fantagraphics Books, 2016), 585. An expanded version of the Gorey book—formless but informative—was published in 2011, and is mentioned often in Mark Dery's *Born to Be Posthumous: The Eccentric Life and Mysterious Genius of Edward Gorey* (NY: Little, Brown, 2018).

once complained to me that a magazine editor once rejected an essay of his because he didn't want to have to copyedit the reference-heavy piece, so I told Alex that if he were ever in that situation again, I would do it for free. (I had spent eight years as a copyeditor at the *Review of Contemporary Fiction*/Dalkey Archive Press, where I published Theroux's *The Lollipop Trollops and Other Poems* and edited a special issue of *RCF* on him in 1991–92.) Groth called me one night in spring 2005 to make sure my pro bono copyediting offer was still good, and came to a verbal agreement with Theroux. (Theroux was sent a contract in October 2006 stipulating a $15,000.00 advance, but put off signing it until 2007, demanding a royalty rate that only the biggest of bestselling authors get. Fantagraphics lost money on the book.)

Thereafter Groth stayed out of the editorial process, aside from some proofreading notes on the first 200 pages of the bound galley, which suited Theroux fine. As he told Calvin Reid of *Publishers Weekly* in 2006, "I've had New York publishers look at my books and ask, 'Can you cut 200 pages?' I ask them, 'Which 200?' I hate the business side of publishing."[29] When the book was finally published, Theroux told literary critic Anthony Miller of the trouble he had had finding a publisher and his relief at finding one who would leave his editorial hands off it:

> "I have no agent. I never really could get in touch with one," he tells me. "I'd sent my long novel to a bunch of New York publishers. Two returned it virtually unread. Another complained literary novels don't sell. One was worrying about the cost of paper. A publisher in Cambridge, Massachusetts, found the novel too controversial, a fat, swithering neutral who refused to send my full typescript back and still has it. . . . Fantagraphics alone was willing to publish the full manuscript without carping or cozy abridgements."[30]

By the time the book went into production in 2005, the manuscript had grown by around 200 pages—the equivalent of roughly 90 typeset pages, and would grow by another 90 pages over the next two years. Before I describe the nature of those additions, let me enumerate the stages the manuscript went through:[31]

29 "Theroux Goes Indie," *Publishers Weekly*, 2 October 2006, 24.

30 "The Satirical Intellectual: Alexander Theroux on the paradoxes of love and the importance of plenitude and redemption," *Los Angeles City Beat*, 15–21 November 2007, https://web.archive.org/web/20080120142328/http://www.lacitybeat.com/cms/story/detail/the_satirical_intellectual/36/

31 All of this material is currently in my possession but eventually will be placed

1. First draft version, dated 2000 on the final page. Printed out on Alex's word processor—described in the draft as "an old putty-colored Dec-mate I computer with exterior disk-drives which jumped to a hum like a vacuum-cleaner whenever he booted it up with his out-of-date eight-inch diskettes, the size of barn-shingles" (84–85, replaced by "an old typewriter" in *LW* 64)—and hand-numbered in the upper-right corners. The final page is numbered 916, but the page count is closer to 920 because of the occasional insert (e.g., 68a, 534a, never more than a page) and one deletion (no p. 180). This is the version sent to agents and publishers (and to me) in 2001–2, and was accompanied by a photocopy of his desired cover art and a four-page "precy" introducing the work as "an encyclopedic novel on the nature of modern love and sex."

2. Submission manuscript to Fantagraphics, dated 2005. The last page is likewise numbered 916, but this version has around 200 pages of inserts. Since Theroux's diskettes were incompatible with Fantagraphics' systems, they scanned the manuscript with an early optical character recognition program that wasn't very efficient (e.g., "willing" came out "VIlm8"), and sent the garbled results to me on several compact discs.[32]

3. First copyedited version, created in summer and fall of 2005, and sent to Theroux in mid-October. I copyedited it onscreen while repairing the Fantagraphics scans, which were so bad in places I wish I had simply typed the whole manuscript from scratch. (They also forwarded to me revisions that Theroux was sending to them, for some reason, rather than to me. Throughout this process, I must say, Theroux was very sympathetic to my plight.) To save space, I printed it out on legal-sized paper with 1.5 line spacing, amounting to 556 pages. Theroux hated the look of it: "I pray the novel isn't published in such a long-framed format, as the book becomes even harder to take with sheets of pages coming at you in such big attacking phalanxes" (letter dated 26 November 2005). I explained the idea was to get him to look at his overly familiar pages with a fresh eye, the better to spot errors, overly long paragraphs, and so on.

---

at a research library.

32 As I set to work on them, Theroux married painter Sarah Son on 16 July 2005 at the Our Lady of Hope Chapel near his residence in West Barnstable, Massachusetts. Shortly after he added the dedication page to the manuscript; "*ab imo pectore*" means "from the bottom of my heart," and is attributed to Julius Caesar.

4. First revised version, incorporating Theroux's corrections (and additions—always additions, rarely deletions), dated 5 December 2005, which I again printed out and mailed to him—Theroux didn't have email—along with his marked-up copy of #3. I emailed it to Fantagraphics as well, thinking that my part of the job was over and that Fantagraphics would take it from there, which caused Theroux some alarm since he felt much work was still needed and he couldn't trust the staff at Fantagraphics to make all the necessary changes. (I was also growing exasperated that Theroux seemed more concerned with adding more material, most of it superfluous in my opinion, than with finessing what he had.) I also sent Fantagraphics catalog copy for the book, which was used, slightly revised, for the back cover of the bound galley (#6) and for the dust-jacket copy of the finished book.

5. Second revised version, produced August 2006, incorporating Theroux's revisions sent to me and to Fantagraphics (handled by Kristy Valenti, who input them into the file I had sent in December) between late December 2005 and July 2006—23,000 words longer than #4.

6. Bound galleys, 824 pages, produced from #5 in September 2006 and sent out to reviewers, with an announced publication date of 15 April 2007. (Additional copies of galleys were produced in November.) It contains numerous errors and even some formatting glitches left over from the original scans. Theroux wrote me: "It is almost heart-stopping to think that these will be given to a list of well-known writers for comment. I cringe" (27 September 2006). I hand-corrected a copy of it from September to October 2006, then sent it to Theroux, who revised it from October to December 2006, and sent it to Fantagraphics, where Kristy Valenti and Ilse Driggs dutifully inputted all the corrections, then sent the galley back to me to check against the new electronic file (and to add any new material not yet entered). Meanwhile, Theroux continued to send insertions to both Fantagraphics and me, and was often in the dark as to whether they were made. At this point, publisher, author, and copyeditor were all exasperated and on edge.[33]

33 And not for the first time. In an essay defending his alleged plagiary in *The Primary Colors* (1994), Theroux wrote: "in the period before final galleys, and much to the great grief of my editor at Holt [Allen Peacock], I made repeated additions and emendations" ("Hateful, Hurtful and Hellish," *San Diego Reader*, 1 June 1995. In an email to me (22 October 2018), Peacock added: "he really could be terribly difficult on matters large and small. Last minute manuscript alterations, yes. Pretty darn fussy on jacket art and other

7. Third revised version, a typescript of 724 8½ x 11 pages completed 26 December 2006, incorporating all the corrections and additions made to the bound galley, as well as the large number of corrections and changes Theroux had mailed me between August and December (and/or mailed to Fantagraphics, which forwarded them to me). At that point, when the text stood at a little over 329,000 words, I told the author and publisher I couldn't take it anymore, convinced Theroux was making his novel worse, not better. (Plus I had interrupted the writing of a book of my own to take on what I assumed would be a two-month project, which by that time had spread over a year and a half.)

8. Finished book (6500 copies) published November 2007, 878 pages (i.e., 54 pages longer than the bound galley of a year earlier), incorporating further changes Theroux had sent directly to Fantagraphics between January and summer 2007, inserted without copyediting (and often without accuracy) by staff members. Most of the novel's nearly 200 typos and typesetting glitches originate from this period. Though copies were available in November, the books didn't reach some stores (the Borders chain, for example) until the week after Christmas, missing the all-important holiday buying season because of Theroux's endless expansion.

Theroux's revisions and additions from 2000–2007 fall into four categories. The first and only beneficial one consists of word changes and improvements in diction. For example, the first draft's "He had such odd thoughts about himself" became "He harbored such renegade thoughts about himself" (689), replacing two bland words with stronger ones. "I seem to recall" is sharp-focused to "I distinctly recall" (293). In other cases, skeletal sentences were fleshed out with details: "It was a drab neighborhood" became "It was an area of drab old wooden three-deckers crowded into a neighborhood of low-income housing with punch windows" (63). There are hundreds of small improvements like these. He also made a few global changes: *Cups* to *Quink*, Nova Scotia to Newfoundland as Mrs. Shqumb's final destination, and *Nemesis 4: Cry of Angels* (aka *Death Angel*, 1996) to *The Night Porter* (1974) as Laura's favorite movie.

He also made Eugene more complicit in their toxic relationship. To

---

design details. (The art director at S&S once threw jacket comp at my head Odd Job style when I rejected a fifth iteration on his behalf.)" Peacock edited Theroux's *An Adultery* for Simon & Schuster; for a tabulation of all the additions Theroux made to the bound galleys of that novel, see pp. 53–56 above.

the sentence that ends ". . . she was neither honest nor committed to him or in fact to anything. Not even to herself," Theroux added: "And he was no better. To whom however was he himself honest? Committed?" (491). Whether this was because Theroux had softened his attitude toward Laura Markley over the years, or because he wanted to complicate their relationship, this is to the good, though the large number of such additions reminded me of the endless ruminations of Marcel over Albertine in the later volumes of *In Search of Lost Time*, for me the most tedious sections of Proust's great novel. Theroux removed from the first draft nearly every reference to Eugene and Laura's sexual relations, jettisoning the autobiographical to heighten the novel's theological contrast between chastity and promiscuity, between *agape* and *eros*. As previously noted, he also replaced many real names with invented ones, less to avoid possible legal repercussions than to establish that these are literary characters with qualities and personalities of their own, often in stark contrast to their originals. (I've met John Wronoski, for example, and he has zero in common with Chasuble.) The outlandish names he chose (Ratnaster, Discknickers, Gnorm, Mutrux, Duxbak) heighten their fictitiousness.[34] All to the good, indicating that he was aestheticizing his raw materials, which became less of a concern later on.

Similarly, Theroux rethought and revised some of the personal attacks against his extended family. He juggled some insulting references to his brother Paul (deleting some, adding others), and deleted one particularly scabrous reference to his nephews Louis and Marcel, though in one instance he merely switched generations. In chapter XXXI, Eugene and Laura duck into a Los Angeles bookstore where "a tallish, spotty-faced, middle-aged novelist with a British accent was giving a diffident reading from his new book that relied as to both title and theme on Sherlock Holmes" (473; cf. 132–33, an earlier reference to the same novel). This would be Marcel Theroux's *The Confessions of Mycroft Holmes: A Paper Chase* (2001), featuring a "quintessential eccentric uncle" based on Alexander that so infuriated him that he scrapped his original account of a reading by Paul so that he could kill off Marcel on the page.

The second category of changes, unfortunately, consists of excessive, unnecessary verbiage at the sentence and paragraph level. "He had not seen her since Thanksgiving" became "He reflected that he had not in fact seen her since Thanksgiving" (855) inserting the very words that any editor would instinctively delete. Originally noting that Marilyn Monroe "was entombed in her favorite green Pucci dress," Theroux unnecessar-

---

34 Duxbak's first name is Datus in the original—a rare Latin prename meaning "act of giving"—but it doesn't appear in the published book.

ily added "entombed at death" (40)—when else would a person be entombed? After the bound galleys were produced, in a paragraph introducing Jane Austen as a *novelist*, Theroux felt compelled to change "wrote in
Mansfield Park" to "wrote in her novel, *Mansfield Park*," which not only
added an unnecessary identifier but also mistakenly punctuated it (524;
Theroux, like many writers, doesn't understand the difference between
restrictive and nonrestrictive clauses, and I had to adjust hundreds of
such lapses). Earlier in the same chapter, in another example of providing superfluous information to his reader, Theroux added "The American
'Bill of Rights' (1791), the first ten amendments of the Constitution, . . .";
I was able to talk him out of the unnecessary quotation marks and date,
but not the explanatory phrase (515; nor does this insertion about privacy
belong in a chapter tabulating sexual oddities). In chapter 2, Theroux
originally wrote: "Eyestones recognized the poor beggar by sight but had
no idea what he wanted," but changed it to: "Eyestones recognized the
poor beggar by sight, he had seen him before, but had no idea what he
wanted." I pointed out that if he recognized the beggar by sight, it goes
without saying that "he had seen him before," so it was redundant to say
so. He changed that slightly to "he had seen him often" (18), which is
marginally better though still unnecessary, but too many of his changes
were along those wordy lines.

As an extended example, I've highlighted in boldface the additions
Theroux made to a passage in the original:

> Something of a homophobe for having lived for years in San Fran-
> cisco, Mutrux was thin and tall with the pulled snout of a steelhead
> trout. An **odd** toothy grimace with which he sought to outface peo-
> ple revealed the curious dentition of an off-center midline of **dental
> numbers** eight and nine that gave him the look, **by way of his teeth,**
> of a house with a badly placed **front** door. **Nor was his nose exactly
> in the center of his face, which added to that.** "I've seen more fat
> variations of that type in Twinkietown, aka 'The City by the Bay,' than
> you can imagine," he said. "Weirdies, beardies, fairies, and queer-
> ies." A scary trait of his, **a physiological oddity,** was that he almost
> never blinked, a fact that gave him in any face-to-face conversation
> a stubborn, **dug-in,** combative air, imparting to any communicant **of
> his—not without the frisson of confronting a machine**—a distinct
> unease and even collapsing vigor. **He constantly logged people's
> mistakes, which vivified him, and his laborious and dogged man-
> ner proved that the crudest malice is perpetrated by those who
> take things seriously.** (27–28)

The final clause is splendid, a good example of Theroux's way with aphorism, but everything else is redundant. A "toothy grimace" is understandably "odd" without inserting that adjective, and after mentioning "dentition" it's unnecessary to add "dental numbers," and even more superfluous to add "by way of his teeth." Readers will assume the door to a house means the front door unless told otherwise—no need for the adjective—and while the detail of the off-placement of his nose is fine, the concluding "which added to that" isn't. "A physiological oddity" is likewise superfluous (and repeats the unnecessary "odd" earlier), and "dug-in" isn't really necessary, nor is "of his." There are hundreds of expansions like this throughout the novel, adding dozens and dozens of pages to its bulk, which Theroux regarded as improvements but which only cluttered up and slowed down the narrative. To be sure, Theroux is a maximalist, those who exult in amplification and elaboration, but there's an art to maximalism, to "the art of excess" (as Tom LeClair calls it in a fine book of that title) that he didn't always practice. In the headnote to his mission-statement essay "Theroux Metaphrastes," Theroux proudly admitted he had an amplified prose style, but made "a distinction between two rhetorical terms: *inflatio* and *amplificatio*. *Amplificatio* is not a fault," but *inflatio* is, and runaway inflation characterizes most of Theroux's changes to the original *Laura Warholic*.[35]

The third category is the extended rants and set pieces that crop up throughout the novel, few of which are relevant to the novel's themes. To the first draft version Theroux added Warholic's 4½-page exposé on Jesus' parsimony (chap. V); a few pages of new material to Eyestones's index cards on sex (chap. VI) and sex questions for future magazine columns (chap. VII); around 18 pages to "The Controversial Essay" (chap. XII), nearly doubling it;[36] thrice as many entries to the list of female "creatrixes" (chap. XIII); lots of new material on Marilyn Monroe wherever she appears (chaps. IV and especially XVII); around 5 pages of additions to "Mutrux's Confession," mostly in his diatribe against San Francisco (chap. XX); about 4 pages added to the diatribe against Boston (chap. XXIV); a page or two of further mockery of the 1970s and Eugene's

---

35 Appendix to *Three Wogs* (Boston: David Godine, 1975), unnumbered p. 2.
36 Originally entitled "The Offending Essay" and complete in one issue of *Quink*, I pointed out that the 23,000-word final version was too long for a single issue of any magazine, so Theroux added some references to it being spread out over a couple of consecutive issues. In a letter to me dated 20 June 2005, Theroux wrote: "The fact is, it just grew and grew over the years, and I had no scruples in adding to it with occasional ideas."

3-page reverie of the early twentieth century (chap. XXVIII); most of the essay against democracy (chap. XXX); a good deal of new material to the cross-country trip, which I find the most tedious section of the novel (chaps. XXV–XXXV); maybe half the 40-page chapter on sexual oddities (chap. XXXIII);[37] a couple pages more here and there from Harriet Trombone contra white people (especially chap. XXXIV); Eugene/Theroux's 7-page diatribe against contemporary America (chap. XXXIV); nearly all of R. Bangs Chasuble's narrative in the first half of chap. XXXVIII; much of Ratnaster's diatribe against God and the universe and Discknickers's against the Jews (chap. XLI); about half of Laura's rant against Eugene (chap. XLIII); about 6 pages to the lesbian nightclub scene (chap. XLVI); and another 6-page diatribe against the Jews by Discknickers (chap. XLIX)—nearly 140 pages of new material, some of it entertaining and enlightening, but little of it adding anything essential to the first draft's focus on "the nature of modern love and sex," as Theroux announced in his précis, and much of it contrary to his promotion of Christian charity and forgiveness. Most set pieces are merely occasions for Theroux to sound off on topics that interest him or, more often, infuriate him. At one point Theroux sent me a new chapter he wanted to insert during the cross-country car trip in which Laura asks Eugene to tell her what he hates, which consisted of several pages of his (Eyestones/Theroux's) pet peeves. I was able to talk him out of that one, but not into shortening the other set pieces, to which he kept adding until the end. The result is a Janus-faced, Jekyll and Hyde of a novel—or better yet an Incredible Hulk of a novel—where Eugene's calm Proustian analyses and Christian meditations are periodically interrupted by the author's volcanic rages and verbal bullying, his intemperate displays of misogyny, anti-Semitism, body-shaming, ethnic bigotry, homophobia, slut-shaming, misanthropy, and very unChristian intolerance.

There are precedents, of course, for such self-indulgence in the genres Theroux works in: the Menippean satire and the encyclopedic, learned novel. Both genres allow for the inclusion of erudite digressions, lists, comic shenanigans, formal variety (the inclusion of poems, essays, fables, documents), and a satirical point of view that revels in exaggeration and grotesquerie. Theroux's "dense prose," like Eyestones's writings,

---

37 Theroux would send new factoids to the women at Fantagraphics and ask them to stick them in anywhere! He sometimes forgot and sent the same material twice. I considered the title "What in Love or Sex Isn't Odd?" awkward, and suggested "Love Is Strange"; since several of Theroux's chapter titles are named after songs or albums, I thought that 1956 Mickey and Sylvia hit would be better. He disagreed.

"suggested a point of view: diverse, adorned, amused, premeditated, filled with details, highly inclusive" (65). All this worked fine in the first draft version, where there was a balance between the straightforward narrative sections and the rhetorical showpieces. But I feel the novel became unbalanced as Theroux included more and more of his personal crotchets and prejudices, favoring his concerns over the novel's. The worst examples of this constitute the fourth category of additions to the original.

As noted earlier, *Laura Warholic* is based on Theroux's relationship with Laura Markley between 1995 and 1997. When he finished the first draft in 2000, there was nothing to indicate that the novel's events took place any later than that, as to be expected, and in the fall of 2005 Theroux even added this Christmas Eve toast by Minot Warholic to the growing manuscript: "And a Happy New Year—year 5760 for the Hebrews!" (821).[38] The new year 5760 = 1999, which means the novel ends on New Year's Eve 1998. However, by that time Theroux had already added some post-1998 references, and continued to do so. I pointed some of these out to Theroux, but he didn't think they mattered. In his letter of 26 November 2005, he said he was trying "to keep the time-frame of the novel limited to the year 2000, with a few key exceptions where I may end up referring to something in 2003 or 2004 but don't care, because in those cases I've decided I am making a more important point. I expect to get away with it." That shocked me, because I couldn't believe he was more interested in getting in a few more satirical jabs than maintaining the temporal integrity of his novel—and that he didn't think anyone would notice. (Since then other readers have noticed.) Here, in chronological order, are the additions that Theroux felt were so important that it was worth breaking the novel's time-frame:

1999: At their Thanksgiving dinner in November 1998, Laura mocks Eugene for worshipping "the late Queen of Jordan" (697). Queen Noor (mentioned earlier on p. 9) didn't relinquish the throne until after her husband died in 1999.

2000: In his "Controversial Essay," Eugene cites a male doctor's opinion on "the *Today Show* on July 10, 2000, that a woman's 'periods' are not even necessary . . ." (167–68).

2000: In the same essay, Eugene includes Condoleezza Rice among those whose gap in their front teeth is aesthetically pleasing (137). Rice first attained national attention in December 2000 when she

---

38 The Hebrew calendar is based on the belief that the world was created on 6 October 3761 BCE, a Saturday night to be specific.

became National Security Advisor to the incoming president George W. Bush.

2001: In the same essay, Eugene refers to "a television show in 2001 in which fifty single women competed to marry a millionaire" (160).

2001: A reference to the 9/11 attacks appears on p. 521, noting hijacker Muhammed Atta's misogyny.

2002: There's a reference on p. 528 to Russ Kirk's 2002 book *Psychotropedia*, which reported that a 1981 novel by Lynne Cheney (wife of then-Vice President Dick) is filled with "disfiguring violence, animal cruelty, feminist thought, and among other things, several instances of taking the Lord's name in vain."

2003: Regarding Laura, Eugene asks himself, "Why did he put up with all this shock-and-awe?" (253). Though the phrase had occasionally been used earlier, it went mainstream during the 2003 invasion of Iraq. There is another reference to the Iraq (and Afghanistan) war on p. 568.

2004: "As of May 17, 2004, by judicial fiat from four unelected judges, the Commonwealth of Massachusetts deems that any and all male homosexuals and lesbians can now officially get married, an option chosen and an act performed often not out of love but as an existence-assertion in an attempt on their part to feel vindicated, as if to say, 'I am not a freak'" (570).

2005: "In 1974 the United States developed 70 percent of the world's advanced technology, by 1984 it was down to 50 percent, and by 2005 it was as low as 3 percent" (571, source not given).

2005: To the chapter on sexual oddities, Theroux added: "In the film *Brokeback Mountain* [released December 2005], the homosexual 'cowboys' are not cowboys at all, as is commonly repeated, but sheepherders, leading inevitably to the subtext of barnyard carnality, ages old . . ." (514–15).

2006: There is a passage on p. 532 noting Flaubert's reaction to Egyptian prostitutes that cites Frederick Brown's biography of the French author, which was published in 2006.

And there is one undated reference: "It is so last-millennium" Laura says of Eugene's gift of a typewriter (587). I'll let the reader decide how crucial any of those are to the novel.

All of this additional, unnecessary, sometimes contradictory material is the main reason why many readers wondered if the book was edited (not really) or even proofread (in the early stages, yes, but later, no). Mark Burstein addressed this in a blog essay entitled "On Editing the

Novel (a Primer): Laura Warholic by Alexander Theroux."[39] After detailing the damage done by the absence of an editor, Burstein concludes, "Had Theroux only allowed one 'to hew away the rough walls that imprison the lovely apparition' [as Michelangelo said], readers would be treated to the taut, elegant, exhilarating 700-page beauty lying within"— which accurately describes the first draft version I read in early 2002.

In the beginning, Theroux was amenable to editing. In a letter to me dated 26 May 2005, Theroux said it would mean a lot to him "if you would be frank and tell me what excisions you'd make, what you find uninspired, sentences, paragraphs or whole pages, even chapters I suppose, if you feel so moved." But later when I made such suggestions, he adopted "a stubborn, dug-in, combative air," and not only kept what he added, but argued that he was making the novel better, not worse, and quoted Anthony Burgess on the importance of revision. He sidestepped my objection that revisions should be done *before* a novel goes into production, not during, and would not heed my warning that he was damaging his novel, not improving it. Among his additions, ironically enough, are some self-defensive justifications for his additions: Theroux *expanded* his description of Harriet Trombone's "powerful tirades that she gave so often, for her creative explosions, sheer mayhem, involved the sort of hyperbolic rhetoric she delighted in to tweak and to entertain" (307). Giving Chasuble a lengthy aria in chapter XXXVIII—amusing but largely irrelevant to the novel's concerns—Theroux *added* this self-conscious remark: "Eyestones patiently listened to Chasuble who talked on and on like Tintoretto painted, to attract attention, often at the expense of coherence" (625). In her accusatory rant against Eugene, Laura "was speaking rapid-fire like an old German MP44 assault rifle, abandoning herself to rhetoric and blue with fury" (635)—*added* at a later time when Theroux himself was abandoning himself to rhetoric and blue with fury. The most supremely ironic statement in the novel appears at the top of p. 81: "Any fool can add; it takes a genius to subtract!"

Theroux wouldn't even allow his choice for cover art to be "edited." The photo he originally wanted to use had to be discarded because the photographer couldn't locate the model for permission (plus he was asking for what Groth regarded as an unaffordable fee), which led to a last-minute scramble for a substitute. Groth came up with some alternatives, but Theroux disliked them and preferred to use an old photograph of actress Evelyn Nesbit, inserting a few references to her after the galley stage to justify his choice, but without identifying her on the jacket or

---

39 https://bookdesigners.com/blog/on-editing-the-novel-a-primer-laura-warholic-by-alexander-theroux, posted 7 February 2010.

copyright page, leaving readers wondering at her identity or relevance. The casual browser in a bookstore could be forgiven for assuming this was a novel about a Gibson girl named Laura Warholic who was a pioneering sexual intellectual of some sort, like Margaret Sanger (who is mentioned on p. 533 of the novel).

Predictably, book reviewers criticized its excessive length, and some of them sensed a shorter, better novel within it. Admitting *Laura Warholic* "is the work of a manic genius," *Library Journal's* Henry L. Carrigan Jr. felt "It's probably too long by 300 pages or so; Laura's insecurities and manias as well as Eyestones's vacillations eventually get tiresome." This was echoed in Theroux's hometown paper, the *Barnstable Patriot*, where Cape Codder Michael Lee called it "bloated" and confessed "I sat in sort of a dumb awe of it—first that the author would not avail himself of editorial privilege and cut the damn thing down by 300 pages and secondly, that the publisher wouldn't do it either." The reliably snarky *Kirkus Reviews* called it "A big, drooly, shaggy dog of a postmodern epic, one that takes up an awful lot of space but doesn't give a lot of affection in return. . . . A bloated *Bonfire of the Vanities* for the pomo set," and in the *Washington Post*, fantasy novelist Jeff VanderMeer criticized its repetitiveness.[40] Even appreciative reviewers expressed doubts about its length; in *Rain Taxi*, Scott Bryan Wilson admitted at the end of his favorable review that "the novel does have some sloppy aspects: a few jokes and similes get repeated, at times it feels overlong, and occasionally a convergence of inflexible opinion and didacticism lend a preachy feeling to the text," and in his excellent review for *TLS*, Paul Quinn politely wondered if the "hateful tirades" of some of his characters "should be allowed such latitude, . . . to take the stage for extended periods."[41] Since then, commentators on Amazon.com and Goodreads have added to the complaint that the apparently unedited novel is too long by far.

40 *Library Journal*, 15 January 2007; *Barnstable Patriot*, 22 May 2008; *Kirkus Reviews*, 15 December 2007; "Looking for Love," *Washington Post Book World*, 20 January 2008.

41 *Rain Taxi* 12.4 (Winter 2007–08): 8; *TLS*, 21 and 28 December 2007, 25–26. These two are among the best reviews the novel received, topped only by Stuart Mitchner's "Reader Beware: Alexander Theroux's Juggernaut Is Here," in Princeton's *Town Topics*, 27 February 2008. Another noteworthy one was novelist Richard Stern's "Linguistic Stylings: Alexander Theroux's long, odd novel is a language feast," *Chicago Tribune*, 26 May, 2007. On June 9 the *Trib* ran a clarification stating that the novel was delayed until September (though it didn't actually come out until December 2007). At least one other review appeared in the summer per the original April 15 pub date, resulting in further lost sales due to the book's unavailability.

This is a shame, because despite its faults, *Laura Warholic* is by any standard an extraordinary novel. Theroux commands a wider vocabulary and linguistic range than almost any living writer, from stately, aphoristic prose to goofy slang, from winsome rhapsody (every time Rapunzel Wisht appears) to flame-throwing invective (against nearly everybody else), with a Shakespearean plenitude of metaphor, one of the last practitioners of an idiosyncratic, logophilic tradition that can be traced back to Joyce and Melville, Sterne, Burton, and Rabelais, all the way back to Petronius and the prophetic books of the Bible. He is smarter and better-read than most novelists, and while many of his reactionary views are dismissible, the others are hard, inconvenient truths. Had the original 2000 version been published, it may have raised some of the same objections—too long, too eccentric, too captious—but I am confident that it would now be regarded as one of the first great novels of the twenty-first century. I'll conclude with my first response to the original version, in a letter to its author dated 22 February 2002:

> I've just finished reading *Laura Warholic* and I must say I like this better than anything you've written since *Darconville*. Maybe "like" is the wrong word, since it's hard to like something so filled with rage, hatred, insults, and grotesque, detestable characters. But the language redeems it: the astonishing vocabulary and Shakespearean range of metaphors and similes. "It left a memory of bleak disillusion she carried about her like a cow-bell ever since" (p. 147 [111]). That cow-bell is so perfect, conveying her bovine complacency, stupidity, clumsiness, the almost physical weight of her fate . . . I could go on for a page praising that single simile, and the novel is filled with hundreds just as good. (Laura's death by typewriter ribbon is a brutally apt metaphor.) And the novel is very funny, though I often felt guilty for laughing, since so much of the humor is cruel: ethnic slurs, making fun of people because of their appearance, comparing them to animals, etc. But this is Bosch's *Garden of Earthly Delights*, not Norman Rockwell, and I reminded myself that you wrote a grad-school paper on the *Dunciad*, not on *Right Ho, Jeeves*. In fact, your novel is a kind of modern Dunciad, a wholesale condemnation of modern America with Laura as the chief dunce. It's an amazing novel. Extreme fiction.

APPENDIX

Laura Markley in San Francisco in 1992.
She mailed this photo to Theroux in 1994, who
wrote a letter back describing her as "winsome."

William T. Vollmann and Laura Markley, San Francisco, 1994

Alexander Laurence (far right) with other members of the *Cups* staff, 1995

"Otter" and "Squishy" in 1992–93 (preceding photos courtesy Alexander Laurence)

Jeff Conolly of the Lyres

had to fight herself fiercely to die, like two people madly racing at each other. A simple quack with foam sounded a cry of unexpected compassion. She looked grey as cindercrete, her skin the misty *truite de bleu* color of a poached fish, bent over at 38 degrees, the first avalanche pitch. Her body lay as she fell on its right side, nose to the baseboard, left shoulder leaning against the wall, right leg up on a table intersecting a loose telephone cord that snaked insidiously between her long, prehensile toes. With open eyes, a look less of bewilderment than utter disgust in that final, futile tableau remained on her face, smeared, stained, the way our tears actually mourn for us.

We are diminished only by our hopes, not when we are led to hope what no hope in this world lets us glimpse, but when we insist futilely that what we dream, what within us we wish in the face of the dark, come true.

We begin to live bravely perhaps when we understand that we can only act only against the truth. When we seek to love and to mate and so dream with a hope of coming to matter in the face of everything we see proves to disappear, we take a terrible risk. It takes place in the blazing wildfire of the heart where, swept into the terrible if incandescent red zone of equatorial passion where a person has two shadows, we are willing to lose ourselves in another as we exchange fates with one whom we love but on whom our heart is nevertheless impaled. Why does that struggle make us a captive? Where is the peace we are due for the penance we give? There is no escape while the mind is attentive to the heart's urges, where fancies are sought and dreams are begot. How sad it is that we should suffer in the very place where we love! Vision constantly calls to us like a seditious angel with what could be. The triumph is that a realm exists, around the corner of our mind, where reality is an intruder and dreams alone, the bad along with the good, have a way of coming true. The fatal and incapacitating truth is that our dreams are often only a matter of the heart. And, paradoxically, of all possibilities a dream is the single thing that none of us can share.

insert one more
line space

West Barnstable, Massachusetts
2005

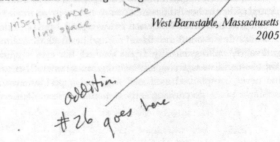

addition
#26 goes here

824

The final page of the bound galley, showing the novel's original conclusion.
(The pencil marks are mine, the addition instruction Theroux's.)

ERRATA FOR *LAURA WARHOLIC*

p. 15, 12 lines up from bottom: FOR managing, to avoid   READ managing to avoid

p. 15, 4 lines up from bottom: de-italicize *Violin Concerto in D major, Opus 61*

p. 20, line 10: FOR rose revealed   READ rose, revealed

p. 28, line 22: FOR raspberrry   READ raspberry

p. 29, line 6: FOR " And   READ "And

p. 29, line 9: FOR Chasuble said   READ Chasuble, said

p. 29, line 25: FOR pasta,   READ pasta.

p. 30, 4 lines up: bad endline hyphenation; should be: Disc-/ knickers

p. 34, line 8:   ditto; should be: Disc-/ knickers

p. 43, line 17: FOR Marysas   READ Marsyas   [as on p. 477: find/correct all]

p. 43, line 24: FOR become   READ became

p. 48, lines 2-5: de-italicize the limerick

p. 49, line 13: FOR farmer.   READ farmer."

p. 52, line 19: FOR eat (Luke 24:41)?   READ eat?' (Luke 24:41).

p. 53, line 22: bad endline hyphenation; should be: *nuch*-/ *shlepper*

p. 54, last four lines: justify, not flush left

p. 56, line 2: FOR *nafkeh*_bitch   READ *nafkeh* bitch   [i.e., delete underscore]

p. 57, 16 lines up: bad endline hyphenation; should be: back-/ scratcher

p. 61, line 4: FOR forf example   READ for example

p. 61, line 9: FOR mesorchium see   READ mesorchium, see

p. 68, line 13: FOR had came   READ had come

p. 79, line 17: FOR la crane   READ le crâne   [as in poetry quotation that follows]

p. 79, line 20: delete deep indent of "De l'Humanité" and align left with previous line

p. 80, line 2: FOR Rene   READ René

p. 101, 4 lines up: FOR icy references she made with irritated references to READ icy references she made to   [i.e., delete "with irritated references"]

p. 125, line 4: FOR "'I love   READ "'I love   [i.e., single quote faces the other way]

p. 127, line 16: bad endline hyphenation; should be: Disc-/ knickers

p. 128, 2 lines up: FOR fore-play   READ foreplay

p. 133, line 9: FOR horn."   READ horn"   [i.e., delete period]

p. 133, 5 lines up: FOR W.B. Yeat' poem, "On Sailing   READ W. B. Yeats' poem "Sailing

p. 134, line 10: FOR costumes cheereleader   READ costumes, cheer-
leader

p. 134, line 17: FOR abundance." (Matthew 25: 29)   READ abundance"
(Matthew 25:29).

p. 135, line 20: FOR fable, *Queen Gloriana's Revenge* which   READ fable
"Queen Gloriana's Revenge," which

p. 139, 5 lines up: FOR St.Denis   READ St. Denis

p. 141, line 16: FOR stunts   READ shunts   [thus in original manuscript]

p. 152, line 6: FOR Wolf   READ Woolf

p. 161, line 10: FOR leading us   READ leading up   [thus in original]

p. 166, line 3: several words missing: FOR themselves, morning
READ . . . themselves stating the obvious! What of the mad hysteria
they show? Those are all women in the morning . . .

p. 186, 13 lines up: FOR shields--women   READ shields—women   [em
dash, not hyphens]

p. 187, line 8: FOR glance black   READ glance back

p. 208, 3 lines up: indent "all a shine, shine, shine" by a quarter inch

p. 211, line 6: FOR plain lonely   READ plain, lonely

p. 211, line 10: FOR "'Blond   READ "'Blond   [i.e., reverse quote mark
and close up]

p. 223, lines 8 and 11: FOR complements . . . Complement   READ com-
pliments . . . Compliment

p. 225, 7 lines up: fraction missing; should read ¾ cup of Parmesan cheese
[capital P]

p. 238, lines 2-4: insert commas after Eyestones and transgressives

p. 238, line 7: insert comma after Laura

p. 242, 11 lines up: FOR minutes.' "Turning   READ minutes.'" Turning

p. 242, last line: FOR Tel-Aviv   READ Tel Aviv

p. 253, 12 lines up: FOR 5X   READ 5%   [thus in original]

p. 257, 11 lines up: indent new paragraph at "To see what?

p. 257, 7 lines up: no new paragraph: run "Wait, may I . . ." into previous
line, so that it reads: and beckoned him. "Wait, may I . . ."

p. 276, line 11: FOR skies."   READ skies,"

p. 284, line 11: FOR "square"   READ 'square'   [single quotes]

p. 285, line 1: FOR 'til   READ 'til

p. 288, line 19: FOR Let me frank   READ Let me be

p. 300, 13 lines up: FOR sleep with?   READ sleep.   [thus in original]

p. 306, line 10: FOR together!'   READ together!'"

p. 327, line 8: FOR One time actually   READ One time he actually

p. 336, 2 lines up: FOR hundred   READ hundreds

p. 338, line 3: FOR unerstand   READ understand

p. 339, line 18: FOR " As   READ "As

p. 351, 13 lines up: FOR Eyestone's   READ Eyestones's

p. 354, line 11: FOR McKeag— "   READ McKeag—"   [reverse and close up]

p. 357, 8 lines up: bad endline hyphenation; should be: Mc-/ Keag   [or bump Mc to next line]

p. 374, line 13: FOR #48LOB   READ #48110B   [thus in original, and historically correct]

p. 376, line 14: FOR Love--?   READ Love—?   [em dash, not hyphens]

p. 379-84: that section was supposed to be set in a different font: Garamond, and in same point size as main text—as long as it ends on p. 385.

p. 389, line 16: FOR bumph   READ bumpy

p. 397, 7 lines up: FOR howls or   READ howls of

p. 399, 5 lines up: FOR *None But The Lonely*   READ *None but the Lonely*

p. 404, line 3: italicize The Midnight Special

p. 428, 8 lines up: FOR then as   READ then, as

p. 436, 8 lines up: FOR to live.   READ to live."

p. 453, line 4: FOR Germany where   READ Germany, where

p. 466, final line of second stanza: FOR love.   READ love."

p. 472, line 20: FOR with 'em   READ with 'em

p. 479, line 20: FPR kreplach—crunching   READ kreplach-crunching

p. 484, line 25: bad endline hyphenation; should be: Disc-/ knickers

p. 485, line 17: FOR dunce   READ dunce,

p. 491, line 19: FOR de-pended   READ depended   [one word in ms. and galleys]

p. 491, 11 lines up: FOR mocked the   READ mocked by the   [thus in ms.]

p. 505, line 14: FOR film, *Quartet*   READ film *Quartet*

p. 506, line 21: FOR Hearst. very   READ Hearst, very

p. 507, 10 lines up: FOR Allen   READ Allan

p. 509, line 2: FOR to or-   READ to or

p. 511, line 23: FOR noticeablespace   READ noticeable space

p. 512, line 9: FOR Latour who   READ Latour, who

p. 512, 14 lines up: FOR Erdös whose   READ Erdös, whose

p. 514, line 13: FOR "The;"   READ "The";

p. 516, line 7: the second Greek word should be spelled: Βάθος   [i.e., correct last two letters]

p. 516, line 11: FOR seven-feet   READ seven feet

p. 518, line 2: FOR in cranky   READ in his crranky

p. 519: extend the lines in the second half of the page all the way to the right

p. 519, 11 lines up: FOR Garcia Marquez's   READ García Márquez's

[i.e., insert accents as well as reverse direction of the apostrophe]

p. 519, 7 lines up: FOR novel, *Robinson*   READ novel *Robinson*

p. 519, last line: italicize Moby-Dick

p. 520, line 6: FOR are, the   READ are the

p. 522, line 14: FOR person, a   READ person a

p. 522, line 23: FOR candy.   READ candy.)

p. 524, line 4: delete the commas before and after *Mansfield Park*

p. 524, line 5: move . . . to next line [so that all three periods are together]

p. 525, 6 lines up: FOR Rougemont in   READ Rougemont writes in

p. 526, line 6: FOR V.S.   READ V. S.   [but keep on same line]

p. 526, 13 lines up: FOR screen were   READ screen, were

p. 527, line 19: FOR 32 READ thirty-two

p. 529, line 7: FOR "The Fall   READ the Fall

p. 533, line 22: FOR novel, *Galatea*   READ novel *Galatea*

p. 534, line 16: delete the commas before and after Paul Tillich

p. 535, line 22: FOR fourteen of   READ fourteen or

p. 540, line 7: FOR 10   read ten

p. 546, 3 lines up: FOR approvall   READ approval

p. 547, line 17: FOR "Cherry Orchard"   READ *Cherry Orchard*

p. 550, line 9: FOR " that   READ "that

p. 553, 10 lines up: FOR "'The   READ "'The

p. 554, line 4: FOR gianlorenzos   READ Gianlorenzos   [capitalized in ms.]

p. 556, line 14: FOR Rectum is   READ Rectum Is

p. 556, line 15: FOR "'Hear   READ "'Hear

p. 556, line 16: FOR 'Exile in Guyville'   READ *Exile in Guyville*

p. 558, line 3: FOR 8   READ 8½

p. 568, 13 lines up: insert comma after show-trial

p. 569, 7 lines up: FOR Evangelists   READ evangelists

p. 599, 10 lines up: FOR The she   READ That she

p. 602, line 2: FOR singing-style   READ singing style

p. 603, 17 lines up: FOR finger,_withdrew   READ finger, withdrew   [delete underscore]

p. 604, line 8: FOR habit.' "   READ habit.'"

p. 608, 16 lines up: FOR I want   READ I went

p. 610, line 20: FOR film, *Goodbye*   READ film *Goodbye*

p. 610, line 22: FOR scenes sit   READ scenes, sit

p. 610, line 27: FOR prettier "—he   READ prettier"—he

p. 610, line 29: FOR going by?"—"far   READ going by?—far   [delete both quotation marks]

p. 610, 8 lines up: FOR preposterously-called   READ preposterously called

p. 611, 5 lines up: FOR nineteen thirty-one!　READ 1931!

p. 611, last line: close up　to—　and

p. 612, 13 lines up: FOR love-song　READ love　song

p. 616, line 23: bad endline hyphenation; should be　near-/　illiterate

p. 617, line 6: FOR Capt'N Jacks or the Little Bar　READ Capt'n Jacks or
the little bar　[thus in Theroux's source, Tennessee Williams' *Memoirs*]

p. 619, lines 15-18: all those music titles should be set in plain type, not
italics

p. 622, line 4: FOR *Fire*1941　READ *Fire,* 1941

p. 643, line 16: FOR Jeff　READ ~~Jeff~~　[the name correctly had a strike-
through from ms. up to galley, but someone at late stage deleted it]

p. 644, line 1: FOR that he is trying　READ that ~~he loves me~~ he is trying
[ditto]

p. 644, line 10: FOR singer in a band　READ singer in ~~The Craven Slucks~~
a band　[ditto]

p. 647, line 9: bad endline hyphenation; should be:　Disc-/ knickers

p. 652, 6 lines up: FOR tumors."　READ tumors"　[the correct period is
already in place after the citation]

p. 653, line 8: FOR "I am　READ "'I am

p. 654, 4 lines up: FOR What　READ "What

p. 655, line 14: FOR Only　READ "Only

p. 658, line 12: FOR 'Afterbirth'"?　READ 'Afterbirth'?"

p. 658, line 22: delete quotation marks around *Dies Irae*

p. 661, 7 lines up: FOR kniow　READ know

p. 664, line 2: FOR woodpecker"　READ woodpecker."

p. 664, line 5: FOR *after*the　READ *after* the

p. 665, line 2: FOR boy— "　READ boy—"

p. 665, line 9: FOR rom the　READ from the

p. 666, line 1: bad endline hyphenation; should be:　Disc-/ knickers

p. 667, line 2: bad endline hyphenation; should be:　wedge-/ nouts

p. 667, line 20: FOR "You."　READ "You,"

p. 674, 6 lines up: FOR "'There　READ "'There

p. 690, 11 lines up: FOR " How?　READ "How?

p. 696, line 2: run in next line: not a new paragraph

p. 699, 11 lines up: FOR wrote '10 . . . be '10　READ wrote '10 . . . be '10

p. 701, line 12: FOR flowers of columbine　READ flowers of a columbine
[thus in ms.]

p. 702, line 11: FOR *Khouna . . . Khouna*　READ *Khoung . . . Khoung*
[thus in ms.]

p. 705, line 5: FOR not　READ *not*

p. 709, line 14: FOR all--?　READ all—?　[em dash, not two hyphens]

p. 719, line 9: FOR Tulnals   READ Tuinals

p. 734, line 10: FOR I'm Trudy   READ "I'm Trudy

p. 734, line 25: FOR teeth. I've   READ teeth. "I've

p. 734, 8 lines up: FOR off to you   READ off you too   [thus in ms.]

p. 737, line 4: FOR Lesbos   READ Lefkas   [Lefkos in ms., but Lefkas is correct spelling]

p. 746, 8 lines up: FOR Hollywood." I   READ Hollywood. I

p. 752, 11 lines up: FOR C2H4   READ C_2H_4 [subscripts, as on p. 746]

p. 734, 11 lines up: FOR "Wrestling."   READ Wrestling."

p. 755, line 7: FOR Krauthamaer's   READ Krauthammer's

p. 758, line 4: FOR Laura who   READ Laura who

p. 758, line 5: FOR fox laughed   READ fox, laughed

p. 759, line 8: bad endline hyphenation; should be: Disc-/ knickers

p. 764, line 7: bad endline hyphenation; should be: Mice-/ pockets

p. 769, line 18: FOR paralytic."   READ paralytic.'"   [i.e., insert single quote mark before double]

p. 806, 13 lines up: after "version of" run in next line: not a new paragraph

p. 807, 10 lines up: decrease length of paragraph indent: align with "Eye-stones" above it

p. 813, line 5: FOR Jeruselem   READ Jerusalem

p. 815, 13 lines up: FOR "'Therefore   READ "'Therefore

p. 817, last word: bad endline hyphenation; should be: hond-/ ling

p. 818, 6 lines up: FOR himself perspicaciously   READ himself, perspi-caciously

p. 819, line 8: FOR Edward said   READ Edward Said

p. 819, line 9: FOR violence'--and   READ violence'—and   [em dash, not hyphens]

p. 819, line 20: FOR out of as   READ out of

p. 820, line 4: FOR false,'said   READ false,' said

p. 823, 6 lines up: bad endline hyphenation; should be: Disc-/ knickers

p. 824, line 4:   ditto

p. 830, 10 lines up: FOR " Do   READ "Do

p. 848, line 22: FOR rage?" Laura   READ rage? "Laura

p. 854, line 8: bad endline hyphenation; should be: Disc-/ knickers

p. 856, line 5: FOR war- bonnet   READ war bonnet   [no hyphen]

p. 865, 12 lines up: FOR Ann Elisabeth   READ Anna Elisabet

p. 873, line 9: FOR Eyestone's   READ Eyestones's

p. 873, line 22: FOR nonexistence flats   READ nonexistence in flats   [thus in ms.]

Collected Stories

A Note on the Text

THEROUX had wanted to publish a collection of his short stories ever since 1985, the year he applied for a Guggenheim Grant; in his Statement of Plans, he stated that he had completed seven stories, and projected six more. The grant was turned down. In a letter to me dated 30 April 1987 he wrote that he had just signed a contract with Simon & Schuster for *A Woman with Sauce and Other Stories*, to be published the following year, but that book never materialized. He continued to write stories and fables over the next three decades, and in November 2016, at the age of seventy-seven, Alexander Theroux emailed me two manuscript collections of his short fiction, published and unpublished, writing "if anything ever happens to me, you will have these in hand maybe to see published." They were divided into stories and fables, as follows:

> *Madonna Pica and Other Stories*
>   A Woman with Sauce
>   Watergraphs
>   Blackrobe
>   Envenoming Junior
>   Summer Bellerophon
>   The Copernicus Affair
>   Scugnizzo's Pasta Co.
>   Madonna Pica
>   A Wordstress in Williamsburg
>   Finocchio, or The Man with the Long Nose
>   An English Railroad
>   Fark Pooks
>   Mrs. Marwood's Spunkies
>   The American Tourist Home
>   A Note on the Type

Julia de Chateauroux; or The Girl with Blue Hair and Other Fables
  Julia de Chateauroux; or, the Girl with Blue Hair
  Summer Bellerophon
  The Schinocephalic Waif
  Captain Birdseye's Expedition
  The Great Wheadle Tragedy
  Master Snickup's Cloak
  The Wragby Cars
  A Christmas Fable
  St. Malecroix
  St. Winifred's Bells
  The Loneliest Person in Scituate
  Queen Gloriana's Revenge
  Song at Twilight: A Tale of Ancient China
  Zoroaster and Mrs. Titcomb
  Blackrobe
  The Enthronization of Vinegarfly
  The Schafenzoyer Diamonds

The fictions are not in any discernible order, and some appear in both collections, blurring the distinction between genres. (I suspect he did so to enlarge the otherwise thin collection of fables.) Theroux envisioned two separate books, and vehemently rejected my proposal at the time to combine them into one book, which Jim Gauer's Zerogram Press was willing to publish after I recommended the project. In November 2017 he sent me two more stories: what he called a "corrected" version of "Envenoming Junior," and a new story, "Grasso Sovrapesso and the Bent Nail."

All that year he had tried but failed to interest Little, Brown, and Farrar, Straus and Giroux in the collection. In March 2018 he emailed me a new fiction, a parody of an Acknowledgements note, and in September of that year renewed his efforts to find a mainstream publisher as an alternative to publishing it with Fantagraphics Books, mostly because he assumed his longtime editor Gary Groth would be unwilling to give him the larger advance that he wanted, namely $6,000 as opposed to the more likely $2,000. I offered to pay the $6,000 advance myself if he would allow me to present the texts as I thought best, an edition that would include all his short fiction arranged chronologically in three sections. Groth was onboard ("Of course I'd do it" he emailed me on 18 September), but Theroux rejected my proposal because he did not want to include (as I did) his first published story, "Over Edom Will I Cast Out My Shoe," nor did he want to present what he regarded as his weakest stories first.

Over the next four months he emailed me a few more new stories and fables, and in February 2019 emailed me a new complete manuscript, organized into three sections as I originally proposed (but in achronological order), which contained some revisions/expansions of older stories as well as a new one, "The Nemesis of Jawdat Dub." (Earlier I had cautioned him against revising older stories; as a textual purist I felt their original form should be honored and retained—as do almost all authors when reprinting their stories in book form—but he didn't share my concern for the historical record.) He continued to work on the text throughout the spring, revising but mostly expanding, as usual (he never shortened anything), and on 15 May 2019 he emailed me what he called the final version of *Collected Stories*—15,000 words longer than the complete version he had sent me three months earlier. I copyedited it during the last two weeks of May 2019, assuming from his remarks he had made arrangements with Groth to publish it the following year. No sooner did I finish than he started making further additions to the text; in addition to revising the earlier stories, he resumed work in June on a story he had begun earlier in winter, "Genius," and the same month I discovered that among Gordon Lish's papers at the Lilly Library (Indiana University) was a 41-page fiction entitled "Herbert Head, Gent." (see appendix), which he had submitted in the 1970s to Lish (fiction editor at *Esquire* 1969–77), who turned it down. Theroux had forgotten about this, but reluctantly agreed to add it to the new collection, along with a few new stories he wrote that summer. (The prospect of publication has always inspired him.) In August 2019, by which time Groth had lost interest in the book, Theroux resumed his search for a different publisher. He continued to send me updated versions of the manuscript, and as of this writing, it remains unpublished.

What follows are notes on the short fictions (excluding the verse narratives, available in Theroux's *Collected Poems*), arranged chronologically, as I had originally proposed, along with the ones he wrote after rejecting that proposal. The dates of composition for some of the earlier unpublished fictions were emailed to me by Theroux on 1 March 2019, though a few proved to be inaccurate.

EARLY STORIES

"Over Edom Will I Cast Out My Shoe": First published in *Canticle* (St. Francis College, Biddeford, ME) 8.1 (1964): 9–17; reprinted in *Plume & Sword* (University of Virginia) 7.4 (Summer 1967): 2–8. The title is from Psalm 60:8: "Moab is my washpot: over Edom will I cast out my shoe," a prophecy of ownership. Theroux earned a BA at St. Francis College in 1964, and an MA (1965) and PhD (1968) at the University of Virginia. He contributed poems, plays, and essays to both school magazines.

"Hubert Head, Gent.": Written in the summer of 1972, previously unpublished. See the second appendix to this book for details.

"An English Railroad": First published as "Beware the Cheshire Cheese, Home of the Mad Train Maven." *New York Times*, 11 February 1973, "Travel and Resorts," 1, 13. Just before the image of the train, the *Times* version read: "and here he drew this diagram (0-6-0/T) from the palette of a sticky beer ring on the bar in front of him"; asked about the missing diagram, Theroux decided to insert a photograph instead of recreating the diagram. At one point Theroux quotes from George Augustus Nokes's *The Evolution of the Steam Locomotive (1803 to 1898)* (1899). In 2019 Theroux gave his Major Tryps enough additional blather to triple the length of the story.

"The American Tourist Home": First published as "The American Tourist Home: In the World, but Not of It." *New York Times*, 20 May 1973, "Travel and Resorts," 1, 51. Expanded in early 2020.

"Fark Pooks": Published nearly simultaneously in *London Magazine* 13.2 (June/July 1973): 48–56, and *Esquire*, August 1973, 104, 126–27. Theroux visited Russia in April 1969. As *Esquire* was considering it, Theroux "was told James Dickey, visiting their offices at the time, went into howls of laughter over the phrase 'breast of it, please.' Maybe that is the only reason they took it" (email 27 February 2019). By the time Theroux sent the 2016 manuscript to me he had inserted two references to televangelist John Hagee's ludicrous 2006 book *Jerusalem Countdown*. Those additions transported the story's setting from the late 1960s to the early 21st century, creating anachronisms (such as "the recent decamp of Stalin's daughter" in 1967) and interrupting the dramatic flow of a crucial scene. I talked Theroux into deleting them. The goofy names of the porn magazines differ slightly between the various versions.

"Finocchio, or the Tale of a Man with a Long Nose": First published in *Massachusetts Review* 17 (Summer 1976): 234–42. *Finocchio* is the Italian equivalent of faggot. "Fark Pooks," "Finocchio," and "Mrs. Marwood's Spunkies" (in that order) originally comprised a manuscript Theroux entitled *De tribus impositoribus*, after the *Treatise of the Three Imposters*, an anonymous medieval attack on Moses, Jesus, and Mohammed, ascribed to various authors and later adapted as an 18th-century hoax.

"Mrs. Marwood's Spunkies": First published in *Antæus* 11 (Autumn 1973): 90–96. The Keightley mentioned several times is Thomas Keightley (1789–1882), Irish author of books on folklore and mythology. Expanded by 1600 words in fall 2019.

"A Wordstress in Williamsburg": First published in *Antæus* 13/14 (Spring/Summer 1974): 346–51; partly recycled in *Darconville's Cat* (Garden City, NY: 1981), pp. 72–74. Theroux added some new material to this in 2019.

"Scugnizzo's Pasta Co.": First published in *Encounter* 43.3 (September 1974): 3–7. *Scugnizzo* is a Neapolitan word meaning guttersnipe, ragamuffin. This is probably the story Theroux meant when he told me that he sent a third story to *Antæus*' editor, Daniel Halpern: "one these slim stories offended his feminist girlfriend at the time—I don't remember which story it was and of course never knew or wanted to know the girl—and he refused to publish it. ('She'll kill me,' he said), so I told him I'd never [send] any more stories to him" (email, 25 February 2019).

"The Copernicus Affair": First published as "A Polish Joke" in *Paris Review* 20, no. 74 (Fall/Winter 1978): 90–100—their choice for the title, not Theroux's.

"Watergraphs": First published in *Boston Globe Magazine*, 9 October 1983, 10–11, 16, 22, 24, 28, 30, 34. Reprinted in the limited edition *Watergraphs* (Boston: Base Canard, 1994).

"A Woman with Sauce": First published in *Boston Globe Magazine*, 13 January 1985, 10–11, 18, 20, 22, 24, 26, 28, 30, 32, 41–42. Theroux told me this story "was prompted by my then girlfriend, Patricia Scoppa—I met her in 1974 in Cambridge, who later figured as the lovely but wistful girl in the novel, *An Adultery*, named Marina—and a bossy mother from Avelino who was extremely cruel to her" (email 25 February 2019).

FABLES

"The Schinocephalic Waif": First published as a booklet (Boston: David Godine, 1975), illustrated by Stan Washburn (1943–). A year earlier, Theroux published his first essay on Edward Gorey, a major influence on Theroux's early fables ("The Incredible Revenge of Edward Gorey," *Esquire*, June 1974).

"The Great Wheadle Tragedy": First published as a booklet (Boston: David Godine, 1975), illustrated by Stan Washburn.

"The Wragby Cars": This was intended to be published in book form by Godine shortly after the preceding two; Godine assigned it an ISBN and a publication date (0-87923-137-8, 1976, according to the 1976 ed. of *Books in Print*), but cancelled the volume, apparently because of a disagreement over Washburn's illustrations. The same edition of *Books in Print* lists what was to have been a paperback omnibus edition of all three entitled *Trilogy of Adult Fables* (0-87923-162-9), priced at $3.95, also scheduled for 1976. The text, sans illustrations, was eventually published in the *Mississippi Review* 15.3 (no. 45)(Spring/Summer 1987): 101–3. In 1993 I proposed publishing the trilogy of fables in a single volume at Dalkey Archive Press, but the author and illustrator once again fell out: Washburn had created a new set of illustrations for "The Wragby Cars," which Theroux disliked, and Washburn refused to allow the use his original illustrations, which we liked. The materials for this unrealized edition are now among my papers at the Harry Ransom Center. The *OED* defines "cars" (more often spelled "carse") as "The stretch of low alluvial land along the banks of some Scottish rivers"; Wragby is a small town in Lincolnshire.

"Master Snickup's Cloak": First published as "Lynda van Cats" in *Antæus* 19 (Autumn 1975), 47–51, and reprinted in the first *Pushcart Prize* annual the following year. It was published in book form in 1979 by Paper Tiger Books (Limpsfield, Surrey) and Harper & Row (New York), illustrated by Brian Froud (1947–), and then reprinted (sans illustrations) in *Darconville's Cat*, pp. 140–44, where it functions as a parable of the relationship between Alaric Darconville, Isabel Rawsthorne, and her future husband Gilbert van der Slang. The *Collected Stories* text favors the last version, where, for example, the brothel called De Zwarte Hertogin (The Black Duchess) replaces the earlier De Valk Gravin (The Falcon Countess).

"St. Winifred's Bells": First published in *Boston Monthly* 1.2 (June/July

1979) (per Theroux; not seen). St. Winifred's Well, mentioned in the fable, is a pilgrimage site in Wales. The music, handwritten by Theroux, is from a setting of a poem by Richard Watson Dixon (1833–1900). This tale of Prince Alexander and the maiden Patricia seems to have been prompted, like "A Woman with Sauce," by his relationship with Patricia Scoppa.

"Captain Birdseye's Expedition": First published in *Hard Scuffle, Folio /79* (1979): 48–49, reprinted shortly after in *Iowa Review* 11.2/3 (Spring/ Summer 1980): 35–38. Throughout 2019 Theroux expanded the original 1200-word story to nearly 7000 words.

"A Christmas Fable": First published as a limited edition booklet, privately printed in 1983 for friends of the author. The fourth line of the traditional carol the orphans sing usually ends "we will *drink* to thee." Theroux added cartoons to it for inclusion in an anthology edited by Steven Heller entitled *The Ultimate Stocking Stuffer*, which A & W Publishers planned to bring out in December 1983, but apparently it never appeared. Photocopies of illustrated page proofs are in my Theroux collection at the Harry Ransom Center. In 2019 Theroux more than doubled the length of the fable.

"Julia de Chateauroux; or, The Girl with Blue Hair": written in 1993; previously unpublished. The "Also by Alexander Theroux" page in *The Primary Colors* (1994) includes *Julia de Chateauroux; or, The Girl with Blue Hair and Other Fables*, which was to have been published by Dalkey Archive in 1994 (consisting of this and the seven preceding fables), but was canceled due to the author's refusal to simplify the wordy, triple-tiered title. (Theroux's refusal to compromise with editors, or to see matters from their viewpoint, is one reason why so many of his books have gone unpublished.) For the cover of that book (and perhaps the inspiration for the story), Theroux planned to use *Caterpillar's Mushroom* by Brian Froud, who had illustrated *Master Snickup's Cloak*. Some of the medieval details come from G. G. Coulton's classic *Life in the Middle Ages* (1910; several editions thereafter).

"Queen Gloriana's Revenge": First published *Conjunctions* 36 (June 2001): 221–25; reprinted with additional material in *Laura Warholic; or, The Sexual Intellectual* (Seattle: Fantagraphics Books, 2007), pp. 379–85, though the 2016 manuscript (and *Collected Stories*) uses the earlier version. The music near the end is from an Elizabethan song called "Fortune My Foe," which begins "Fortune, my foe, why dost thou frown on me?" Theroux chose this to replace the music in the *Laura Warholic* version (pp. 383–84), namely, "When That I Was a Little Boy," sung by the Clown at the end of Shakespeare's *Twelfth Night*. The *Conjunctions* version had two bars of piano music that would be unplayable on a mandolin, as I later pointed out to him. He accepted my suggestion to use the Shakespearean song instead, and I believe I sent him "Fortune My Foe" at the same time as an alternative. Both are from *Songs from Shakespeare's Plays and Popular Songs of Shakespeare's Time*, ed. Tom Kines (NY: Oak Publications, 1964).

"St. Malecroix": Date uncertain: Theroux told me 1981, but that may have been a slip for a much later date due to (a) its placement in *Collected Stories* and (b) for the presence of the character named Paul Nosedocks: see Theroux's poem of that name (*Collected Poems*, 70; first published in 1996). Previously unpublished. The Latin line in the first paragraph is a schoolboy pun that comically translates, "Where O where is [my] underwear?" (It usually reads "*meus sub ubi*," but when asked, Theroux replied, "back in my seminary the word was—intentionally—left out" [email 25 May 2019]). Theroux originally had "*Fidem scit*": literally "He knows the faith" but sounding like "Feed 'em shit," which he used in "Madonna Pica" instead. The setting resembles that story, which is why I suggested it should be grouped with the stories, but Theroux decided to place it with the fables.

"Song at Twilight: A Fable of Ancient China": Written in 2001, expanded in 2019. Previously unpublished. Theroux uses older spellings for such names as Qin Shi Huang (third century BCE).

"The Enthronization of Vinegarfly": Written in 2002, expanded in 2019. Previously unpublished.

"The Ratmansky Diamonds": Written in 2006 (and updated later), previously unpublished. On the contents page of the fables manuscript, the title is "The Schafenzoyer Diamonds," and then Theroux changed it to "The Wroclaw Diamonds" before settling on the present title. The reference at the beginning to "Nedda Nipps Wolfsblatt—she later wrote a book about it" originally read "Irene Weisberg Zisblatt—she wrote a book about it called *The Fifth Diamond*," which was published in 2008.

"Rolf Vowels": Previously unpublished. Emailed to me on 1 October

2018, and a revised version the next day. Expanded in 2019. When I told Theroux I thought the ending hokey, he defended it by writing: "The Son of Sam came to God, while, paradoxically, a mother of one of the girls he shot came to despise God, religion and church" (email, 30 October 2018).

"The Missing Angel; or, Seven Blackbirds Stand for a Secret That's Never Been Told": Previously unpublished, emailed to me on 22 November (Thanksgiving) 2018. Expanded in 2019–20. This struck me as a fable, certainly more so than "Rolf Vowels," but Theroux grouped it with his later stories in the proposed book.

"The Oxholt Violin": Previously published. First draft emailed to me on 15 August 2019 (two days before Theroux's eightieth birthday), asking my opinion of the ending, which he wasn't sure of. Revised version emailed 21 August.

LATER STORIES

"Summer Bellerophon; or, The Agonies of James Querpox": Previously unpublished. The first whispered remark by Querpox is the opening lines of Edith Wharton's poem "Summer Afternoon." In the 2016 version of this story, the paragraph enumerating Summer's classmates who hate her used the real names of Theroux's former girlfriends, including the three female antagonists of Theroux's novels. Theroux said he wrote this and all the remaining stories (except for "Blackrobe" and "A Note on the Type") "since 2013" (email 25 February 2019), but later dated this story 1987 (email 1 March 2019). Further expanded in 2019.

"Blackrobe": First published as a memoir entitled "Camp Cedar Crest" in *Conjunctions* 37 (Fall 2001): 374–80. Theroux expanded it twofold and then included it in both his stories and fables manuscripts. Interestingly, he deleted a reference in the *Conjunctions* version to his future wife; after the sentence "I had six rolls of Wheatsheaf pennies," the paragraph ended: "A beautiful Korean girl named Sarah with an angel's features once gave me a valentine that I still have in a drawer. I wanted to know and I needed to feel and I felt I had to know the meaning of everything" (375).

"Envenoming Junior": Written in 2001 (but expanded in subsequent years), submitted to but rejected by *Conjunctions*; previously unpublished. This petite roman à clef alludes to (a) Theroux's poem "Insect" (from *The Lollipop Trollops and Other Poems* [Normal, IL: Dalkey Archive Press, 1992], p. 80, reprinted in *Collected Poems*, pp. 477–78); (b) his nephew Marcel Theroux's novel *The Confessions of Mycroft Holmes: A Paper Chase* (2001), which includes a character based on Alexander; and (c) to several novels by his brother Paul Theroux. Marcel's novel is alluded to on pp. 132–33 of *Laura Warholic*, a passage that is more revealing in the early manuscript version: "Mr. Fattomale who hated his brother was so driven to equalizing revenge that he forced his easily intimidated older son, Marcel, a spotty, deceitful little Blifil with a face like a handpuppet and a reptilian need to please his father, to hate his uncle as well and to write a novel ridiculing him with lies" (173). The *Laura* manuscript has details about Paul that, years later, Alexander added to the story to revenge himself on them both. He obviously sent a copy to his brother at some point, for the story is quoted and discussed in Paul's *Mother Land* (Boston: Houghton Mifflin Harcourt, 2017), pp. 151–52, after the publication of which Alexander sent me a revised, longer version of the story he had sent me the previous year. He continued to expand it, adding more than 3000 words between November 2017 and October 2019, including more pointed criticism of *Mother Land*.

"Madonna Pica": Previously unpublished, written in 2011 (per Theroux's email). St. Barnabas's Seraphic Seminary is apparently based on St. Joseph's Seraphic Seminary in Callicoon, New York, which Theroux entered in 1960 at age twenty-one. He studied Latin there, which is on display throughout this lengthy story (18,600 words), which Theroux greatly expanded between 2016 and 2019.

"Grasso Sovrapesso and the Bent Nail": Previously unpublished, written in late 2016 and early 2017. Further expanded in 2019. The protagonist's name could be translated Fatty Fat. The passages about oysters comes from Andrew Beahrs's article "The Decades-Long Comeback of Mark Twain's Food," *Smithsonian Magazine*, June 2012. The English translation of Tosca's famous aria is by Rebecca Burstein.

"Chosen Locksley Swims the Tiber": Previously unpublished; written in 2018 and emailed to me on 31 October 2018. The title alludes to the Roman legend of Cloelia, who escaped captivity by swimming across the Tiber River. Expanded in 2019–20.

"The Brawn of Diggory Priest": Previously unpublished; written in 2018 and emailed to me on 31 October 2018. Greatly expanded with historical detail in 2019–20.

"The Nemesis of Jawdat Dub": Previously unpublished; written fall/winter 2018–19 and emailed to me on 17 February 2019. For St. Pretzel, see chapter 51 of *Laura Warholic*.

"Genius": Previously unpublished. Begun in the winter of 2018–19, resumed in June, and emailed to me on 9 July 2019, with a slightly revised version following on 13 July. Further expanded in 2019. The setting evokes Theroux's graduate school days at the University of Virginia.

"An Interview with the Poet Cora Wheatears": Previously unpublished. Written immediately after "Genius," Theroux emailed me the first draft on 12 July 2019, then greatly expanded it over the next month, emailing me a final version on 22 August 2019. Further expanded into 2020.

"Acknowledgments": Previously unpublished. Theroux emailed this parody to me on 16 March 2018, saying he wrote it for the story collection that Little, Brown was considering then, but rejected shortly after. Further expanded in 2019–20.

"A Note on the Type": First published in the *Review of Contemporary Fiction* 11.1 (Spring 1991): 41–42; reprinted in *The Pushcart Prize XVII: Best of the Small Presses 1992–1993*, edited by Bill Henderson (Wainscott, NY: Pushcart Press, 1993), 268–70; and in *Watergraphs* (Base Canard, 1994). For its original appearance in *RCF*, I obtained Theroux's permission to print the three sections in different fonts. It may have been inspired by Ray Russell's "A Note on the Type," *Paris Review* no. 92 (Winter 1981), which may in turn have been influenced by the concluding "A Note on the Type" in Richard Grayson's *With Hitler in New York and Other Stories* (Taplinger, 1979). Grayson read the *Pushcart* version of Theroux's endpiece and alerted *RCF* of the similarities.

Poems on Sundry Occasions

ALEXANDER THEROUX HAS been writing and publishing poems all his life. The first literary journal he contributed to contained one of his poems, and the first published book he contributed to contained two of them. While still in graduate school he placed poems in such places as *Poetry Bag, Transatlantic Review, Latitudes,* and *Georgia Review.* He published only a few poems in the 1970s and '80s, but by 1992 he had enough to fill a 167-page book, *The Lollipop Trollops and Other Poems.* By the end of 1996, he had two more volumes ready for publication, *Maud Blessingbourne's Temptations and Other Poems* and *Ghosts in the Rain and Other Poems*—"100 poems to each book" Theroux told me in a letter—but he couldn't find a publisher for them. Most of those and hundreds more went into his *Collected Poems* of 2015, which contains around 750 poems. Since then he has been compiling a new collection, *Godfather Drosselmeier's Tears and Other Poems*—around 300 at last count—as well as a book-length collection of quatrains entitled *Truisms.* Poetry clearly constitutes a major facet of his work.

But what to make of this mass of poetry, especially his *Collected Poems,* a huge, unorganized jumble that veers from exquisitely crafted verse to doggerel (his word), from subtle aesthetic statements to crass kiss-offs to former girlfriends, from "The Consolation of Philosophy" to "The Mind That Moved The Hand That Broke The Hood Ornament Off My Mercedes"?[1] Fortunately there are a few documents that suggest how best to approach Theroux's poetry.

First there's his self-defining essay "Theroux Metaphrastes" (1975), where on pages 21–22 he may be recalling his fellow contributors to *Five Poets* (privately printed in 1966 in Charlottesville, Virginia):

---

1 Caps *sic.* Neither Theroux nor his copyeditor knows the rules for the capitalization of titles.

I am personally acquainted with crapulous and incompetent "poets" for whom poems are nothing more than the little maimed ends of life, bald confessional snippets flung to us ragged, unworked—assembled carelessly rather than *written*—and hastily misaccomplished for no other motives than to diarize their dull lives, crab about fate, muscularize a vita sheet, and/or enfirm a job. They inflate, don't amplify,[2] who, like fowls, have ten distinguishing sounds and nothing more—all of these, overmedicated little philophasters and slim attitudinising ghosts who feel a polysyllable dishonest, an analogy criminaloid, and a pre-1970 allusion more than a body can bear. . . . If W. B. Yeats is given the title of poet, why then what shall we call the thrice-encountered-a-day belly-busters, arch-scribblers, louts, and antichrists of wit from this generation who crowd our bookstores and lecture halls, shelling out for some kind of commemoration, and proudly signing, some of the worst fistfuls of jingle written since Colley Cibber got inspired?

Then there's the introduction to his earlier, slimmer, alphabetically organized collection, *The Lollipop Trollops*.[3] After giving a little background and noting the similarities between poetry and artistic prose, Theroux asks "Why did I turn to poetry?" and then answers: "Ideas of a certain kind, thoughts of a certain nap, can properly be expressed in no other way, not merely one-take ideas, rather substances requiring a specific form, the way brandy suitably calls for a snifter, absinthe a drip glass, and champagne an eight-ounce 'tulip'" (xi). He enjoyed poetry from childhood, and later on the rhythmic language of Catholic liturgy. He names some favorite poets: "Shakespeare, of course. Milton, especially. The Jacobeans. Middleton. Tourneur. John Webster. Pope. Swift. Keats. Dickinson. Yeats. Wallace Stevens. Philip Larkin" (xii). And he insists, "I take poetry seriously. I wrote none of these poems merely as a diversion" (xiii).

Though his list of favorites was not intended to be exhaustive, it's worth noting that there are no poets later than Philip Larkin, whose best work was published between 1955 and 1974. He was contemptuous

2 The essay begins with a headnote distinguishing the rhetorical terms *amplificatio*, a virtue, from *inflatio*, a fault.

3 Published in August 1992 by Dalkey Archive Press; it was preceded by a limited edition entitled *History Is Made at Night*, published by Aralia Press in March of that year. The latter contains fifteen poems, all of which were included in *The Lollipop Trollops*, just as all of its poems were eventually included in *Collected Poems*. I was an acquiring editor at Dalkey then, and offered to publish it after another publisher (perhaps Aralia) changed its mind about doing it.

of Beat poetry, especially that of Allen Ginsberg, and in 1997 lambasted modern poetry in general when the *Los Angeles Times Book Review* invited him to review Ecco's omnibus edition of John Ashbery's first five books, *The Mooring of Starting Out*. Three weeks later, the newspaper published Ashbery's letter to the editor complaining of the review, as well as Theroux's reply, a compact and valuable position paper that not only clarifies his dim view of modern poetry but illuminates the aesthetic guidelines he follows in his own poetry.[4]

After thanking Theroux for the few positive things he says about his work, Ashbery notes that Theroux expresses his overall disapproval of his poetry by lumping him with (as Theroux described them) "the likes of Ezra Pound, Gertrude Stein, the queen of tautology, and yam-in-the-mouth Charles Olson, a total fraud, and Louis Zukofsky of whose uncircumscribable poem 'A' critic Hugh Kenner once admiringly pronounced, 'Critics will take a thousand years to solve it'. . . . he meant this as praise." Ashbery continues: "Theroux goes on to say that certain works of mine that he considers 'impenetrable,' like theirs, are 'nothing less than irresponsible.' In my case: 'for a writer to write codswallop? Jabber? . . . can become nothing less than infuriating, I would even assert it is morally indefensible.'" The poet concludes his letter with: "Rather than trashing Stein, Pound, Olson, Zukofsky and Berryman *en passant*,[5] it would have been more enlightening for the reader if Theroux had outlined the nature of his case against them a little more amply, then and only then dropping the shoe of the morality issue. . . . I for one would have been interested to learn why a writer of Theroux's stature has it in for a handful of America's great modernist poets." Theroux obliges with an 800-word response.

He objects principally to the incomprehensibility of so much modern poetry, and does so in his best Corvine manner:

> I am unaware of shooting at any bêtes noires in my review of his books other than those who practice the crapulous and farcically self-defeating act of offering bad or half-made work under the guise of serious poetry to be pondered, when it remains in fact impossible to be understood. . . . Willful obfuscation in a writer is completely indefensible simply because, like jealousy, it mocks the meat it feeds on. It is the ugly matching bookend of that other moronism, the greeting card verse of simple-minded hacks. . . . Obscurantism is morally

4 *Los Angeles Times Book Review*, 3 August 1997, 9, and 24 August 1997, 10.
5 In his review Theroux criticized "the late poet John Berryman's impossibly dull literary criticism, impenetrable walls of gibberish and jargon."

wrong precisely for the lie it tells in the pretense of coming forward with the truths it simultaneously—and always posturingly—refuses to divulge. . . . While I believe a good bit of incomprehensibility in a poet is often the result of attempted flight rather than of sheer ineptitude, a good deal of it is caused by the vice of intellectual snobbery and the assumption that whatever one writes is good, what Robertson Davies once referred to as the "shame of brains." . . . Only a fool would try to insist that poetry be easy to write or easy to read. No one who treasures such poets as Gerard Manley Hopkins, W.B. Yeats and Wallace Stevens, as I do, can possibly fail to acknowledge the unavoidable fact that difficulty increases with candlepower and vision. An incoherent poem is, nevertheless, no more tolerable than a drunkard's rant, except that it is more disgraceful.

Theroux has sometimes been criticized as a "difficult" writer, but only because of his large vocabulary—always deployed for lexical precision and "candlepower,"[6] not for willful obfuscation—and the complexity of some of his moral calculations, though it must be admitted he is occasionally guilty of "the vice of intellectual snobbery and the assumption that whatever one writes is good." And though his prose is always clear and comprehensible, some of his poems can be "difficult," but are never willfully obscure or incomprehensible.

Finally, there are Theroux's own self-evaluations of his poetry in the jacket copy he wrote for *The Lollipop Trollops* and *Collected Poems*. Making allowances for the carnival-barking exaggeration common to most jacket copy (along with editorial tweaking by their publishers), they enumerate what Theroux regards as his strengths as a poet. The one for *The Lollipop Trollops* argues that his poetry forms, along with his other works, "a single vision, the unfolding drama of a mind in action." He goes on to praise the "complex of styles, his versatility," justly, in my opinion, though he gets a little carried away at the end:

> Here are occasional poems that explore secret moments of passion as well as sonnets, simple unadorned lyrics, blank verse, jingles, and, along with some masterful Therouvian "triplets," much scarifying satire, forms in their plenitude including everything from closed couplets to bold free verse, from the dissonant to the deeply meditative to the elegantly lyrical. There is mad exactness here, great insight, rapier wit. Theroux has a commanding genius, whether writing of love or sketching a profile or fitting out thoughts like weapons with tips

6 Let's pause briefly to marvel at Theroux's choice of that term.

barbed with ferocious signifiers. With his love of words and penetrating way of seeing things like no one else, whether pastoral or political or polemical, he conjures poems out of his fingers like miraculous birds with an instant singing life.

The jacket copy for *Collected Poems*, which reads like Theroux's dream of an ideal review as well as a preemptive strike against hostile readers, is likewise accurate, though overblown, and again rightly insists on his versatility:

> Theroux works with words the way Bulgari, Chopard, and Piaget did with jewels. In the capacity of poet, his versatility is conspicuous not only in the beauty of his softer, if intense, and dazzling lyrics but also in his flaming invective. His *saeva indignatio* is a correct part of his satire. A good deal of his caricaturing ferocity clearly serves as a balancing need as much to keep his readers sharply awake as to maintain his candor and honesty. In much of his work, he is not so much fleeing from himself in his unsparing attacks as looking to justify various points of view or arguments that are kryptonite to the politically correct, cagily off-limits to the earnest, the faint-hearted, and the brainlessly conventional. Many of his poems tell stories, have plots, reveal great dramatic force. He can be a hard marker, with a lacerating command of language and Juvenalian sense of attack.

True, all true. Repeating the image of poems issuing from the poet-magician's fingers, the ringmaster announces the variety of poetic acts performing in his circus:

> Theroux can do it all, as he flashes as if from the tip of his fingers a bold and resourceful collection of ballades, villanelles, odes and epodes, sonnets and nonnets, elegies, *vers libre*, lyrics and love poems, elegies [redundancy sic], pastorals, doggerel, couplets, song lyrics, gravely measured romantic reveries, epithelemia [sic], narrative poetry, stately tributes and comic *jeux*, stark, implacable satires, and no end of conversation and confessional poems.[7] He prefers succinct and compact, self-contained forms, as did Edgar Allan Poe, William Blake, Emily Dickinson, and in music Frédéric Chopin who designed his *études* out of stylish invention, almost as an exercise.

---

7 By "conversation" he means "the conversation poems of Coleridge" (*The Lollipop Trollops*, xii).

The grandiose concluding lines of the jacket copy overstate the value of *Collected Poems*; I sincerely doubt it will "serve as a rich and astounding introduction to a new generation of readers," nor is it "nothing less than a watershed in modern poetry . . . and a major contribution to American literature." Serious readers of poetry would probably feel there are too many weak poems to support that claim, too much doggerel (again, his word) and trifling ("comic *jeux*"), too many outrageous statements, too much pettiness and crankiness, too much anti-Semitism and racism, and way too many verbal assaults on women. But for the rest of us it provides a fascinating tour of the world according to Theroux: his likes and dislikes (make that his *loves* and *hates*), opinions and pet peeves, his views on art and religion, examples of his stylistic variety and virtuosity, and versifications of numerous incidents and people in his life. It is not exactly an autobiography in verse, but close.

Do the poems measure up to his extravagant praise? Since my specialty is prose fiction, I haven't kept up with contemporary poetry; consequently, I read the latest edition of *The Best American Poetry* (2018, edited by Dana Gioia and David Lehman) to see how Theroux's poems measure up to what is considered the best today. I'd say at least half of those in *Collected Poems* are as good as most of those in that annual. Theroux uses rhyme and traditional meters more often than those Best American Poets, and is certainly more allusive and referential than they are (which I'll discuss below). Where he differs is his willingness to publish poems on topics professional poets wouldn't touch with a ten-foot line. I can't imagine any of the 75 contributors to the 2018 annual writing, much less publishing, poems entitled "Never Date a Woman with Big Teeth," "All Roys Are Fat," "All Actors Are Mentally Ill," "No Jews Can Actually Be Found in Japan," "Richard Simmons's Hair," "Why Do Homely Women Buy Expensive Clothes?," or "Departmental Secretaries at Yale," which begins, "You were both death on a bun, / Two bitches with bums spinnaker-fat. . . ."[8] None of them would dream of writing, even in jest,

> Jewish women are bilious cranks
> Who'd step on God to score a bargain hat
> They have profiles long as foot-long franks
> And will squeeze a narrow dime 'til it shits fat.
> They utter not a word they do not whine,
> Rush with delight to every goy malign,

8 After this appeared in *The Lollipop Trollops*, novelist David Markson wrote me to express his shock that anyone would write such a petty, spiteful poem.

Spit at every Arab face in Palestine.

—and that in a poem entitled "Bigotry is Ugly," which certainly lives up to its name. I can't think of any poet who would evoke "God's unalterable edict that / a woman actually cannot have a baby unless / she is also pretty" (CP, 223). I doubt any respected, anthologized, prize-winning poet would dare publish a loony lampoon entitled "A Fat Woman's Blocked My Passage All My Life," with such verses as:

> Move it, porky! Shift that fat caboose!
> I've a gun! And you're a grazing moose!
> Want to learn the meaning of a goose?

much less compare himself to Jesus while doing so. And while some occasionally dabble in light verse, few professional poets would expend their talents on such trifling subjects as pedestrian crossing signs, beauticians, guys named Roy, Little League parents, funny city/state names, local newscasters, lottery tickets, the difficulty of singing "The Star-Spangled Banner," of driving in Vermont, tarpon vs. tuna fish, *Gourmet* magazine, pitchers who deliberately hit batters, King Farouk's diet, misbehaving kids on trains, Canadian names, Christmas cards, or on who is uglier, Woody Allen or Alan Dershowitz, or who is the "biggest mook," Leon Uris or Herman Wouk. Few would write, much less publish, a three-page poem rattling off a hundred pet peeves along the lines of

> television is killing the national soul,
> Spanish in places has English replaced,
> going on welfare is everyone's goal,
> all seven seas are filling with waste,
> rap music is now considered harmonious
> the crappiest books are best-sellers,
> feminist rants are now seen as euphonious
> fish sold in markets are all bottom-dwellers,
> ("Goodbye to All That," 597)

—which is not a deliberately outrageous impersonation of an old right-winger's cranky complaints but a venting of Theroux's own views, as indicated by his other writings.[9] And while some might privately write a vicious poem on an ex-lover for their own grim satisfaction, they wouldn't

---

9 His unpublished *Truisms* is a 320-page compilation of observations in the same meter and rhyme scheme.

actually publish it if it was as harsh and venomous as those in *Collected Poems*. Nor would they always share with their reading public flowery poems written for private occasions, such as births, christenings, birthdays, and weddings. Mae West famously said, "When I'm good, I'm very good, but when I'm bad, I'm better"; when Theroux is good, he's as good as any poet in *The Best American Poetry 2018*, but when he's bad, he's worse, which prevents *Collected Poems* from being the historic achievement trumpeted by its jacket copy.

※

To understand poetry's place in Theroux's work, it might be best to start with what he identified in his introduction to *The Lollipop Trollops* as "the fistful of poems" addressing poetic theory: "Ars Poetica," "Fiction's Fun to Feign," "The Lollipop Trollops, "Padre Todopoderoso," and "The Way to Cedar Rapids."[10] The first compares the composition of poetry to goldsmithing, transforming "moron metal" into "gilded monstrances" such as those Benvenuto Cellini created. He emphasizes the "fluidity" of the process, and in the poem's last four lines enacts fluidity by way of enjambment and the absence of commas: "Poems are hammered and distinct // Of what once of course was molten / Precious and fluid and light and sweetly gold / As sesame oil in Szechwan." Alliteration runs rampant throughout "Fiction's Fun to Feign," where Theroux notes how "duplicitous" some works are, providing as examples religious holiday favorites (Dickens's "A Christmas Carol," Berlin's "Easter Parade" and "White Christmas," Dr. Seuss's *How the Grinch Stole Christmas*) that mask secular gripes. It concludes "All writing is confession, duplicity in session, / Our imagination's never more than anything our creed."

"The Lollipop Trollops" begins mysteriously "Matsu, spread out your netsukes, / A good one has no sharp points,"[11] but then in plainer terms goes on to make several observations on poetry:

> The poet is a veteran of the night,
> Method the soul of his management,
> Drawing lines that you might dream,
> . . . .
> A poem must reach, as a blowing wind

10 As this book and *Collected Poems* have indices, I won't supply page numbers for quotations hereafter.
11 Matsu is a sea goddess in Chinese mythology; netsukes are small sculptures worn with traditional Japanese costumes.

After constant rain manages somehow
To bring summer somehow in again,

. . . .

But poetry should please as well,

. . . .

As trollops singing "Zuk Zuk Zuk!"
Heedless as their clients are un-,
Poems to that extent are fun.

. . . .

A simple lyric makes us as unaware
Of time as time is of itself passing.
Can't sense be made of only what we feel?

The pleasure that we seek in them
And often find makes poems like boxes
Lovely as Italian bijouterie.

. . . .

We are never twice ourselves,
Whether read for sensuality or sense
A poem must disturb,

Badly remind you, spintry
And spintressa, of your need to be
Surely more than what you are.

That last tercet seems to echo Rilke's famous line in "Archaic Torso of Apollo" about the impact great art can have on the right viewer/reader: "You must change your life." But as the long poem progresses, the sheer fun of poetry begins to dominate ("Jubilo! Jubilo! Jubilo! / Skip into sheets of driving rain with me / So we can lick our faces and laugh!"), seen in silly rhymes (-un/fun) and personified by "the painted trulls in heels" of the title, who were cheekily rendered by Edward Gorey in the cover art for *The Lollipop Trollops*.[12]

12 We used it as the cover for Dalkey Archive's Fall 1992 catalog, the same season we moved from Naperville, Illinois, down to Illinois State University in Normal. We put a catalog in the mailbox of every member of the English Department to introduce ourselves, but soon heard complaints of sexism and pornography. Welcome to academia! Gorey also drew a cover for Theroux's *Collected Poems*—adapted from an earlier one for an unpublished collection entitled *Maud Blessingbourne's Temptations and Other Poems*—but the Gorey Estate denied permission to use it. He also did a striking one for *Godfather Drosselmeier's Tears and Other Poems*, which was posted online

"Padre Todopoderoso" evokes Stephen Dedalus's notion of the artist as "a priest of eternal imagination, transmuting the daily bread of experience into the radiant body of everliving life."[13] Padre Todopoderso (Spanish for "all powerful") is "A cleric transubstantiating hosts with a *hoc* and a *poc*" who takes immense pleasure in his writing abilities: "Ink's a drug. / I have titquills, paper, hands / Strong as a fruit tramp's / To wield a pen to circumscribe / The fat round wholeness / Of the vast compossible." (Compare Darconville's exuberant recovery of his writing powers in chapter XCVI of *Darconville's Cat*, "Quire Me Some Paper!") "The Way to Cedar Rapids" is his most enigmatic *ars poetica*, and was apparently modeled on Stevens's "Thirteen Ways of Looking at a Blackbird." In twelve (rather than thirteen) numbered stanzas of irregular lengths, Theroux's poem begins with an epigraph from Sir Thomas Browne: "We carry with us the wonders we seek without us; there is all Africa and her prodigies in us." For Africa Theroux substitutes Cedar Rapids, Iowa, of all places, as a geographic symbol for the aesthetic urge, both the urge to create and to appreciate art: "What Cedar Rapids waits / for you depends on who you are / and what you want." Art is not for everybody—"Not to have to go / to Cedar Rapids and being there / is much the same"—nor is everyone interested in art capable of a thoughtful response to it:

> Among the more irritating
> ideas are that those who go
> whistling off to Cedar Rapids,
> like small retailing Nebuchadunsaw[14]
> with his train schedules,
> grow large.

Such people "have not seen a city or a soul, / neither transfigure nor adopt, only verify," language that recalls the religious terminology of "Padre Todopoderoso." The poem concludes with the need to transfigure reality into art:

> In real Cedar Rapids
> a spirit that is stricken
> makes the bones dry, too. My gaze
> is for that grace unaware of itself, imagining pale alexandrites,

---

in 2019.

13 *A Portrait of the Artist as a Young Man* (1916; New York: Penguin, 2003), 240.

14 When I asked who this was, Theroux set me a riddle: "Starts with P, end[s] with T" (email 17 February 2019).

say, in skylight.

"That grace unaware of itself" is the subject of many of Theroux's kinder, gentler poems, and "alexandrites" (a gemstone) of course puns on the name of the poet-gazer. Theroux placed this poem third in his *Collected Poems*, announcing in a beguiling, riddling manner what he expects of himself and of his readers.

Does he accomplish what these artistic mission statements promise? As an example of Theroux's graceful manner, and of the response it can elicit from someone who has gone to Cedar Rapids for the right reason, consider "Ceylon's Isle," which is short enough to be quoted in full:

> I dreamt I had a glimpse of you
> As if with the beauty of a child
> running in the blowing soft
> wind of Ceylon's isle.
> But when I woke, I came to see
> As though I'd seen a child depart,
> The blowing wind on Ceylon's isle
> Had blown away my heart.

My old Denver friend Maurice Cloud, himself a published poet, once told me what this poem meant to him:

> That poem was something of a lifesaver for me all those years ago when I had moved to California. My marriage to my boys' mother was dead and she had decided, quite out of the blue, that I was a monster who was unfit to parent anything and was on the warpath. In those difficult times I often took refuge in the library at the Univ. of the Pacific which, fortuitously for me, carried the Denver Quarterly in which this poem appeared. The first time that I read it I felt that I had been thrown a lifeline, too it was special for me that it was in the DQ which was in fact another lifeline (I hated living in Ca. and was over-the-moon homesick). Anyway, I have a deep and constant bond with this poem and will always be grateful for his having written it.[15]

15 Email of 26 December 2017. "Ceylon's Isle" first appeared in the Fall 1997 issue of *Denver Quarterly*, along with "African Reflections." My first book publication was the afterword to Cloud's poetry collection *From Pine to Wave* (Francestown, NH: Golden Quill Press, 1976). He also read drafts of the new chapters of this book and made many valuable suggestions for improvement. He too is a longtime Theroux fan.

Three of these five artistic statements are in free verse, but more often than not Theroux works with traditional components of poetry—rhyme, meter, established forms and genres (announced in his jacket copy)—far more than most contemporary poets do. For that reason, many of his poems have an old-fashioned feel: "Willow Tree" might have been written by Sara Teasdale in the 1920s, and others evoke her contemporaries (A. E. Housman, Edwin Arlington Robinson, Elinor Wylie[16]). There's little here in the high modernist manner of Pound or Eliot—though Theroux greatly admires Stevens, he wisely doesn't attempt to imitate him[17]— or the wild Beats of the 1950s, or the sedate academic poets of the 1960s.

The one thing Theroux has in common with Pound is the plethora of people named in his poems. *The Cantos* contains hundreds and hundreds of references to people both famous and obscure, and *Collected Poems* likewise names names more often than most poets do. As the index at the end of this essay indicates, his poems are populated with actors, artists, authors, aviators, characters from novels, Shakespeare, and the Bible, feminists, journalists, literary agents, musicians and singers, photographers, poetry editors,[18] politicians, psychologists, saints, scientists, socialites and celebrities, sports figures, and television and radio broadcasters, as well as his parents and siblings, friends and in-laws, ex girlfriends, local acquaintances, and his wife and daughters. By contrast, there are only a half-dozen poems in *The Best American Poetry* that refer to public or historical figures. The subject index to *Collected Poems* looks like it belongs to a wide-ranging work of cultural criticism, which in a sense it is: there's critical commentary on literature, movies, politics,

16 Theroux quotes Wylie's entire poem "Velvet Shoes" (1921) in his introduction to *Feelings: Soft Art*, ed. Loren Olson (New York: Skira Rizzoli Publications, 2015), 7.

17 The unctuous narrator of Theroux's story "An Interview with Poet Cora Wheatears" (2019) surely speaks for Theroux when he learns the interviewee doesn't like Stevens: "It caused me middling despair. I worshipped that poet, loved his images, revered the boldness of his uncompromising wit, valued the conscious meiosis of his phrases, the ringing invention of his place-names, his breadth, the daring neologisms, the line breaks, the crisp exactness of his mind, to say nothing of the tightness of his stanzas, the *mise-en-page*, neat, taut, calculated, balanced."

18 Specifically, those who rejected his poetry submissions: see "To the Poetry Editor of *Yankee* Magazine Ms. Jean Burden," and perhaps the poetry editor at the *New Yorker* (575). As the bibliography at the end of this book indicates, Theroux was able to place many of his poems with magazines, but (like most poets) he also received a number of rejections, and eventually gave up sending his poems out.

the Bible, and culture at large, as well as the more usual poetic fare.

If arranged chronologically, the poems would almost function as a journal, first responses to events in the world as well as those in Theroux's personal life. Wordsworth famously defined poetry as "the spontaneous overflow of powerful feelings: it takes its emotion from moments recollected in tranquility" (preface to *Lyrical Ballads*), and for Theroux poetry has always functioned as a vehicle for spontaneous reactions to things, positive and negative. For example, on 11 September 2001, before the culprits were identified, Theroux wrote "What's that black odor? / I distinctly recognize / Religion / there" ("Twin Towers"). In Paul Theroux's autobiographical novel *Mother Land*, when the mother learns that the Alexander-figure has been jilted again—this time by a woman from New Jersey who works for a pharmaceutical company—she unsympathetically says, "Maybe he can write another poem about it."[19] And indeed he did, not one but several: see "Counterparts," "Thanks for the Memory," and perhaps "A Daughter's Confession."[20]

Often poetry is a first response to a topic Theroux would expand upon in prose. When Camille Paglia refused to provide a blurb for *The Lollipop Trollops*, Theroux quickly wrote a poem about her ("Passacaglia for an Italian Witch") before writing a lengthy review of her latest book (see pp. 152–54 below). As soon as his affair with Laura Markley ended, he wrote a withering series of poems on her before composing *Laura Warholic* (see pp. 61n10 above); one of them, "Laura Sparkley Takes Her Sketchpad to a Café," seems so fresh and spontaneous that he can barely put it in poetical form; it's basically prose cut up into captious couplets. In these cases, poems were like sketchpads that Theroux would later fill out in his prose in "moments recollected in tranquility" (if an edgy guy like him is ever actually tranquil). For example, "Whenever I see Egon

19 *Mother Land* (Boston: Houghton Mifflin, 2017), 57.

20 Her name was Cathy Weeks; she is also alluded to in *Laura Warholic* (pp. 146–47, 228, 293), and is mentioned twice by name in Theroux's essay "Nerd University," *New England Monthly* (October 1986), 62, 64. (When two friends and I met Theroux in 1985, it was at her apartment in Cambridge; she arrived near the end of our visit.) In his unpublished story "Summer Bellerophon," (1987) she shares space with Dale Atkins, the model for Farol Colorado in *An Adultery*: the passage that currently reads "Homely rubber-lipped Dale Weeks, who was known for stealing, boosted her hockey stick out of sheer jealousy. Fat, short unprepossessing Cathy Atkins, schadenfreudedly delighted, once saw the girl trip and invidiously cried out, 'Bust!'" originally read: "Homely rubber-lipped Dale Atkins, who was known for stealing, boosted her hockey-stick out of sheer jealousy. Fat short Cathy Weeks once saw her trip and invidiously said, 'Bust'!"

Schiele's *Nude With Crossed Arms* / you yourself pencil-thin and homely
descend to cry again" (from the sketchpad poem) was much improved
when converted from poetry to prose for *Laura Warholic*: "He only saw
Egon Schiele's *Nude with Crossed Arms*, a true refrigerant, grotesquely
thin, hipless, soulless, sexless, with her pointed nose aimed like a low-
class cheat in the direction of only another cornfield" (706).

As the subject index indicates, ex girlfriends are a frequent topic in
the poems. A few are nostalgic, but most are contemptuous. "Bouquet
for an Ex-Girlfriend" is a clever catalogue of foul-smelling flowers and
plants, and an acrid odor hangs over most of the ex-girlfriend poems.
After Laura Markley, the one who gets the most lines is a woman he calls
"Lubricia," with whom he was involved around 1993–94. (If Laura hadn't
come along in early 1995, Theroux might have written a novel about
her instead.) She appears of course in the poem of that title, one of the
longest in *Collected Poems*, as well as in "Litany for Lubricia," "Childless, Dogless, Manless, Empty" (another long poem), "Richie the Third,"
"Mrs. Fishcrane Caught Again in the Act of Betrayal," "Curse of a Dying
Harlot," "Trouant's Island," and "Telephone Conversation on November
6, 1994." The viciousness in these poems, as in the Laura poems, is hard
to bear. I'm sure in grad school Theroux read Alexander Pope's "Epistle
II: To a Lady," which could be described as a diatribe against women
if not for the empathy he shows for his gallery of ladies. It's unfair to
compare any poet to Pope, but Theroux is as harsh on women as Pope
is, but without his worldly understanding of their plight—or, it must be
admitted, Pope's poetic complexity. Theroux is so focused on narrative in
"Lubricia" that he neglects the poetry:

> A look in her eyes of panic
> Led her straight to the door,
> And I saw mounting the porch
> A bald man extremely cocksure.

A look can *accompany* someone but not lead her—a better poet would
have written something like "She went straight for the door"—and door/
cocksure is a false rhyme. "Childless, Dogless, Manless, Empty," has
some better stanzas—

> You light candles. Cold hearts find hope
> In candles lit against the sentimental night
> To fight the shadows of their lives.

—but others just heap up insults:

> Your gray hair dyed a plastic helmet,
> Wobbling thighs, flaccid body, half-made leg
> And over-perfumed self revolted me.

"Mrs. Fishcrane Caught Again in an Act of Betrayal" makes effective use of the snake as a controlling metaphor, but all these poems seem to aim no higher than trolling a woman in public by publishing her alleged faults, real and imagined, in as coarse a manner as possible. For the student of Theroux's novels, it is yet another example of his (i.e., his protagonists') puzzling habit of falling for women who are clearly unsuitable for him, which he addresses near the end of "Lubricia":

> Where does that leave me here?
> What sin is mine, you may ask?
> My sin was the vain assumption
> I could do an impossible task,
>
> To construct a human Babel,
> With mortal shovel and pail,
> And seek with pride to foster
> A relationship doomed to fail.
>
> The writer's vice, overreaching,
> Is what I loathed in such lice.
> And yet I found in her duplicity
> Myself—and wearing her vice.
>
> I saw myself quoted exactly
> And confess in my sin to say
> Upon my first seeing that woman
> I should have hastened away.

While the ex-girlfriend poems supplement his novels, the ones on writers extend his body of literary criticism. In "Theroux Metaphrastes," he enumerates the writers who have influenced him; in "A Poem in Which Is a Celebration by Negation Or, a Repartee on Jeopardy," he includes mostly the same names in a sillier setting:

> If on a friend's bookshelf

You cannot find Joyce or Sterne
Cervantes, Rabelais, or Burton,

You are in danger, face the fact,
So kick him first or punch him hard
And from him hide behind a curtain.

There are perceptive poems on Baudelaire's poetry, especially "The King
of a Rainy Land," while "The Raven" is not only a superb parody of Poe's
poem, but also a critique of Poe's poetics as well as a commentary on
birds in poetry. In "The Whirligigs of Pretense" Theroux challenges critic
Robert Hatch's negative view of Genet's play *The Maids*[21] with a more
insightful reading of it. There is a tasteless attack on Allen Ginsberg
written just after his death, consistent with the low opinion expressed in
his prose criticism (see p. 143n23 below), and remarks on a wide range
of writers from Auden to Yourcenar. There are also a large number of
poems on artists and photographers, to supplement the art criticism
Theroux has been writing most of his career. Of special note is his poem
"Peasant Festival," a textbook example of *ekphrasis* in which Theroux
creates a poem even more crowded and bumptious than the Breughel
painting he describes.

Two other topics stand out in the subject index: the entry for "biblical characters" demonstrates Theroux's close familiarity with the Bible,
expressed in tones ranging from the pious to the sacrilegious. (And as
that entry says, *see also* God.) Theroux's views on religion is a topic
for another day (and for another critic; as an atheist I can't take them
seriously). The other is the long entry for Jews, which seems to support
those who have accused Theroux of anti-Semitism. But it's worth noting
his views are not racial but cultural and political; he doesn't hold with
those benighted bigots who are convinced Jews are racially and mentally inferior to Caucasians, he simply doesn't like their manners, their
chutzpah, their self-aggrandizement (self-proclaimed "chosen people"),
or their political ideology, particularly the way they've treated Palestin-
ians ever since 1948. Besides, it's not just them: Theroux is a "panfurious" misanthropist (to use one of his words), for in his poetry there are
slurs against almost everyone—see index under "misanthropy." In his
autobiographical poem "Godfather Drosselmeier's Tears," he calls himself an "anthropophobe" (one who dislikes humans), which makes him
anti-everybody—except for his wife Sarah, the subject of several sweet
poems.

21 *The Nation*, 28 May 1955, 469–70.

That superb poem is a kind of *apologia pro vita sua/ars poetica* by way of Hoffmann's Nutcracker fable with Theroux in the role of the mysterious Drosselmeier, and is one of the finest poems he has written. It touches upon Theroux's feelings of neglect by the literary establishment, the topic of two other poems. In "Neglected" he puts a brave face on it by proclaiming "Whereas once I had no other choice but to accept it, / now I like it over here in the shade and write for myself. / Being granted no recognition sharpened my quill."[22] He blames the neglect on critics, "little hunchy villains whose calumnies pointed nose-like / to their own insufficiencies," but goes on to spread the blame to "Reviewers, agents, editors who by whim alone selected / which will *not* be the chosen people, which are the Jews"—an odd analogy given his attitude toward them. The bitterest poem on the topic is "Epitaph for Alexander Theroux," where he laments "he was envied by *les pauvres* // Who kept him from public recognition, / Never mind fame. / Such is the malignity of dwarves." As might have been predicted, *Collected Poems* was neglected by the review media and didn't sell well.[23]

※

A longer, even better version of the Drosselemeier *apologia* appears in *Godfather Drosselmeier's Tears and Other Poems*, the unpublished manuscript Theroux has been compiling ever since *Collected Poems* went to the printers in early 2015, along with a handful of earlier unpublished poems, one dating back to 1965.[24] It's a more mature collection, befitting a man in his seventies, with far fewer poems on trivial topics, though there are a few (Mickey Mouse, easy-listening music), and none on ex girlfriends. (However, the departmental secretaries at Yale receive an-

---

22 Theroux's sentiment echoes that of Henry David Thoreau, whom he quotes in *Estonia* on the commercial failure of *A Week on the Concord and Merrimack Rivers*: "Indeed I believe that this result is more inspiriting and better for me than if a thousand had bought my wares. It affects my privacy less and leaves me freer" (Seattle: Fantagraphics, 2011, p. 121—amended).

23 For the record, Theroux had a tendency to blame others for problems he created himself due to his obstinate, demanding, self-entitled insistence on having his own way, and his contemptuous disregard for the realities of publishing. He alienated virtually every editor and agent he dealt with, and turned down many publishing offers because the proposed advance wasn't as big as he felt he deserved.

24 The longer version, along with Gorey's cover for the collection, was posted online by *Conjunctions* on 13 August 2019 in commemoration of Theroux's 80th birthday (on the 17th).

other round of insults.) Poetry continues to function as a first responder to events, such as a poem on celebrity chef Anthony Bourdain written the day he committed suicide, and the two dozen or so charming poems on his twin daughters sound like spontaneous reactions, not recollected in tranquility: apparently there's little of that when they're around. There are several poems on Henry David Thoreau that were prompted, I'd wager, by a re-reading of *A Week on the Concord and Merrimack Rivers*.[25]

The collection includes new poems on several lifelong concerns of his: on Catholicism (pro and con), on Jews (with special malice for those celebrities who change their names), and on irritating neighbors. There are poems on a variety of birds, especially crows (his spirit animal?), on plants and flowers, on painting (pro Corot, con abstract expressionism), and on old movies. And like his earlier collections, there are poems about a wide-ranging number of people: actors,[26] politicians (four poems alone on Nixon), and writers (Balzac, Bukowski, Chandler, Kafka, his brother Paul [see p. 209–10 below]). There are further references to biblical characters, especially Jesus, including one on the many prostitutes in his lineage that begins "Is it any wonder Jesus was gentle to tarts?"

A poem entitled "Sexual Misconduct" addresses the charges that surfaced in 2016 that Theroux was guilty of misbehavior when teaching at Phillips Andover in 1982, along with four other faculty members. One former student, Marie Sapienza, attempted to sue him for damages in April 2017, but the case was dismissed "with prejudice" in March 2018. Theroux told author/publisher Jim Gauer that "this was a 'boundary' issue, nothing to do with sex," and dramatizes his version of the story in the poem in his usual caustic manner. He also wrote a new poem on the faculty at Phillips Academy—the school had barred Theroux from campus and Andover events—castigating them for "fearing light where truths govern."[27]

Godfather Drosselmeier's Tears and Other Poems is a fine collection that deserves to be published someday. Few would say the same for Theroux's other poetry manuscript, *Truisms*. This is a collection of rhymed observations Theroux has been working on for years (the first version he emailed me arrived on 27 February 2009). Although he described it to me in 2013 when emailing an expanded edition as "a book that will one day

---

25 Eight were published in the online journal *The Rupture* in June 2020.
26 There's a lovely epithalamium on *Buffy the Vampire Slayer* alumna Eliza Dushku, who in 2018 married Peter Palandjian, mentioned in *CP*.
27 His story "Summer Bellerophon" seems to allude to this episode. In a later story, "Grasso Sovrapesso and the Bent Nail," the character Odiosa Sapienzina was originally surnamed Sapienza.

be a true classic, if an eccentric one. . . . Quatrains, [rhymed] *abab*, all truly original perceptions," those he has shown it to haven't agreed. As an example of the work itself, and of an unsurprising reaction, here is a passage that was cut from Theroux's 2011 essay on cartoonist R. Crumb:

> I once took the initiative to send him, with a view to his illustrating it, a manuscript of mine entitled *Truisms*. I was astonished to find it not only returned but annotated by a Luddite, an earnest and flat-footed herbert, immune to irony, with neither a sense of humor nor a concept of either the tropological or the figurative. A few of my truisms follow—they were composed in quatrains—with Crumb's comments in brackets:
>
> A handshake's more than anything a code [—?huh??]
> You rarely see a pretty woman walking [not true! I seen lots of pretty
>   women walking—thousands of them, so what are you talking
>   about??]
> Dryness never figures as a concept in a toad [silly]
> There's lassitude in every rumpled stocking. [??]
>
> Baseball writers are always sentimental [—?]
> It is vulgar to smear jelly over bread. [snobbism]
> Commitment is avoided by a rental [? not necessarily]
> Texans like buckles as big as their heads. [silly]
>
> Eating coffee-grounds will kill a dog [nah . . .]
> Impotence is common among sports fans. [conjecture, snobbism]
> The act of voting is like feeding hogs [who says?]
> A ballerina's beauty's in her hands [No, in her legs!!]
>
> Chaplin was a bore compared to Keaton. [opinion]
> Mountains always range from north/south. [??]
> A good biscuit's never overbeaten. [you don't beat biscuits]
> Bad teeth slubber a pretty mouth. [slubber?]

He submitted the manuscript to his longtime editor at Fantagraphics, Gary Groth, who rejected it, telling Theroux "I think it would get us all excoriated on social media and would do more to destroy you and your reputation than anything I can think of—assuming anyone read it carefully" (email 4 October 2018).

Perhaps due to such harsh responses, Theroux added a subtitle ("Are

Generalizations Accurate?") and a 2100-word preface to a later version
he emailed me (30 October 2018), justifying the work. He writes, "Any
truism can often likely seem subjective, arbitrary, biased, peculiar, too
obvious, sometimes profound, and to a large degree politically incorrect.
One's characteristic reaction recapitulates what Alexander Pope stated
in his *Essay on Criticism*: 'True wit is nature to advantage dress'd/What
oft was thought but ne'er so well express'd.'" But as the above examples
show, these truisms are neither witty or well-expressed. He provides a
brief, well-informed history of apothegms and epigrams, but there's a
world of difference between the examples he furnishes from Fielding,
Ossian, Emerson, and Thoreau, and this quatrain plucked at random:

> Reality TV is all manipulation.
> In extremis man will search for God.
> Superstition animates a Haitian.
> Bankruptcy cases thrive on fraud.

I can't decide if the forced rhyme of "manipulation/animates a Haitian"
is ingenious or cringeworthy, or both, but I like the perhaps unconscious
rhyme of "God/fraud." Theroux concludes his prologue on a defiant note:

> Goethe said, "All writing is confession." I do suspect that for its strong
> opinions, without which no list of original truisms can exist, this book
> constitutes a kind of autobiography. But you could also call it a joke
> book or a litany of laments or an examination of culture. I do not
> shrink from self-revelation. . . . I am sorry, but, taken altogether, this
> is the way I see the world. I bequeath my observations to you.

For that reason alone, the Theroux admirer will want to mine this collection for insights into its author if/when it is published.

Theroux's poems are not really "a watershed in modern poetry . . . and
a major contribution to American literature," as the jacket copy of *Collected Poems* claims. Their real value is the light they shine on Theroux's
multifarious mind, and (as he put it) "the unfolding drama of a mind in
action."

INDEX TO *COLLECTED POEMS*

actors, 591–94. *See also individual names*
Adams, Ansel, 333
Afghanistan, 178–79
Aivalikles, Diana, 225
alcoholic drinks, 499–501
Alaska 327–28
Aldington, Richard, 433
Alexander the Great, 420, 484–85
Allen, Woody, 404
Alliluyeva, Nadezhda Sergeevna, 617
Ames Brothers, 82
Amish, 252–53
Andersen, Hans Christian, 313
Anthony, Susan B., 579
anthropophobia, 201–2, 398
Anza-Borrego Desert, 130
Arabs, 117–18, 167, 309, 354, 436, 503
Arnold, Matthew, 88
asyndeton, 565–67
Attack of the Puppet People (film), 144
Auden, W. H., 282, 402, 427
Augustine, Saint 169, 367, 399
Austen, Jane, 571
Austin, Gene, 573

Bacall, Lauren, 167–68
Baldwin, James, 369–70
ballet, 45
Balzac, Honoré de, 244
bananas, 562
Bánky, Vilma, 151–52
Bara, Theda, 216
baseball, 7–9, 77, 625–26
basketball, 58–59
Baudelaire, Charles, 317, 397, 413–14, 604
bear-hunting, 307–8
Beast of Yucca Flats, The (film), 143
beauticians, 254–55
Ben-Hur (film), 152
Bennett, Arnold, 507
Benny, Jack, 138
Berle, Milton, 295

Berlin, Irving, 460
Bernatonis, 614
Bernini, Gian Lorenzo, 561–62
Berry, Chuck, 240
Bhagavad Gita, 169
Bianco, David, 571
biblical characters: Abraham, 303–4, 315; Absalom, 370–71, 397; Adam and Eve, 612; Ahasuerus, 600; Ahilud, 562; Amaziah, 49, 568; Amos, 49, 567–68; Baana, 562; Baanah, 562; Balthazar, 389–90; Damaris, 210–12; Daniel, 601; David, 399, 562, 604; Dives, 463; Eli, 270; Eli's sons, 7; Elijah, 621; Elisha, 404; Elkanah, 271; Enoch, 621; Esau, 32; Ezra, 16; Esther, 600; Goliath, 604; Hannah, 270, 271; Herod, 86; Herodias, 86, 320–21; Isaac, 303–4; Isaiah, 355–56; Ishbosheth, 562; Jeremiah, 476; Jeroboam II, 49; Jezebel, 553; Job, 389, 478–79, 535, 551–53; ; John (apostle), 348; John the Baptist, 86; Jonah, 40; Joseph, 306, 513, 601; Judas, 451, 453, 535; Lazarus, 315, 347–48, 475; Lydia, 368; Mary, 297, 348, 426–27, 603; Mary Magdalene, 347; Matthew, 367; Michael, 271; Mordechai, 600; Moses, 326, 399, 494–96; Nehemiah, 385; Noah, 512; Pontius Pilate, 86, 282–84; Rachel, 306; Rechab, 562; Rimmon, 562; Salome, 86; Samson, 255; Sarah, 304; Satan (aka Lucifer), 56, 63, 96, 131, 271–73, 630; Saul, 562; Simon of Cyrene, 140; Solomon, 562; Tobit (and dog), 69; Timothy, 368; Titus, 368; Uzziah, 385; Zacchaeus, 367; Zebedee and sons, 322–23; Zechariah (and wife), 55. *See also* God; Jesus; Paul
Big Bopper, The (J. P. Richardson), 46–47
Big Knife, The (film), 338

bigotry, 117–18
bin Laden, Osama, 335–37
Billy the Kid, 297, 428
birds in poetry, 512
Birkin, Jane, 585
Bivens, Heidi, 230
Bjerre, Jens, 309
black (color), 46, 82–83, 221–22,
    268–69, 554–55
Black Torment (film), 144
Blaise, Saint, 466
Blake, William, 441
blue (color), 408
Blue Dahlia, The (film), 394–95
Bodfish, Nelson, 415–16
Bogart, Humphrey, 167–68
Bolaño, Roberto, vii
Bonhoeffer, Dietrich, 473
book thieves, 95
Booth, John Wilkes, 151
Borden, Lizzie, 138; and family, 310–12
Borneo, 207–8, 329–30
Bosch, Hieronymus, 174
Boston, 75–77; girls of, 120; Irish
    politicians of, 431–32
Boston Bruins, 396
Boston Globe, 87, 400
Botswana, 414–15
Brahms, Johannes, 158, 434
Brain That Wouldn't Die, The (film),
    142
Brandsma, Titus, 473
brevity, 244
Brillat-Savarin, Jean Anthelme, 404
Brontë, Emily, characters in, 129
Bronzino, 247
Brooks, Louise, 246–47
Broonzy, Big Bill, 476
Brown, Buster, 476
Brown, Harriet, 441
Brown, John, 250–51
Browne, Thomas, 1
Brueghel, Pieter, 313, 505
Bryant, William Cullen, 512
Bunyard, Edward, 404
Burden, Jean, 144–45
Burke, "Circle," 444–45

Burton, Richard Francis, 81
Burton, Robert, 509
Bush, George W., 294; and Adminis-
    tration, 601–2
Byrd, Euple, 525

California, 331. *See also* Hollywood
Calvino, Italo, 559
Campbell, Roy, 453
Canadian names, 129
cannibalism, 309–10
Cape Cod, 89, 111, 415–16; Hurricane
    Bob and, 223
Capote, Truman, 590
Carnera, Primo, 73
Caroline of Ansbach, 231–32
"Carroll, Sean," and "Jim O'Connell,"
    75–78
Cassatt, Mary, 193
Castellano, Paul, 590
Çatalhöyük, 610
cat noises, 440–41
Causley, Charles, 585
Caxton, William, 620
Ceaușescu, Elena, 320
Cellini, Benvenuto, 426
Cervantes, Miguel de, 509
Ceylon. *See* Sri Lanka
Chamonix, 412
Chang (Chinese surname), 187
Chapel, Don, 525
Chaplin, Charles, 274, 401
Chaucer, Geoffrey, 254
Cheap Trick, 190
Chekhov, Anton, 313, 485
Cheney, Dick, 174, 601–2
children on trains, 56
children's parks, 478
Chirico, Giorgio de, 442–43
Chomsky, Noam, 357
Christmas, 184, 188–89, 458, 596;
    Christmas cards, 132, 262–63;
    "White Christmas," 460
christening poems, 135, 213, 508–9
Church, Frederic Edwin, 306
Churchill, Winston, 531
circles, 555

city/state puns, 485–87
Civil War battles, 43, 256
Clinton, Bill, 177
cocaine, 445
Cochiti people, 446
Coleridge, Samuel Taylor, 512, 609
collecting, 177
Collins, Sue, 473
Colouris, George, 224
communion (Catholic rite), 447–49
compound consonantal sounds,
     517–18
Confidential Agent, The (film), 114
"confrontation freaks," 630
Confucius, 237, 407
Conolly, Jeff, 190–91, 195
Corey, Wendell, 337–39
Cosell, Howard, 531
Cousy, Bob, 58–59
Coward, Noël, 396
Coward McCann, Inc., 265–66
Crawford, Joan, 338
Creature from the Black Lagoon,
     The (film), 144
Creech, Edna Mae, 565
crime and women, 453–54
crows, 141–42, 388, 403–4, 454–55,
     512, 578, 626
Crusades, 61–62
Cummings, E. E., 456

Dada, 480–81
Dante Alighieri, 461, 463, 601–2
Davis, Bette, 239, 370
death, 71, 246, 405, 417, 424, 472, 506,
     621
Degas, Edgar, 554
Delacroix, Eugène, 231, 591
de Menil, John and Dominique, 405
de Mille, Agnes, 248–49
Denali (Mt. McKinley), 84–85
de Putti, Lya, 113
Dershowitz, Alan, 404
Devil Bat, The (film), 142
Dickens, Charles, 368, 460, 538
Dickinson, Emily, 160, 458
Diddley, Bo, 340

dolphins, 330
Donne, John, 199
doo-wop, 532–33
Dostoevsky, Fyodor, characters in,
     112, 371
Double Indemnity (film), 323
Doughty, Charles M., 219
Drake, Betsy, 227
dreams, 170, 225
Duccio di Buoninsegna, 631

Earhart, Amelia, 64, 421–22
Easy Street (film), 401
Eddy, Mary Baker, 579
Edwards, Ralph, 525
Einstein, Albert, 158–59
Eisenhower, Dwight, 176
Eliot, T. S., 324, 475
Ellington, Duke, 107
Embalmer, The (film), 143
englyn (Welsh poetic form), 189
Epicurus, 576–77
epithalamiums, 112, 204, 259–60, 554
Eratosthenes, 139
Eric, 72
Estonia, 314, 382, 386, 390–91
Eugene Onegin (opera), 493–94
Eurydice (author), 196
Evelyn, John, 418–19
ex girlfriends, 4–5, 14–15, 17, 19, 22,
     101, 118–19?, 257–59, 487–88,
     563–65, 622; Camille Petacci, 15;
     Catharine, 441–42; Cathy Weeks,
     15, 450–51, 455–56?, 526–27; Dale
     Atkins (aka Mixter), 497, 518–20,
     537; "Lubricia," 18, 23–29, 91–92,
     102–4, 538–49, 550–551, 568–69.
     See also Markley, Laura

Farouk I, 115–16
Farrow, Mia, 213–15
Faster, Pussycat, Kill! Kill! (film), 199
fasting, 493
fat people, 107, 114, 131, 153, 265,
     314–15, 336, 341–42, 405, 424–25,
     444–45, 457, 459, 493, 503
Fessenden School, 260–62

Fields, W. C., 287
Fish, Evelyn, 406
fishing, 620–21
Fitzwater, Marlin, 503
Fixx, Jim, 491
Fizeau, Hippolyte, 585
fleas, 174
flowers, 128; buttercups, 614; dahlias, 395, 589; daylily, 581; dandelions, 608–9; lobelia cardinalis, 594; night-blooming cereus, 524–25; persicory, 181; roses, 140–41; tulips, 1
Fontanne, Lynn, 147–48
food, 115–17, 146, 168, 203, 358–59, 518–20; crows as, 403–4; Malcolm X and, 268
football, 126–27
Ford, Harrison, 317
Formby, George, 573
foxes, 223
Francesca da Rimini, 461
Francis of Assisi, 483
Franco, Francisco, 462
Freud, Sigmund, 154, 282, 370
Friedrich, Caspar David, 591
friendship, 485
Frietchie, Barbara, 66
Froman, Jane, 239
Frost, Robert, 233–34
Fucci, Vanni, 463
Fuller, Buckminster, 589

Gaitskill, Mary, 196
Garbo, Greta, 83–84, 128, 246–47
García Márquez, Gabriel, 313
Genet, Jean, 559–61
George II, 231–32
Ghoom (India), 40–41
Ginsberg, Allen, 177–78
God, 413, 460, 465, 474–77, 577–78, 616; in Old Testament, 49, 270, 271–73, 326
Goethe, Johann Wolfgang von, 437–38, 506
Goings, Oscar, 389–90
Goldstein, Baruch, 67–68

Gottlieb, Adolph, 586–87
Gould, Glenn, 54
Gourmet magazine, 38–40
Grable, Betty, 127
graduate students, 7
Graham, Martha, 248–49
grebes, 528
Greece, 168, 225, 456–57
Gringoire, Pierre, 399
Guest, Jennifer, 379

Harriet Craig (film), 338
Harris, Wynonie, 476
Harvard College, 467–68
Hatch, Robert, 559
Hawk, Solange, 354
Hayward, Susan, 239
Hayworth, Rita, 287, 446
Hazlitt, William, 570
H.D. (Hilda Doolittle), 433
hell and damnation, 315–16, 408, 601–2
Hemingway, Ernest, 392, 506
Hennedy, Hugh, 602–3
Henry IV of Navarre, 187
Henry, Clarence "Frogman," 430
Heraclitus, 492
Herbert, Victor, *Babes in Toyland*, 19–20
Hillary, Edmund, 366
Himmler, Heinrich, 321
Hitler, Adolf, 409, 572, 589, 591, 623
Ho Chi Minh, 400–402
Hoffer, Eric, 191
Holiday Affair (film), 338–39
Hollywood, "old-style," 113, 127, 351–53, 471–72
Holocaust, 326
Homer, 442, 472–73
Hood, Mickey, 168
Hopkins, Gerard Manley, 199, 465–67, 512
Howard, Henrietta, 232
Humperdinck, Engelbert, 487

incest, 477–78
Ingersoll, Robert G., 300

interviewers, 87–90
Irish people, 90, 253–54, 444; Boston Irish politicians, 431–32
Israeli–Palestinian conflict, 67, 118, 167, 354, 494–96, 601

Jackson, Melanie, 395–96
James, Henry, 200, 434, 535, 579
James, Joni, 479
James, William, 556
Japan, 97–98; wood in, 607–8
Java, 304–5
Jefferson, Thomas, 46
Jerusalem, 385
Jessel, George, 117
Jesus, 41, 62, 131, 140, 211, 282, 297, 300, 314, 318–19, 347–48, 362–63, 385, 399, 427, 475, 476, 595, 604, 613, 652
jewels, 553
Jews (and Judaism), 68–69, 117–18, 127, 177, 217, 219–20, 258, 291, 301, 304, 308–9, 310–11, 314–15, 326–27, 353–54, 355, 374, 385, 410–11, 436, 460, 589, 601; "Hebrew" vs. "Jewish," 136–38; Kissinger on, 563. *See also* Israeli–Palestinian conflict
Joan, 215–16
Joan of Arc, 433
Johnson, Philip, 325
Jones, George, 525
Jong, Erika, 117
Joyce, James, 509
juries, 180–81

Kaaren, Suzanne, 143
Kafka, Franz, 576
Kahane, Meier, 117
Kahlo, Frida, 221–22
Kant, Immanuel, 620
Katrinka, 161–62
Keats, John, 512
Keinholz, Edward, 173–74
Kelly, Grace, 239
Kepler, Johannes, 161
Kipling, Rudyard, 90

Kissinger, Henry, 563
Kreskin, the Amazing, 262–63

Labor Day, 295
Labre, Benedict Joseph
Ladd, Alan, 394
La Falaise de la Coudraye, Henry de, 352
Lahr, Bert, 381–82
Lahr, John, 591
Lake, Veronica, 394
Lamarr, Hedy, 629
Lao-Tze, 59
La Rochefoucauld, François de, 300, 568, 586
La Rocque, Rod, 151–52
Latude, Jean Henri, 46
Laurel, Stan, 310
Laurence, Alexander, 110
lawn mowing, 6–7, 89, 296
Lawrence, D. H., 433
lawsuits, 58
Lebowitz, Fran, 381–82
Lee, Stanislaus, 182
Leigh, Janet, 339
Leonardo da Vinci, 48
Lewis, Jerry, 295
limericks, 314, 516–17
limes, 355
Lincoln, Abraham, 580
literary agents, 395–96, 508
Little League parents, 481–82
logic, 78
lottery tickets, 490–91
Louis XV, 43–44
Lowell, Amy, 432–34
Lubinsky, Hyman, 310–12
Luce, Leila Hadley, 225
Lucian, 179
Lugosi, Bela, 143
Lukas, Paul, 324
Lunt, Alfred, 148
Lycurgus, 299
lying, 69

Macomb, Hardin, 354
magpies, 303

Main, Marjorie, 410
Makow, Henry, 623
Malcolm X, 268
Malthus, Thomas, 368
Mancini, Henry, 516
Manet, Édouard, 369
Mantovani Orchestra, 571
Mao Zedong, 146
maracas, 60, 440
Marian apparitions, 269
Mario, Father, 461–63
Markley, Laura, 182–83, 189–202
marriage, 64, 244, 469–70
Marsh, Ngaio, 395
Martha's Vineyard, 200
Marx, Karl, 308, 398
Masaccio, 612
Masereel, Frans, 614
Matto Grosso (Brazil), 80
Mature, Victor, 571
Maya peoples, 36, 42, 388
Maxwell, Elsa, 293
McCarthy, Joseph, 94
McDonald's, 518–20
Mdivani, Serge, 352
memory, 188
Miller, Henry, 355
Miloşovici, Lavinia, 145
Milosz, Czesław, vii
Milton, John, 91
misanthropy, 57, 180–81, 330–31,
    335–37, 387, 588, 612
Mitchum, Bob, 338–39
Mobutu Sese Seko, 168
Modotti, Tina, 228
Mohammed, 562
Molière, Tartuffe in, 132
Monet, Claude, 45–46, 251, 369, 595
Monk, Ray, 488
Monroe, Marilyn, 203, 239
Mont Blanc, 412
Montherlant, Henry de, 45–46
Moore, J., 166
Moore, Steven, 499
More, Thomas, 408
Mormons, 483
Mott, Lucretia, 578

Mrs. Miniver (film), 286
Muslims, 117–18. *See also* Arabs
Mussolini, Benito, 142, 255, 498–99
Myerson, Bess, 629

Nabokov, Véra, 393–94
Nabokov, Vladimir, 393–94, 625
natal poems, 32, 348–49
National Public Radio, 375–76
NATO, 131
nature, 411, 608–9
Nebraska, 604–6
Negri, Pola, 113, 352
Nevelson, Louise, 371–73
New Guinea, 309–10
news broadcasters, 516–17, 531–32
New Yorker, 575–76
Nietzsche, Friedrich, 66
9/11 attacks, 256, 337
novels, literary analysis of, 559
Nutcracker, The (ballet), 396–99

O'Brien, Dave, 143
O'Connor, Flannery, 397
Of Human Bondage (film), 370
Oklahoma, 411
Oklahoma! (musical), 248, 269–71
Oppenheimer, Robert, 316
Ortega y Gasset, José, 465
owls, 331, 388

Pacino, Al, 591
Paglia, Camille, 504
Palandjian, Madelon, 213
Palandjian, Peter, 260
Palestine. *See* Israeli–Palestinian
    conflict
Paley, Babe, 134
Park, T. Peter, 465
Pascal, Blaise, 443
patriotism, 503
Paul (Saul of Tarsus), 56, 210–11, 368,
    474, 475, 477
Pavese, Cesare, 559
pedestrian crossing sign, 53–54
Pelosi, Eleanor, 571
Pepys, John, 418–19

Perkins, Frances, 579
Persepolis, 68–69
Peru, 34
Phillips Academy, 423
philosophy, 55
photography, 241–42, 407, 437–40, 572
Pinelli, Ralph Arthur "Babe," 7–9
Pissaro, Camille, 554
Plath, Sylvia, 269–71
Plato, 131, 481
Poe, Edgar Allan, 88, 334, 511–12, 628–29
Pointe-aux-Trembles (Canada), 43
Polonnaruwa, statues of, 12–13
Pompadour, Madame de, 44, 46
Pound, Ezra, 199, 433
Poussaint, Alvin, 429
Powell, Dawn, 64
prayer, 160, 162–63, 174, 188–89, 251, 363, 473–77
prefixes, 185–86
priests, 461–63, 622–23, 628
Pritikin, Nathan, 491
Proulx, Annie, 79
Proust, Marcel, 550
Provincetown, gays of, 589, 606
psychologists, 429

Rabelais, François, 509
Ravel, Maurice, 158
Raveloe, 57
ravens, 84–85, 183, 511–12, 604
Ray, Johnnie, 70
Rear Window (film), 339
red (color), 365–66, 409
Reich, Wilhelm, 158
Renoir, Auguste, 174, 554
Reynolds, Burt, 525
Rhages (Persia), 69
Ricardo, David, 368–69
Richey, George, 525
rich people, 357–58, 368–69
right-wing conservatives, 255
Ritter, Thelma, 238–39
Rivera, Diego, 221?
Rivers, Joan, 117–18
Robertson, Dick, 573

Rochester, John Wilmot, Lord, 535–36
Rolfe, Frederick, 142
Rollins, Sonny, 230–31
Romanoff, Michael "Prince," 351–52
Romanticism, 590–91
Romard (Robert Mardirosian), 515
Rome, 57, 116, 631
Roosevelt, Theodore, 158
Rorem, Ned, 376
Rothko, Mark, 342–46, 405–6
Rouault, Georges, 101
Rousseau, Jean-Jacques, 535
Roy, men named, 114
Russell, Ada, 432–34
Ryder, Winona, 629

Sade, Marquis de, 64
salmon, 290–91
Samoa, 340–42
Sanborn, Franklin Benjamin, 250
San Juan (Puerto Rico), 68
Santa Fé, 423, 428
Santayana, George, 556
Sappho, 433
Sargent, John Singer, 579
Savages from Hell (film), 143
Schiele, Edith, 408–9
Schiele, Egon, 193, 408–9
Schiff, Stacy, 393
school commemorations, 260–62
Schopenhauer, Arthur, 480
Schubert, Franz: "Serenade," 250; "Winterreise," 204
Scoppa, Patricia, 502
Screaming Skull, The (film), 143
Seuss, Dr., 47, 124, 321–22, 460
Sexeny, Julie, 435
shadows, 179–80
Shaftoe, Lord, 326
Shakespeare, William, 199, 307, 394; characters in, 47, 79, 219, 417, 451
Shamir, Yizhak, 494
Shearer, Norma, 286–97
She Beast, The (film), 143
shoplifting, 95, 629
Shelley, Percy Bysshe, 512, 535
sibling rivalries, 284–86

silk, 181–82
Simmons, Richard, 156
Simon, André, 404
Sinatra, Frank, 239
Sitwell, Edith, 20–21
smells, 98–100, 563–65
Smith, Patti, 228
Snowfire, Mary, 488–89
song lyrics, 44–45, 120, 125, 147, 163–64, 280–81, 333–34, 430–31, 471–72, 573–74, 611
Son, Young, 363–64
Son-Theroux, Sarah, 205, 207, 235–37, 240, 242–43, 251–52, 306–7, 333–34, 359–60, 363, 382–83, 392–93, 529; portrait of husband, 267–68
South Africa, 170–72, 510, 555–56
South Pacific (movie), 14–15
Sparta, 298–99
Spiller, Hortense, 93
Sri Lanka, 12–13, 70, 134
Stalin, Joseph, 572, 617
Stanislavski, Konstantin, 330
Stansell, Alec, 620
staring, 119
"Star-Spangled Banner, The," 521–22
Steele, Barbara, 143
Stein, Gertrude, 95
Stephenson, June, 453
Stepp, A. G., 525
Sterne, Laurence, 509
Stevens, Wallace, 199
Stevenson, Robert Louis, 538
Stewart, Martha, 319–20
Stieglitz, Alfred, 89, 242
Stone, Lucy, 578
Stroheim, Erich von, 352
sun, 585
Susann, Jacqueline, 117
Swenson, May, 128

tarpon and tuna, 583–84
Temple, Shirley, 227
Tennant, Stephen, 528–29
Teresa, Mother, 526
Teresa of Avila, Saint, 105–6, 561–62
Ternan, Ellen, 537–38

Terror of the Bloodhunters (film), 143
Thailand, 181–82, 208–10, 225–27
Thalberg, Irving, 287
Thatcher, Margaret, 253
Theroux, Albert E. (father), 63, 73–74, 89, 204, 275, 371, 623–25, 632–33
Theroux, Alexander, 87–90, 289, 300, 357, 468, 476; bedwetting problem, 288, 406, 461–62, 623–24, 627–28; boyhood, 73–75, 109–10, 216–18, 265–66, 320–21, 464, 513–15, 534, 604, 618–19, 623–25, 627–28; college years, 465–67; epitaph for, 402; literary neglect of, 402, 410–11; nail-biting problem, 371, 623–25; name, 420; on poetry, 425, 482–85; stutter, 47; suicidal thoughts, 412; teen years, 14–15, 46–47, 142–44, 175–77, 358–59, 390, 406–7, 449, 487, 488–89, 565–67, 571; Trappist years, 577–78; wife's portrait of, 267–68
Theroux, Anne (mother), 85, 89, 204, 263–64, 275–79, 292, 406, 514
Theroux, Ann Marie and Mary (sisters), 85–86, 263–65, 275–79, 292, 313, 358–59, 373, 477–78
Theroux, Joseph (brother), 516
Theroux, Louis (nephew), 416; and Nancy Strang, 204
Theroux, Marcel (nephew), 215, 415
Theroux, Paul, 70, 477–78, 507–8
Theroux, Shiloh and Shenandoah (twin daughters), 581–82, 631
Theroux family, 107–8, 262–63, 275–79, 284–86
This Is Your Life (TV series), 525
Thomas, Edward, 520
Thoreau, Henry David, 380, 398, 505, 556, 620
Three Degrees, the, 337
Thurber, James, 335
Tibet, 149–50, 528
tigers, 391–92
Tijuana, 157
Titterington, Eric "Titters," 115–17
Toklas, Alice B., 95

Tone, Franchot, 227–28
torture, 174, 298, 602
Tosca (opera), 128
Toynbee, Arnold J., 505
transvestism, 528–29
trees: buckthorn, 42; copper beech, 10–11; mahogany, 146; poplar, 42, 162, 481; tamarisk, 42; willow, 61, 162
Truro (Cape Cod), 136
Tunis, 249–50
Turandot (opera), 439
Turkana people, 530–31
Turner, J. M. W., 570–71
Twain, Mark, characters in, 485
20,000 *Years in Sing Sing* (film), 370

Ungaro, Emanuel, 294
University of Virginia, 465–67, 511
Updike, John, 306
Uris, Leon, 117, 416–17

Valéry, Paul, 240
van den Bossche, Aert, 444
Van der Goes, Hugo, 613
Van Gogh, Vincent, 141–42
Venus (planet), 584
Vermont, driving in, 233–34
Vietnam War, 360, 529–30
Violated (film), 143
Virgil, characters in, 250, 566
Virginia State Song, new version of, 44–45
Voltaire, 175
Vreeland, Diana, 135
vultures, 165

Wagner, Richard, 307, 589
Walter, Bruno, 159
war, 505
Warhol, Andy, 550
Warren, Earl, 595

Watch on the Rhine (film), 324
water, 328, 492; lochs and lakes, 378–79
Waugh, Evelyn, 375
Weil, Simone, 251, 410
Weinstein, Harvey, 382
Wells, H. G., 593
Wesley, John, 332
white (color), 183–84, 251, 268–69, 376–77, 380, 412, 524–25
Whitman, Walt, 241
Wilde, Oscar, 618
Winnie-the-Pooh (Milne), 307
Wise, Kelly, 438–40?
witch hazel, 328–29
Wittgenstein, Ludwig, 434, 488
Wizard of Oz, The (film), 224–25, 381–82
womandrakes, 305–6
women's rights advocates, 578–79
Wood, Mary, 579
Wordsworth, William, 142, 406, 534–35, 591, 609
Wouk, Herman, 416–17
Wright, Frank Lloyd, 325
Wrist, Susan, 78–79
Wynette, Tammy, 525–26

Yale University, 59, 189, 457–58, 509
Yankee magazine, 144
Yeats, William Butler, 199, 380, 512
Yegorova, Galya, 617
Yemen, 229
Yosef, Ovadia, 118
Yourcenar, Marguerite, 128

Zasulich, Vera Ivanovna, 112
Zodiac Mindwarp and the Love Reaction, 533
Zoroaster, 69, 122–24
Zungomero (Africa), 629

The Novelist as Critic

IN 1987 I invited Alexander Theroux to contribute an essay to a special issue of the *Review of Contemporary Fiction* that I had been asked to guest-edit, to be called "Novelist as Critic" (published in the fall of 1988). I've always felt that novelists often make better critics than academics for the obvious reason that they know what it's like to actually write a novel: they've struggled with conceiving and developing an idea, finding a form, breathing life into characters, plotting the narrative, revising and aestheticizing their work, and finally seeing it through the press, sometimes even defending it from doubtful editors. They've walked the walk, and consequently are far more qualified to talk the talk than professors or book-reviewers who have never tried their hand at fiction, and thus have only a theoretical notion of what goes into writing it. Theroux certainly bears me out; he declined my invitation for reasons I no longer recall—he either had nothing to offer just then or perhaps felt the $200 fee was too low—but over the last 55 years he has produced an impressive, sophisticated body of literary criticism. Theroux has voiced his views on literature in over a hundred essays, introductions, and book reviews; while only a few are on his own work, they all reflect literary standards and preferences that are useful in evaluating his own fiction, and it is those criteria—rather than the nominal subjects of these writings—that I want to focus on.

Theroux's earliest published literary criticism appeared in St. Francis College's literary magazine, the *Canticle*, where in 1964 he reviewed James Baldwin's *The Fire Next Time* and Günter Grass's *The Tin Drum*. His first sustained work of criticism was his 1968 PhD dissertation "The Language of Samuel Beckett," an expanded version of his 1965 Master's thesis, "Samuel Beckett: The Emunction of Language (an Approach to the Epistemology of Words)."[1] By any standard, it's a dazzling disserta-

---

[1] Which I've not read. "Emunction" means "the act of blowing one's nose,"

tion: Theroux demonstrates his command of the theories of language, from the Greek *logos* and Johannine *verbum* to the latest linguistic studies, as well as his thorough familiarity with Beckett's work and criticism thereon. He quotes from virtually all major philosophers, alludes to an extremely wide range of poetry and fiction—especially experimental twentieth-century fiction (chap. 4)—and is *au courant* enough to cite both Roland Barthes and John Barth's just-published "The Literature of Exhaustion." He traces the gradual loss of faith in language's relationship to reality from ancient times to the present: for "the Greeks, there was no gap between reality and language," and for Europeans before the seventeenth century, there was the "belief that words, handled with requisite precision and subtlety, could bring the mind in accord with reality" (2, 6). But after that, "a strange, perhaps frightening, idea arises: language is a product of the mind." We now occupy a world where there's often "a veil spun by language which shrouds the mind from reality," when it's doubtful "whether there is any verifiable relation between the word and fact, between mind and reality" (2)—and Beckett is the great geographer of that world.

Theroux identifies "five salient features" of Beckett's language: "(1) The language calls attention to itself; (2) The language avoids subject matter; (3) The language has little referential power; (4) The language suppresses reality; and (5) The language exists in a void" (18). Only the first of these features applies to Theroux's own fiction, and for that and other reasons Beckett seems an odd choice for Theroux, rather than someone like Alexander Pope (whose "idea of 'words-as-moral-adjunct'" he cites).[2] At the time, PhD candidates were discouraged from writing about living writers, and Beckett's absurdist antinovels are diametrically opposed to the kind of fiction Theroux was already starting to write. Having identified the salient features of Beckett's language and the theories behind it, Theroux proceeds to give a creditable account of Beckett's difficult work. (He took a copy of his dissertation to England in 1968, where

---

which Theroux found in Beckett's *Molloy* (1955): "For that would have allowed me, before parading in public certain habits such as the finger in the nose, the scratching of the balls, digital emunction and the peripatetic piss, to refer them to the first rules of a reasoned theory" (*Novels*, vol. 2; The Grove Centenary Edition [NY: Grove Press, 2006], 21).

2 Martin Battestin, one of his professors at the University of Virginia, reports that Theroux wrote a "brilliant," A+ essay entitled "Words in *The Dunciad*: An Approach to the Evil of Verbal Inanity"; see "Alexander Theroux in Virginia and London, 1964–1973," *Review of Contemporary Fiction* 11.1 (Spring 1991): 50. The anecdote that follows about taking his dissertation to England is from p. 62.

he tried to interest Beckett's publisher, Calder & Boyars, into publishing it, but without success.)

There are aspects of Beckett's style that clearly appealed to Theroux and that he would deploy in his own fiction (if he wasn't already doing so), beginning with the use of rare and unusual words. In the first six pages of Beckett's first published novel, *Murphy* (1938),[3] one finds "iridescence," "auscultated, percussed," "ebullition," "sublation," "tetrakyt," "conarium"—and they don't end there. Beckett would greatly simplify his language in later years, but even in his last novel, *How It Is* (1964), there are locutions such as "we let go our hands and turn about I dextrogyre and she sinistro," which even Theroux wouldn't dare. Among other elements of style that can be found in Theroux's work are the Irishman's use of formal discourse for informal, even wacky subjects; the use of lists; fanciful classical allusions and obscure learned references; funny names; set pieces; wildly varying registers of language; epigrams;[4] and nature-based analogies to human behavior (a particularly favorite device of Theroux's), such as "There are pears that only ripen in December."[5] "I like this colourful language," says the narrator of *The Unnamable* (1958), "these bold metaphors and apostrophes,"[6] a linguistic preference that Theroux would take up seven years later in his most significant essay on literature.

※

"Theroux Metaphrastes" is a 32-page essay that was published in 1975 both as a booklet and as an appendix to David Godine's reprint of *Three Wogs*.[7] (It was omitted from Holt's 1997 reprint.) This is the single most important essay that Theroux ever wrote, a white paper on maximalist prose of maximum importance not only for understanding his work but that of all maximalists—including those, like Rabelais, who wrote long

---

3 Beckett's first written novel, *The Dream of Fair to Middling Women* (1932), would not be published until 1992, three years after the author's death.

4 "The epigram incarnates the poetic laconism, the expressive brevity, which only the most thorough command of language can produce" (98).

5 *Malone Dies*, in *Novels*, vol. 2, 254—though Theroux could have found many more of these analogies in Shakespeare and especially John Lyly.

6 Ibid., 429 and 327.

7 Its thesis and many of its sentences were first tried out in Theroux's early essay "The Inarticulate Hero," *National Review*, 24 February 1970, 199–201, which contrasts well-wrought literary language with the near-inarticulate language of student protestors and countercultural spokespeople like Peter Fonda.

before the term came into use.

The *OED* defines "metaphrast" as "One who renders a composition into a different literary form, e.g., by turning prose into verse, or one meter into another; also, a translator." The term is usually associated with Symeon Metaphrastes, the ninth-century Byzantine compiler (another meaning of "metaphrast") of a ten-volume collection of saints' lives, but it has also been used (according to the *OED*) to describe a few others. But for Theroux, who uses a form of the word only once in passing,[8] a metaphrast is one who translates prosaic reality into poetic art: "Writing is life become art, not simply the random copy made out of one's dishwatery day or diary or panfurious whims" (27).

Before he starts, Theroux in a headnote makes "a distinction between two rhetorical terms: *inflatio* and *amplificatio*. *Ampflicatio* is not a fault. I would plump for it being a virtue." Unlike hostile critics and reviewers who regard all elaborate prose as *inflatio* (wordiness, overwriting), Theroux comes "down on the side of *amplificatio*—as did Burton, Montaigne, Rabelais, Sterne, and others memorably innumerable."

The essay was instigated, he tells us on the first page, by a reviewer who complained of the amplified (*not* inflated) style of *Three Wogs*. He doesn't name her, dismissing her instead with comically insulting descriptors—"wood-hewing Gibeonite, the mis-educated snool in factory shoes," "that gib-cat of a critic," "the less-than-informed howbeit (q.v.) who squawked at me in that funge she called a book review"—but it was novelist Diane Johnson, who concluded with "A cautionary word about the style, which at its best, offers happy surprises; at other times exasperation. . . . The language is always interesting and can be rewarding. But you have to be in the mood."[9] Theroux addresses the particular sentence Johnson objected to, then proceeds "to defend elegance for its own sake and to defend knowledge as an end in itself" (28) in a rhetorical tour de force of coruscating brilliance. It is aggressively elitist, deliberately outlandish, and unapologetically masculinist. He offers a master-class demonstration of maximalist writing by way of a fictitious Elizabethan ancestor, Cardinal Pierre Christophe Théroux-D'arconville, author of a writing manual entitled *The Shakeing of the Sheetes: A Yare Treatise on ye Englissh Tongue and Sage Counsel on Clinches, Flashes, Whimzies, & Prick-Songs with Regards to Questions of Style; Or, Put Not More*

8 Hostile readers "shan't force me, I promise you, into either a guilt or self-consciousness that might oppose my metaphrases, symbols, adages, sentences, hieroglyphics, fables, apologues, *suasoriae*, and *controversia*" (22).
9 "Wog Good, Us Bad," *Chicago Tribune/Washington Post Book World*, 13 February 1972, 8.

Inke on Thy Paper Than Thou Hast Braines in Thy Head. Theroux prof-
fers six extended quotations from the tutorial in a rollicking pastiche of
Elizabethan style, reminiscent of Anthony Burgess's *Nothing Like the
Sun*.[10] One passage Theroux concocted makes the most hilariously sexist
defense of "difficult" writing I've ever encountered:

> Sentences Long and Ornamented are oft Scorn'd at First: "Swowns,"
> cries the Gentleman at the Bookstall, what a sentence is this one!
> Yes, they do at first appear difficult; yet, bethink thyself anon of the
> lachrymal Bride who fear'd her Husband for his large Member, for
> she imagin'd hideous Pain upon its Entree into her Temple; yet,—
> tush! the Act is done, consummated, and she yamphs in Delight; if
> thou hast Apprehensions about this amplified Stile, think on the Bliss
> when you have understood, and oft wilt thou return for More and
> More, as did the Bride, newly Wyf, to her manly Husband, and eft-
> soones with squealings. (13)

It's worth noting that in a later passage the prelate praises simple sentences and warns against *inflatio*: "oft do I see a pretty Sentence o'er-
frescoed with Layer and Layer of Bombastic Horrours of needless Word-
ry, with superfluous Adjectives and Clawses all over it like Strings of
flawed Gems round the neck of a Maid" (20). That is, there's an art to
maximalism, what Stephen Dedalus in *Ulysses* calls "the art of surfeit"
(9.626). It is not an excuse to get word-drunk and make a spectacle of
yourself.[11]

Joyce is among those whom Theroux identifies as his mentors in a key

10 In his review of Burgess's *A Dead Man in Deptford* (*Chicago Tribune*, 16 July
   1995), Theroux wrote: "'Nothing Like The Sun' (1964), Burgess's fantastic
   speculation on Shakespeare's love-life, is more compelling than 'A Dead Man
   in Deptford,' not because Shakespeare outshone Marlowe but because the
   premises of Marlowe's personality are not as dramatic, gossipy or fascinating." Later in this essay I'll describe the unusual circumstances behind this
   review.

11 It's mostly a male genre, but on the distaff side there are (to mention a few)
   Djuna Barnes, Frances Newman, Elizabeth Smart, Marguerite Young, Brigid
   Brophy, Christine Brooke-Rose, Rikki Ducornet, Kate Braverman, Carole
   Maso, Gabrielle Burton, Helen DeWitt, Greer Gilman, Zadie Smith, Pola
   Oloixarac, Karen An-hwei Lee, and especially Georgiana Peacher, whose
   Mary Stuart's Ravishment Descending Time (1976) Theroux quotes at length
   in the yellow section of *The Primary Colors* "for, among other things, the
   edification of those undermedicated hacks, shameless book-a-year novelists,
   and jug-headed commercialist yahoos whose predictable prose comes crank-
   ing out of the trafila of their heads like streams of common pasta" (104).

paragraph, with some surprising inclusions and omissions:

> The Chinese have a place they call The Hall of Manifest Origins—as do I, in my mind. And of the writers whom I think might legitimately people it, for having taught me some of the ruses of the trade, I would name the following: Homer; the Cicero of the Letters to Atticus; Rabelais; Shakespeare; Milton; Aubrey; Proust; Dostoevsky; Dickens; Frederick Rolfe; Joyce; Saki; and a man whom I place last only for emphasis, a realist, oddly enough, and a harsh one, but no less than my mentor: Decimus Junius Juvenalis. (23)

I wouldn't have expected Homer (though see below for Odysseus), Cicero, or John Aubrey, and I'm surprised at the absence of Pope, Sterne, or Beckett (though they are mentioned elsewhere in the essay, and apparently taught him things other than "the ruses of the trade"). Saki (H. H. Munro) is a delightful surprise, whose influence is perhaps best seen in Theroux's short fiction. Conspicuous in their absence is anyone later than Joyce, reinforcing his earlier statement that he might be suspected of "finding everything after Joyce an impertinence" (9).

There is a crucial passage that would have meant little to the reader of *Three Wogs* but that, in retrospect, announced the major motivation for his later fiction: revenge. (Ironically, Theroux's mentor Juvenal condemns revenge in his thirteenth satire.) Note how the word creeps through the quotation that follows, italicized for emphasis near the end. Unlike the hack writer,

> the true writer is a crucial clinician of self, and, notwithstanding Keats's "negative capability," all things begin there. A writer, in fact, is constantly revenging himself against himself. No act of that self, it could be argued, exists for the writer until it is ransacked for its worth, if worthy it is, and then a crazy kind of movement—say dialectic, say revenge—takes place. The artist is a little cosmogener walking around God's World with gripes, smirks, and plans for his own. He is a man who must have a great sense of revenge himself, just as his characters do: Odysseus, Achilles, Beowulf, Hamlet, Satan, Quixote, et cetera. Allow a question: has it ever occurred to you, as it has to me more than once, that *revenge* in point of fact is the single most prevalent disposition in literary characters down throughout history? Shunt about your abacus. You'll prove me correct. (11–12)

As he typed those words, Theroux was composing his great novel of revenge, *Darconville's Cat*, which is prefigured at one point: "And how could the hero fall in love with that ugly tit named Linda?" (30). In later years he would publish both an essay and a poem on the topic of revenge, and in his third avenging novel the protagonist, speaking for his creator, would claim "Prospero is Hamlet who gets his revenge through art."[12]

I've already quoted several other passages from "Theroux Metaphrastes" in my essay on learned wit, so I'll resist the urge to quote further from this wonderful work. ("Someone somewhere say wonderful," he states with deserved self-congratulation after one of the Cardinal's passages [26].) Theroux not only blazons his style and influences, but in the second half also expresses his cranky annoyance with American culture, which would grow more intemperate over the decades. He feels the majority of the American public is too dumb to appreciate novelists like him, and he is especially exasperated with the book-publishing business, which he will likewise rail against all his life.[13] Theroux realizes that choosing to write maximalist fiction has financial implications, for it's not the kind of fiction that sells, with rare exceptions (Joyce, Pynchon, Wallace), and consequently publishers are reluctant to waste advertising dollars on something written "for a very small audience."[14] As an introduction to Theroux's aesthetics and worldview, "Theroux Metaphrastes" is essential reading.

Theroux began writing book reviews of new fiction around this time, but he wouldn't write another essay on literature until 1988, by way of one on the seventeenth-century Dutch painter Jan Vermeer.[15] His essay "The Sphinx of Delft" (*Art & Antiques*, December 1988) begins and ends with the importance of Vermeer to Marcel Proust, who wove numerous references to him throughout *À la recherche du temps perdu*. Theroux displays a close acquaintance with the French writer—his biography and minor works as well as the great novel—and closely identifies with Proust's style and attitude toward art.[16] For Proust, literature was a ve-

12 The essay "Revenge" appeared in *Harper's*, October 1982, 26–31, and the poem "The Revenge of Art" on p. 313 of Theroux's *Collected Poems*. The concluding quotation is from p. 199 of *Laura Warholic*.

13 This portion of "Theroux Metaphrastes" was published in the April 1975 *Atlantic Monthly* as "Divvy Up Dollars and Eat More."

14 In William Gaddis's maximalist novel *The Recognitions*, a character reacts to the author's metafictional description of this novel with "—Good lord, Willie, you are drunk. Either that or you're writing for a very small audience" (NY: Harcourt, Brace, 1955, 478).

15 Theroux has written a number of essays and introductions on art over the decades, but in this chapter I want to confine myself to his literary criticism.

16 In his dissertation Theroux occasionally mentions Beckett's short book on

hicle not for revenge but for redemption, even immortality, an attitude that tempers Theroux's vindictiveness. In a remarkable passage cut from the published version—one that begins to emulate Proust's style as it progresses—Theroux wrote:

> Proust surely found in Vermeer's painting what was confirmed in the theory and study of his own work: in those rare moments, those entirely fortuitous moments which the conscious will can do nothing to evoke, our being, momentarily released from the one-dimensional Time to which in actual life it is tied, becomes "real without being actual, ideal without being abstract." Proust had experienced nothing less than a glimpse of himself in eternity. He had touched a point in the fifth dimension. He had relived an isolated moment in its crystal purity, free from the strain of anxiety and the blight of habit which in real life can so often sully experience and make it nebulously unreal. He had relived it, this time, with insouciance because his being recognized it as real and ideal. Utterly real, with nothing in it to abstract from simultaneous realization, the moment was also the ideal of contemplation. Man no longer stood in his own shadow. The duality had been bridged.
>
> They are there, these essences of things and states of being, vials, each filled with a special perfume, its own climate, suspended in the vortex of memory, there sheltered and withdrawn from Time, perpetuated in eternity. And at a sound, a secret touch, we involuntarily tap these vases, which release their fragrance to make us breathe a new air. The air of paradise it is, new only because we had already breathed it in the forgotten years. Forgotten, eternity had preserved it for us in its pristine purity, no longer cloyed over or distorted by our fears, habits, or intentions, in the full beauty of its infallible proportions of light and shade, which vouchsafe its authenticity. These involuntary bursts of memory that assail us so seldom but so powerfully are like sudden raids into the treasure-house of the resurrected life. That is why, for Proust, art was more urgent than life, since it not only revealed life to itself, but resurrected its very essence, translating intimations of immortality into the facts of the dynamic medium which for him was words, for Vermeer, paint.[17]

Proust (1930), and, as noted earlier, Proust is included in the short list of writers who have taught him "some of the ruses of the trade."

17 The original essay is entitled "Vermeer's Secret," and contains much more on Proust than the published version does, including some trivial personal details on his clothing and diet. Since the essay was written for an art magazine,

Theroux found in Proust the motivation to expand *Darconville's Cat* from a satirical work of revenge into a grand meditation on art and the imagination, and found in Proust's stand-in, the writer Bergotte, the proper attitude toward the "dynamic medium" of words. When Bergotte views Vermeer's *View of Delft*, he says, "That is how I ought to have written. . . . My last books are too dry, I ought to have gone over them with several coats of paint, made my language exquisite in itself, like this little patch of yellow wall." That's Theroux's justification not only for his maximalist style but for his endless revisions (in defiance of deadlines). Proust's majestic, ruminative style and his extensive use of metaphors and analogies are characteristic of Theroux at his best.

Proust makes one observation in particular that clearly spoke to Theroux: noting that none of Proust's sexual relationships lasted for more than about eighteen months, he quotes this apothegm from *La prisonnière*:[18] "Desire, reaching out always to what is most opposite oneself, forces one to love what will make one suffer. . . . It is a mistake to speak of a bad choice in love since as soon as there is a choice, it can only be a bad one." By 1988 Theroux had written two novels dramatizing that dismal thesis, and ten years later would begin writing a third.

Like Proust, Theroux is an autobiographical writer, and he adopts Proust's defense for transmogrifying real-life experiences into larger-than-life art:

> Like Proust, Vermeer doesn't distort reality; instead, he transfigures it, in a way transubstantiates it, and finds in it a patch of yellow wall, a tiled roof, or a girl's yellow turban the means of expressing the highest poetry. . . .
>
> Proust, of course, well understood Vermeer's method, which renders things neither photographically nor too imaginatively—and, especially for that, he felt secret affinities to him, for Proust always extolled the art of hiding art. It was Proust, after all, who taught us that art by no means represents a copy of reality, rather that it creates a truer, a nobler, a more poetic reality. Vermeer and Proust shared this same vision. They were men determined to get the last ounce of what Ruskin called "fact" into their work, but who, to secure that end, had

---

his editor obviously felt justified in trimming some of the Proust material to keep the focus on the Vermeer.

18 "The Wife of God" (in *Three Wogs*) was originally entitled *La prisonnière*. Theroux's manuscript is with the Martin Battestin Papers at the University of Virginia Library.

no fear of the transforming imagination.

And like Proust, Theroux frequently moralizes upon his materials, pan-ning like a gold-miner for philosophical nuggets and universal truths in the incidentals of his story material and the actions of his characters. In both the scope of his work and its stylistic extravagance, Theroux was as inspired and influenced by Proust as the Frenchman was by Vermeer.[19]

I became an editor for the *Review of Contemporary Fiction* around this time, and in 1990 asked Theroux to submit an essay for a special issue devoted to him and Paul West. He first sent me an essay on pop music lyrics, but when I asked for one more focused on literature he sent me "The Detours of Art," which was intended as the introduction to a collection of essays he hoped to publish soon (which failed to material-ize). After explaining how the necessity to earn a living as a journalist and teacher has created detours from his pursuit of writing, and after airing the frustrations of being a novelist-professor among committee-loving academics, Theroux returns to his childhood to tell how he be-came an author. He then provides a brief overview of the essays he's written over the years, noticing that they are "curiously dark and betray, in places, you may think too many, a rather lingering disquiet over the nature of man."[20] It's a disjointed, half-hearted effort, which he probably would have expanded if the proposed book had gone through. Indeed, he expanded on some of this material to much greater effect in an essay published five years later in the *San Diego Reader*, which I'll discuss below.

Shortly after, he wrote another introduction at my request that *was* published. In *The Lollipop Trollops and Other Poems* (1992), Theroux discusses the place of poetry in his writings, but also took the occasion to defend himself against charges of racism, which put an end to his teaching career. Outraged at news reports of a gang rape in Central Park in April 1989 by some black teens, Theroux "had the audacity to call six rapists 'monkeys'—I was using the word in the sense of '*moitié singes*,' as Voltaire sarcastically described the French," and then wrote a blister-ing letter to a "black psychologist from Harvard named Alvin Poussaint

19 Theroux's reverence for Proust would persist: years later he reviewed (unfa-vorably) William Carter's thousand-page biography of Proust, complaining that the author was "too indifferent to the ongoing psychological need Proust had in using literature to revise his life," a need Theroux shared. See *Review of Contemporary Fiction* 21.2 (Summer 2001): 177–78.
20 "The Detours of Art," *Review of Contemporary Fiction* 11.1 (Spring 1991): 39–40 (correcting the final phrase from "nature of the man").

[who] within the week went on a television talk show and said the rapists, who were also black, were 'angry' (his word), implying, at least to me, not only that their actions involved a sort of social protest but that they were somehow relatively blameless or misunderstood."[21] Poussaint went after Theroux in turn, denounced him as a racist to his superiors at Yale, which then got picked up by the *Yale Daily* and the *Boston Globe*. No one at Yale supported Theroux, and let him go when his contract came up for renewal in 1991. He complains that it didn't "occur to any of them to read my novels, *Three Wogs* and *Darconville's Cat*, which, among other things, are wholesale vilifications of prejudice, bigotry, and racism" (xiv–xv). Nonetheless, charges of prejudice, bigotry, and racism would dog Theroux throughout his career.

A few years later, the Woodrow Wilson Center (Washington, DC) invited Theroux to give a talk on "The Novel of Learning" on 20 January 1994, but the event was canceled due to the extreme cold. He offered it to me instead, and I added it to the Summer 1994 issue of the *Review of Contemporary Fiction*. Repurposing some material from "Theroux Metaphrastes" and even his Beckett dissertation ("Language alone was always the living organism that formed the perfectly wedded relationship between Mind and Reality"), Theroux begins by praising the learned novel, and laments that "We live in an age where such books seem more and more an anomaly." He spends the rest of the essay updating his complaints about American culture with fulminations against political correctness, multiplying media distractions, declining readership and educational standards, current American fiction, the tendency of his magazine editors to simplify his prose, "the Disneyfication of American life," talk-radio shows—condemning all of it as "a circus taking place in a kind of ongoing Dunciad."

This relentless airing of grievances, here and in so much of his subsequent work, is puzzling and tiresome; it's not as if any intelligent reader needs to be informed of falling reading scores or the inanity of talk-radio, yet Theroux, unlike any other major writer, feels compelled to enumer-

21 Like nearly everyone at the time, Theroux and Poussaint were wrong. The five (not six) teens confessed to the murder, but later said they were coerced into doing so. In 2002 it was revealed that the rape was committed by a seventeen-year-old Hispanic named Matias Reyes. *The Lollipop Trollops* includes a poem about Poussaint entitled "Black Racist"; when Theroux prepared it for inclusion in *Collected Poems*, he dedicated it "to Dr. Pouce, child spychologist" and added a few more lines of justified outrage. Among the nuns who torment the title character in Theroux's fable "Julia de Chateauroux" is "Sister Alvina Poussaint, a sawn-off little rocking horse of stupidity, [who] viciously calumniated her with charges of meeting a Moor in the woods."

ate his endless complaints in a manner suggesting he is exposing alarming, hitherto unnoticed truths about modern culture. A dispirited rehash of his earlier proclamation, "The Novel of Learning" lacks the splendid swagger and stylistic panache of "Theroux Metaphrastes," understandable after twenty years of disappointment with both his career and his country.

Just as he was finishing *Laura Warholic*, Theroux published two more literary essays worth noting. "James Joyce: A Reverie and a Reverdie" appeared in the Fall 1999 issue of *The Recorder: The Journal of the American Irish Historical Society*, and mostly concerns Theroux's visit in the summer of 1966 with Joyce's friend and biographer Frank Budgen (1882–1971). It is clear that even at that early date Theroux was besotted by Joyce, familiar with all his works, and it is equally clear to any reader of the profound influence Joyce had on Theroux's fiction, both formally and stylistically. Writing in 1999, Theroux confesses he can no longer separate what he learned at Budgen's house from "a half-lifetime of copious reading by, on, and about James Joyce, books, memoirs, reveries, whatever," but the brief memoir celebrates the fourth key writer who— along with Beckett, Proust, and Rolfe—would encourage Theroux's literary vocation and shape his style and attitude toward literature.

In October of the same year Theroux published an opinion piece in the *Wall Street Journal* on creative-writing programs, and predictably gives the back of his hand to them.[22] Deploring the belief that anyone can write—"encouraged by quackmasters like Allen Ginsberg, who published virtually everything he put down on paper"[23]—he mocks those who think they can become writers by attending a few classes. He uses as a case in point Tom Grimes's anthology *The Workshop: Seven Decades of the Iowa Writers' Workshop*, which had just been published. Theroux pronounces a few of its stories "splendid," but dismisses the rest as "monochromatic": "Realism prevails. Safe, smooth pasta rolling through the trafila. . . . workmanlike, autumnal, droning, deliberate, efficient." Convinced that no one "can find a 'voice' by studying. Or a 'point of view' by critical exchange. Or a 'style' by sharing thoughts in a circle,"

22 "Tolstoy Need Not Apply," *Wall Street Journal*, 22 October 1999, W15.
23 Ginsberg was a frequent target of Theroux's scorn: he wrote a dismissive review of the poet's *Journals Mid-Fifties* (*Chicago Tribune* (11 June 1995), a hateful obituary in verse (*CP*, 177–78), and in his essay "Plaid" (*Yale Review*, July 1998), he wrote: "Regarding beatniks, I once saw Allen Ginsberg, that total fraud, wearing a plaid vest in the 1960s and, with his wisps of horrible scraggly hair blazoning out, thought he resembled a huge scrubbing pad, like Brillo, which by the way is something of a plaid object all by itself!"

Theroux relates a number of anecdotes from his own experiences teaching fiction-writing at Harvard, Yale and MIT ("Reluctantly, in need of a paycheck"). One develops voice, point of view, and style from reading and experience, not from attending class:

> The machinery of literature exacts mature reflection, to say nothing of time and experience of the world. These are precisely what middle-class college students—whose life so far consists mostly of hundreds of hours in classrooms—don't have.
>
> Not that they have knowledge either. I remember, in an undergraduate oral examination at Harvard, one creative-writing student had never heard of Robert Browning and didn't know what a heroic couplet was. Another guy hadn't read *Hamlet*. This is the upshot of granting power to sorcerer's apprentices—of allowing students to spend their time "creating" instead of reading.

He names some "sorcerers"—"I'll dispense with asking what would have happened if such iconoclasts, madmen and unbudging literary originals as, say, Laurence Sterne, James Joyce, Vladimir Nabokov and Nicholson Baker had gone to Iowa and got hooted at"—and urges would-be writers to go it alone: "It may seem abnormal but I advocate solitariness in just about everything: traveling, movie-going, walking, praying, sleeping—yes—and definitely writing. In conceiving what one's going to write. In the act of writing. As Laurel and Hardy used to say, 'You can lead a horse to water, but a pencil must be lead.'"

※

After writing an introduction to *The Lollipop Trollops* in 1992, Theroux began writing introductions to reprints of classics. I asked him to write one to Ford Madox Ford's 1938 compendium *The March of Literature, from Confucius to Modern Times*, which Dalkey Archive published in the summer of 1994.[24] His ten-page introduction is splendid, providing both sufficient biographical background and balanced critical evaluation of Ford's massive survey to prepare the reader for what follows. (Theroux did his homework, reading at least one biography of Ford, Alan Judd's

24 As a small, nonprofit press, Dalkey didn't pay authors for introductions to our reprints, who wrote them pro bono, but knowing that Alex was out of work at the time, I told him we'd pay him $500, then wrote a check to Dalkey for that amount so that he wouldn't know it came from me—otherwise he would not have accepted it.

fine 1991 book.) Stating in his second sentence that "We tend to learn as much about Ford in *The March of Literature* . . . as we do of the work itself," Theroux likewise reveals his views of writing and criticism. Often criticized for his mannered style, Theroux agrees with Ford that

> a passage of good prose is a work of art in itself, exclusive of context, "with no more dependence on its contents than is a fugue of Bach, a minuet of Mozart, or the writing for the piano of Debussy." Along with that he felt that being "slightly mannered" is characteristic of the work of all great writers, an idea that may come as a blow, constructive, one would hope, to the now popular Less Is More school, the Reporter-As-Novelist, today's undermedicated hack, etc.

Echoing the premise of the *Review of Contemporary Fiction*'s "Novelist as Critic" issue, "It was Ford's strong conviction that the tuition of presenting literature 'should be, not in the hands of the learned, but in those of artist-practitioners . . . men and women who love each their arts as they practice them. 'Hot love,' says Ford, as distinguished from 'dry delvings.'" Theroux wholeheartedly agrees with Ford that "the working writer was by far the best judge of literature," and spends a page mocking the academics with whom he worked for twenty years: "I have often seen constantly preferred to good writers eighth-rate academics on the tenure track . . . with narrow monographs and mediocre books of criticism dropping out of their insufficiencies like eggs from battery fowl. . . ." He goes on to mock the "modish criticism" of the day and "the kind of deconstructionist theorists of the sort I met with during my years at Yale with their fatuous poses, unbearable jargon, and sophomoric 'zones of meaning' ('I've got a secret'). The teacher as expositor is often a complete and utter fake, frequently complicating the obvious and obfuscating what he is paid to clarify."

While admiring Ford's personal (rather than academic) approach, Theroux admits the book is "often singularly wrongheaded and even outlandish" and provides several examples of Ford's inexplicable likes and dislikes. ("He takes three pages to sing the praises of the 'great' Jean Paul Richter . . . and proceeds to dismiss James Joyce in a few lines as a word-juggler. . . . He thought Captain Marryat to be 'the greatest of English novelists' but doesn't mention Tolstoy at all. And where is Proust?")[25] As an introduction to Ford's book and a diatribe against minimalist writers and theory-driven academics, the untitled introduction is another valu-

25 I had to look him up: Frederick Marryat (1792–1848), author of several nautical novels, once favorites of boys.

able contribution to understanding Theroux's aesthetics.

The same year, an editor at the Modern Library asked Theroux to write an introduction to Thomas Hardy's *The Return of the Native*, perhaps assuming the author of *An Adultery* would have interesting things to say about Hardy's 1878 novel on adulterous impulses. It too is a model introduction with the right mix of biographical background and literary analysis, but it's half the length of the Ford and lacks any indications of Theroux's own aesthetics. He notes with what can be inferred as disapproval the original publisher's insistence that Hardy add a happy ending to his gloomy story, but resisted the impulse to comment further on this gross imposition of middlebrow tastes on highbrow art.[26]

The Ford and Hardy assignments were not inspired choices—and Theroux is sufficiently well-read that he could write about anyone—but six years later a match was made in literary heaven when New York Review Books invited him to introduce their new edition of *Hadrian the Seventh*, the best-known novel of British writer Frederick Rolfe, the self-styled Baron Corvo (1860–1913). First published in 1904, this fantasy of a slighted writer who is elevated to the papacy is an extraordinary (and/ or extraordinarily ludicrous) work, one that Rolfe's biographers assure us is an accurate expression of his views and self-image. It is mediæval-ly Catholic, arrogantly elitist, ostentatiously erudite, transparently gay (and campy *avant la lettre*), spitefully vindictive, unapologetically misogynistic (and misanthropic and anti-Semitic), regally reactionary (and hysterically anti-socialist), prissily fastidious, rudely supercilious, confidently superstitious, egotistically opinionated, and prudishly humorless, inadvertently exposing the Catholic hierarchy as the silliest boys' club in Western civilization.

Rolfe (rhymes with *oaf*, Theroux informs us) uses this "if I were pope" premise to promulgate his skewed views on politics, religion, journalism, science, male beauty, and the menace of socialism and heresy of equality, among other things. Its only redeeming feature is its style, what Theroux in his introduction calls its "baroque sentences and arcane vocabulary," and what its author calls Hadrian's "quaintly correct and ar-

26 In a footnote on this matter in the added book six, Hardy explains why he wanted to end the novel with book five, then offers a choice: "Readers can therefore choose between the endings, and those with an austere aesthetic code can assume the more consistent conclusion to be the true one." In 1878 the novel genre was still considered mere entertainment by most readers and publishers, so it's historically significant that Hardy insists there is "an austere aesthetic code" that governs fiction as well as poetry and drama (the two "legitimate" genres of literature at the time).

chaic diction."[27] Here and in his other works, Rolfe revels in unusual spellings (Xystine Chapel, Theokritos), self-made neologisms—"taking Greek words from Liddell-Scott and Latin words from Andrews, enlarging his vocabulary with such simple but pregnant formations as the adjective 'hybrist' . . . or the noun 'gingilism'" (4)—and hyphenated verb forms: "He sent-back the guard to his station; but He Himself went-on into the vast obscurity of the basilica" (98).

Near the end of his introduction—a first-rate overview of Rolfe's life and the novel itself[28]—Theroux mentions that he first became aware of him while in London in 1968, where he attended a performance of Peter Luke's play version of the novel. He began reading it and other novels by Rolfe, asking in a letter back home to his University of Virginia mentor Martin Battestin, "Have you read any of Rolfe's (Corvo's) novels? Wow!"[29] Theroux had just begun writing *Three Wogs*, and though his maximalist style was almost fully formed by then—in grad school he had read the novels of Thomas Love Peacock, a smarter, more sensible satirist with an equally learned vocabulary—Rolfe shifted it into overdrive and kept it there for most of Theroux's writing career. The ostentatiously obscure first word in *Three Wogs*, "Picric," appears in *Hadrian the Seventh*—"A

27 *Hadrian the Seventh* (NY: New York Review Books, 2001), xiv, 162. The same style can be found in two more realistic, posthumously published novels by Rolfe, *Nicholas Crabbe* (written 1900–1904, published 1958) and his finest novel, *The Desire and Pursuit of the Whole* (1910–13/1934). A quotation from the latter serves as the epigraph to Theroux's *Lollipop Trollops*: "It is not my fault, I assure you, that things occurred in the order in which they did occur. I am not the regulator of this universe." Rolfe also co-wrote a fantasy novel called *The Weird of the Wanderer* (1912), which is the title of one of Theroux's later poems (*CP*, 142). He first alluded to it in "Herbert Head, Gent." (1972): "The weird, the wanderer, the ways of the rumpopulorum, Herbert Homotaxis noted, had essentialized the long dirty busride that had borne him southward for almost twelve hours down the line of the eastern United States into Virginia."

28 Though one Rolfe specialist has objected to Theroux's assumption that details about Hadrian applied to Rolfe as well, such as his wearing of glycerined gloves; but as one autobiographical author writing about another, his assumption is probably a safe one. See Mirosław Aleksander Miernik, *Rolfe, Rose, Corvo, Crabbe: The Literary Images of Frederick Rolfe* (Frankfurt am Main: Peter Lang, 2015), 111.

29 Martin Battestin, "Alexander Theroux in Virginia and London, 1964–1973," *Review of Contemporary Fiction* 11.1 (Spring 1991): 65. In his introduction Theroux says he saw Luke's play on 10 April 1968, but Battestin quotes from Theroux's letter of 9 October 1968, where he writes, "we see *Hadrian VII* tonight. Review pending" (63).

feeling that His Holiness was dynamic, picric, dangerous, pervaded the assembly" (341)—and many of its sentences are almost indistinguishable from the Englishman's. The following one, for example, could just as easily be from a Theroux novel as from *Hadrian*: "This world is infested by innumerable packs of half-licked cubs and quarter-cultivated mediocrities who seem to have nothing better to do than to buzz about harassing and interfering with their betters" (10). Or this one (also featuring cubs): "That was the gossip of my fellow-students, immature cubs mostly, hybrid larrikins, given to false quantities and nasal cacophonies" (29–30). One more, also using animal imagery: "The cardinalitial mask is as superior (in impenetrable pachydermatosity) to that of the proverbial public-schoolboy, as is the cuticle of a crocodile to that of *pulex irritans*" (73).

Theroux also took over Rolfe's proudly eccentric self-image to an extent; in "Theroux Metaphrastes," in a passage I quoted earlier, he pictures himself very much in Corvine terms, though he's much jauntier than humorless Rolfe: "I am a fearful Jesuit, I don't doubt. I am an antiquary, a pedant, a metaphysical deacon and special student on lease from the University of Padua with a swag-bag filled with ciphers, bolts, and refutations. I am a Roman Catholic, born to its jewels and bulls, and constantly aware of its byzantine smoke, wrought chasubles, traditional liturgies, and litanies infinite. You can find me . . . beclosed, pushing notions around on foolscap with a goblet of mulled wine at my elbow and finding everything after Joyce an impertinence" (9).

Rolfe continued to be a presence in Theroux's life after his 1968 discovery. In his 1978 profile of the Theroux family, James Atlas notes that Alexander possessed "the most valuable collection of Baron Corvo's works I have ever seen," and notes similarities between the two, in particular the revenge motive in their works.[30] Theroux told Atlas he didn't think he was guilty of "Corvine contentiousness," but if he didn't possess that quality then, he certainly developed it later. For those who know him, much of what Theroux says of Rolfe's personality in his introduction applies to him as well. References to Rolfe appear throughout Theroux's writings, and in writings about him: in his nephew Marcel Theroux's 2001 novel *The Confessions of Mycroft Holmes*, the will of the deceased character modeled on Alexander mischievously bequeaths "the complete works of Frederick Rolfe for an illiterate and vulgar niece."[31]

30 "The Theroux Family Arsenal," *New York Times Magazine*, 20 April 1978. Theroux later told me that the books weren't particularly rare; Rolfe's novels were reprinted (or posthumously published) in the 1950s and 1960s and were not too hard to come by back then.

31 *The Confessions of Mycroft Holmes: A Paper Chase* (New York: Harcourt,

✳

As noted earlier, Theroux began reviewing literary books in college, but his career as a professional book reviewer began in the spring of 1973 in William F. Buckley's *National Review* (where he had published one of his earliest essays, "The Inarticulate Hero," in February 1970), to be followed over the next 40 years by a hundred or so reviews in a variety of newspapers and journals.[32] They range from reviews of new books from literary authors (Kathy Acker, Aravind Adiga, Nicholson Baker, Julian Barnes, John Barth, Jorge Luis Borges, Anthony Burgess, Guy Davenport, John Fowles, Carlos Fuentes, Gabriel García Márquez, Jostein Gaarder, Siri Hustvedt, Gary Indiana, Elizabeth Kostava, Milan Kundera, Jonathan Lethem, Tom McCarthy, James McCourt, Bradford Morrow, Vladimir Nabokov, Milorad Pavić, Padgett Powell, Thomas Pynchon, Adam Ross, Will Self, Gary Shteyngart, Philippe Sollers, Paul Theroux, John Updike, William T. Vollmann, Paul West) to literary nonfiction (biographies, letters, and criticism by or about Harold Bloom, Paul Bowles, Stephen Crane, Harry Crosby, Fyodor Dostoevsky, Arthur Conan Doyle, T. S. Eliot, William Faulkner, Patricia Highsmith, Henry James, Jack London, V. S. Naipaul, Marcel Proust, Ayn Rand, Henry David Thoreau, Leo Tolstoy, Thornton Wilder) to poetry (John Ashbery, Allen Ginsberg, the Library of America's *American Poetry: The Nineteenth Century*) to new midlist fiction from such authors as James Carroll, Sue Grafton, Jack Higgins, Louis Begley, Anne Rice, and William Trevor.[33]

The bulk of Theroux's reviews appeared in eight venues: the *National Review* (three in 1973, one more in 1995), *Boston Magazine* (eight between 1976 and 1996), *Boston Globe* (five, 1985–2009), *Washington Post* (five, 1991–94), *Review of Contemporary Fiction* (twelve, 1991–2001), *Chicago Tribune* (twenty-eight, 1994–96), *Los Angeles Times Book*

2001), 34

32 To avoid a trampling of footnotes hereafter, see the bibliography at the end of this book for details.

33 In addition, Theroux reviewed new books on actors and directors (Chaplin, Fellini), on singers and musicians (Frank Sinatra, Patti Smith, the Beatles), on food (by M. F. K. Fisher, Barry Glassner), on painters (Ansel Adams, Leonardo da Vinci), on historical and political figures (Merriwether Lewis, William Bulger), and miscellaneous books like Richard Selzer's *Mortal Lessons: Notes on the Art of Surgery* (1981)—six years later Dr. Selzer provided a blurb for Theroux's *An Adultery*—and John Follain's *A Death in Italy: The Definitive Account of the Amanda Knox Case* (2012), a case that transfixed Theroux for years.

Review (four, 1996–97), and the *Wall Street Journal* (thirty-one, 1998–2014).[34] His reviews before 1991 were a sideline, but after Theroux lost his job at Yale that year, they became one of his few sources of revenue, hence the large number of reviews after that date. I won't discuss them all, but there are several worth noting.

One of the first books the *National Review* allowed him to review was *A Russian Beauty and Other Stories* by Vladimir Nabokov, an author Theroux name-checks throughout his writings. He regards this "fascinating, though sporadically uneven" collection of older stories as "a psychograph of Russian expatriates in the Twenties and Thirties in Germany—a world of very Bad Luck." He says a little about each story, then heaps high praise on "Ultima Thule," which he declares "one of the greatest short stories—may I be cavalier?—in the English language," and which reminds Theroux of Nabokov's "masterpiece, *Pale Fire*." In his concluding paragraph, he reveals what he values most in fiction in general and Nabokov in particular, namely, "his consistently breathtaking and magic prose—*styled*, in the parlance of the watch industry—which always reaches out for the sinuosities of thought and those uncannily accurate observations by which we already know and worship respectfully Nabokov."

Nabokov was still alive when Theroux wrote that review; 36 years later, Theroux was assigned the sad duty of reviewing the posthumously published *The Original of Laura* (2009). He was disappointed with it, as were many reviewers: "The first effect of reading 'The Original of Laura' gives less pleasure than a certain squeamishness," he confesses. "The lineaments of a serious literary undertaking are obvious, too, but only in a few places can one discern even a hint of the technical brilliance, the penchant for parody, the irresistible flippancy that we would recognize as the work of the author of 'Lolita,' 'Pale Fire' and 'Ada.'" Theroux gamely praises what he can in the novel: "There are many moments in the novel unmistakably Nabokovian, with cutting wordplay, ironic description, the fixation with close and immaculately observed descriptions of young girls, supreme wit."[35] But he concludes by condemning Dmitri Nabokov's long-delayed decision to publish the unfinished novel against his father's wishes. Theroux paid his final respects to Nabokov in a re-

---

34 Theroux told me that many of his reviews for the *Wall Street Journal* were shortened by his editor Erich Eichman for space, "sanitized (for political correctness), and in my opinion made worse—gelded of many interesting points, very many" (email, 12 June 2019). See next note for an example:

35 This sentence from Theroux's manuscript was curtailed in the published version to "There are witty Nabokovian moments as well."

view of Lila Azam Zanganeh's *The Enchanter: Nabokov and Happiness* (2011). He doesn't care for Zanganeh's fangirl effusions, but he does offer further opinions of the man and his work. He was "a genius but also a snob and curmudgeon. Nabokov was frequently competitive and unkind, belittling the likes of Faulkner, Tolstoy, Dostoevsky, Conrad, Jane Austen, Cervantes, Hemingway and Henry James." Nor does Theroux care for Nabokov's wife: "In college I once mailed to his hotel in Montreux, along with a gift of butterfly stamps, one of his novels for him to inscribe and was immediately sent back, along with the unsigned novel and rejected gift, a scolding letter from Vera telling me not to bother them."[36] Distinguishing between the man and his work (as we should always do), Theroux concludes with remarks that echo his evaluation of Proust: "What Nabokov valued, perhaps above all else, was what he could preserve in memory and save from oblivion. He located and fixed the past in much the same way that in his lepidopteral experiments he fixed his beloved butterflies."

Another early review caused long-lasting outrage. In 1976 he reviewed Adrienne Rich's *Of Woman Born: Motherhood as Experience and Institution* in *Boston Magazine*, and expresses his dim view of the book in his opening sentence: "The propagandistic title—exaggeration, you assume, for emphasis—doesn't quite prepare one for the sad, monomaniacal lunacies attempting to prop it up in this book, which is less a feminist manifesto than the 'Confessions of St. Adrienne.'" While granting that some of Rich's complaints about women's rights are solid, and sympathizing with Rich's disappointing personal experiences of motherhood, Theroux pushes back against her claim that men are responsible for forcing motherhood on women, dominating pediatric theory and practice, and making them "into negative quantities or bearers of evil" (Rich's words). Such extreme views ruin the book for Theroux: "for the pages of exclusivist and misandrous rubbish in *Of Woman Born*, for the cruel exaggerations that can only further widen the already wide rift between the sexes, for the agitprop, for the sloganeering, for the absurd and crapulous poetry thrown in to support the unilateral myths in the history to which she'd have us subscribe, I can only say I find most of it mercyproof, reasonless, blackhearted, and unfair."

Eight years later, Jane Roberta Cooper reprinted the review in her anthology *Reading Adrienne Rich: Reviews and Re-visions, 1951–1981* (Ann Arbor: University of Michigan Press, 1984), calling it a "willful misreading of *Of Woman Born*," and I assume it has been outraging Rich

36 Theroux versified this incident in "Vera Nabokov Hurts an Animal" (CP, 393–94).

scholars ever since. For Theroux scholars, it's important as a source for some of the views Eugene Eyestones expresses in *Laura Warholic*. In his review, Theroux had quoted Rich's claim that "The ancient continuing envy, awe, and dread of the male for the female capacity to create life [!] has repeatedly taken the form of hatred for every other female aspect of creativity." In Eyestones's "controversial essay" he acknowledges that women who want to create art as well as life often wind up in the frustrating situation faced by the younger Rich, who "simply resented—while feeling guilty for it—the artistically creative chances stolen from her as she tried to conform to the 'patriarchal' conception of motherhood her parents, her mimetic youth, her contemporary experience tried to instill." Eyestones groups Rich with other "extreme feminists" in his essay (189), and in his notes on "frigidity" (for a future magazine column) he mentions "the man-hating lunacies of Adrienne Rich's idea of 'compulsive heterosexuality,' easily the biggest load of bollocks since Andreas Capellanus in his *De remedio* repudiated sexual love" (82–83).[37] Later in the novel, a young women's studies student states, "Adrienne Rich who claims that men are not necessary for women to get pregnant asserts that heterosexuality is not natural" (756). Theroux is often accused of misogyny, but it is primarily these sort of women who set him off.

Camille Paglia is another, and in 1993 he published a blistering review of her essay collection *Sex, Art, and American Culture*, and thereby hangs a tale. Theroux read and admired Paglia's brilliant *Sexual Personae* (1990), and has praised her work. Writing of Botticelli's *Birth of Venus*, he introduces a block quotation from pages 150–51 of her book with "There is no better description of the painting than in Camille Paglia's *Sexual Personae*."[38] In a later essay entitled "The Stendhal Syndrome" (*Art & Antiques*, April 1993, though probably written in 1992), there is this paragraph:

> "Spiritual enlightenment produces feminization of the male," writes Camille Paglia in *Sexual Personae* in one of her coruscating, if slightly cavalier, observations. She quotes with approval Margaret Mead: "The more intricate biological pattern of the female has become a model for the artist, the mystic, and the saint." She goes on to say

37 "Compulsory Heterosexuality and Lesbian Experience" is a 1980 essay by Rich.

38 Theroux wrote about Botticelli's painting in the March 1988 issue of *Art & Antiques* ("Mortal Goddess"); his remarks don't appear there but in the longer manuscript version he sent me in September 2018 (renamed "Simonetta Vespucci"), meaning he added it to his original essay at a later date.

that "intuition or extrasensory perception is a feminine hearkening to the secret voices in and beyond things. [Lewis] Farnell says, 'Many ancient observers noted that women (and effeminate men) were especially prone to orgiastic religious seizure.' Hysteria means womb-madness (from the Greek *ustera*, 'womb')."[39]

He was clearly a fan and consequently asked me in early 1992 to send her a galley of *The Lollipop Trollops and Other Poems*. She sent back an angrily handwritten letter scolding me for intruding on her time, telling me she doesn't approve of blurbs, and claimed she threw the galley in the trash. (Four years later she published a short article in *Publishers Weekly* entitled "The Unbridled Lust for Blurbs," decrying the practice, though without mentioning Theroux.[40]) Theroux's first response was a vicious if cleverly titled poem entitled "Passacaglia for an Italian Witch," dedicated "For Camille," which he added to the book just before it went to press. Then Theroux wrote an insulting 1500-word review of her just-published essay collection *Sex, Art, and American Culture*, which appeared in the spring 1993 issue of the *Review of Contemporary Fiction*.[41] It's less a review than an ad hominem attack, mocking Paglia's public persona at a time when she was giddy with new-found fame. ("People have dishonored me. I want revenge," Theroux quotes her as saying, which must have struck a chord.) Of the book itself, he says, "It is only a worried batch of disparate half-lectures, sniping book reviews, TV interviews, rock essays, inconsequential gasconades, a few pointless cartoons, and a media history of her life made up of a series of nitwittish articles all clapped together to capitalize on the recent attention given her book of literary criticism, *Sexual Personae*." Near the end, Theroux indirectly reveals the motive of his attack: "All this, mind you, from a shill who has the hypocrisy, somewhere in one of these turgid essays, to inveigh against the harmless practice, common in the graceful and

39 I'm quoting from Theroux's manuscript version, which is superior to the published version (76–77); he quotes from p. 45 of *Sexual Personae* (New Haven: Yale University Press, 1990).

40 Reprinted in her *Provocations: Collected Essays* (New York: Pantheon, 2018), 205–7.

41 I was the book-review editor of *RCF* at the time and occasionally sent Alex something to review, but in this instance he just sent it in. If I hadn't been miffed at Paglia—who throws *a book* in the trash!? (Alex doubted she actually did so)—I might have asked Theroux to tone it down. Since then I've become a fan of Paglia's erudite, iconoclastic work, so I'm not proud of publishing this, though I still take guilty pleasure in it, for it's a great example of Theroux in attack mode.

far more generous past, of writers of books asking other writers for a commendation—a blurb—in the hope of garnering wider attention for their efforts." (Theroux always complied when I asked him to supply a blurb for one of Dalkey Archive's authors.[42]) He ends with an extended metaphor: "the book is a circus of self-promotion, a farce of buncombe, dim lights, and horseshit, where Camille Paglia is P. T. Barnum, Tom Thumb, and ticket-taker all at once." As in this book, there is a "Media Chronicle" in Paglia's 1994 essay collection *Vamps & Tramps*, but neither Theroux's poem or review is mentioned, nor are these the only attacks the controversial critic received at that time. And like Adrienne Rich, Paglia wound up in *Laura Warholic*; Eugene is startled by Laura's admission that she's attracted to girlish-looking boys: "Have we descended, he wondered, to oddball feminist Camille Paglia's unwholesome assertion that children are sexy?" (482).

Among Laura's other faults is her ineptness as a book reviewer. On pages 116–17 of *Laura Warholic* we're told that Eugene "encouraged her to study to become a paralegal secretary until he realized she was not dutiful enough, and to write book reviews until he saw how bad they were—once she wrote a review of a biography of Christopher Marlowe that, although assigned him by the *Chicago Tribune*, he had subleased to her because she needed the money, and it was hopeless." This undoubtedly refers to Theroux's then-girlfriend Laura Markley and his intervening review of Anthony Burgess's *A Dead Man in Deptford*, which appeared in the 16 July 1995 issue of the *Trib*. I'm shocked that he would "sublease" a commissioned review to anyone, and wonder if there are others.[43]

A year earlier Theroux wrote another review for the *Chicago Tribune* that is puzzlingly, counterintuitively harsh. He begins his review of John Barth's "novelized memoir" *Once Upon a Time* (1994) with an odd statement coming from the author of three highly autobiographical novels: "Why writers choose to dress up autobiography in the trappings of fiction—Nabokov's "Look at the Harlequins," Paul Theroux's "My Secret History" and Kathy Acker's "My Mother: A Demonology" are three fairly recent examples—is, I'm convinced, a matter as much for the psychologist as for the literary critic. In any case, writers do so under various and sundry guises and usually, I've found, with little success." Hmm. As an author who revels in what academics like to call "intertextuality" (literary

---

42 The two I recall were for Timothy d'Arch Smith's *Alembic* (1992) and Lauren Fairbanks's *Sister Carrie* (1993).

43 Cf. this quatrain in Theroux's "The Gospel According to Laura Sparkley": "I'm forgetting the LA *Times*, / When you let me do book reviews / Because you kindly managed to see / The money I could badly use" (*CP*, 200).

allusions, parodies, quotations, references to other books) it's strange to hear him complain, "The author, as only Barth can, interrupts himself constantly, showing off with what academics like to call 'intertextuality'. . . ." And why would an author who boasts of his own amplified style and arcane vocabulary—a mode that some readers and reviewers have said takes getting used to, and that might be called Therouxese—complain: "Barthese is a language that takes getting used to. And once you get the grammar and vocabulary, come to terms with all the parentheses, collapsed syntax, preening wordplay, self-consciousness, editorializing, Micawberesque flights, false starts and general afflatus—the author will never use the word community, for example, when 'commonality' is handy—a biography begins to loom up out of a handful of multiple selves." One would think he would celebrate a fellow novelist who "loves verbal flourishes and the euphuistic, the kind of rhetoric university professors tend to think of as wit," but no (though Barth is admittedly more playful than Theroux). This isn't the first time I've seen novelists criticize the kind of fiction they themselves write; it is indeed "a matter as much for the psychologist as for the literary critic."

In October 1996 Theroux wrote another vituperative review that received much more attention than the Paglia, this one on his brother Paul's latest novel, which I'll describe in the chapter on the brothers Theroux. It caused a furor and was the last review he wrote for *Boston Magazine*. Similarly, see my chapter on Theroux's poetry for his negative review of John Ashbery's *The Mooring of Starting Out*, which elicited a letter of protest from the poet and a fiercely unapologetic response from the novelist. That was the last review he wrote for the *Los Angeles Times Book Review*.

In 1999 Theroux was given an opportunity by the *Wall Street Journal* to express his lifelong admiration for Jorge Luis Borges in a review of the Argentine's posthumous *Selected Non-Fictions*, edited by Eliot Weinberger. "As a student at the University of Virginia," he notes, "I was once lucky enough to hear Borges give a lecture on Poe, a splendid discourse sans notes, full of insights and strong opinions that in a perfect loop lasted exactly one hour."[44] Theroux admires "the limitless curiosity and astonishing erudition he brought to all subjects," his film criticism, his interest in Buddhism, and especially his essay "Our Poor Individualism," which "addresses the illusions of patriotism and the potential vice of nationalism." Clearly *simpático*, Theroux concludes his review by say-

---

44 They met on at least one later occasion, for there's a photograph of them together on p. 48 of the op.-cit.'ed *Review of Contemporary Fiction* number on Theroux.

ing no one "will be surprised that its author was a man who conceived Paradise to be a kind of library."

Borges was astonishingly erudite, but never willfully obscure. The obscurantism that Theroux complains of in the Ashbery review is the reason for his mixed opinion of Thomas Pynchon, whose work he has reviewed on two occasions, and has mentioned in several other places. In 2012 he told interviewer Paul Maliszewski, "I love Pynchon's sense of humor. I admire his invented names. I treasure his style. I also find him also in too many places pretentious, inaccessible, and even unreadable—I should say incomprehensible. One of the few boasts I believe I can make is that in my fiction I have never written a single line in a single book to obfuscate or to becloud."[45] One of the last books he reviewed for the *Review of Contemporary Fiction* was *Pynchon and "Mason & Dixon,"* a collection of essays edited by Brooke Horvath and Irving Malin (University of Delaware Press, 2000), but unfortunately it doesn't offer a clue as to what Theroux thought of the 1997 novel. (He praises a few essays, but finds "Much grad school gobbledygook elsewhere, hypertextual frenzifying. . . .") Pynchon was much on his mind in those years. After publishing *The Primary Colors* and *The Secondary Colors* in 1994 and 1996, respectively, he wrote two similar ones on black and white, which remain unpublished. *White* gives a few examples of Pynchon's use of that non-color in *Gravity's Rainbow,* and in *Black* we read: "A mysteriously secret compound, the 'Black Vault' of the enigmatic organization, TRW—located in Redondo Beach, California—appears in Thomas Pynchon's novel, *Gravity's Rainbow.* 'Black' is of course a catchall term that the intelligence community applies to any covert intelligence operation." In *Laura Warholic,* written and expanded between 1997 and 2007, there are several unflattering references to *Gravity's Rainbow* (and to Mrs. Pynchon, agent Melanie Jackson), which are described in my chapter on that aggrieved novel. Theroux resented what he regarded as irresponsible obscurity in *Gravity's Rainbow,* and in his unpublished *Anomalies,* Theroux notes: "Vladimir Nabokov, the brilliant author who wrote the complicated novel *Ada,* claimed he could not understand the novel, *Gravity's Rainbow,* by Thomas Pynchon (a former pupil) and 'gave up.'" And in his unpublished *Seacoast in Bohemia, or The Story of Literary and Cinematic Blunders, Howlers, and Flaps,* he scores several hits against the novel (which I'll quote at length partly because it's unpublished, and partly to show how closely he's studied it):

45 "The Back of Beyond: An Interview with Alexander Theroux," *Rain Taxi* Online Edition, Winter 2012/2013.

Thomas Pynchon in his omniversal, highly allusive, to me, sort of comic-book epic, *Gravity's Rainbow* (1973) leaves a surprising trail of gaffes. Since Germany figures so highly in the novel, one is unprepared for some almost elementary bungles on the part of such an otherwise informed writer, all of which are cited by Steven Weisenburger in *A "Gravity's Rainbow" Companion.* Amazingly, Pynchon fails even to get the word *schnauze* right. In Episode 19 of this complicated novel he refers at one point to "*the Judenschnautze.*" *Schnautze* is a nonsense word that, first of all, does not exist in the German language, and Pynchon obviously intended to write *Judenschnauze,* meaning "Jewnose" or "Jewsnout." He also refers to a popular song of the time in Episode 16 when he alludes to "There, I Said It Again." The actual title however is "There! I've Said It Again." At another point in the book, the program "Allen's Alley" is playing over the BBC, when in real life it never did. As Weisenburger demonstrates, Pynchon is also hugely fascinated with a work by Ivan Pavlov called *Lectures on Conditional Reflexes* (Vol. 2)—it is repeatedly referred to as "The Book" all through *Gravity's Rainbow*—and reports that at the end of World War II copies of that book in manuscript-form are passed around, "rotated," as he puts it, as a kind of underground agitprop. Pure melodrama! The book had been translated into English in 1941—did Pynchon know this or did he simply commit a gaffe?—by one of Pavlov's American collaborators, Dr. Horsley Gantt. There can also be found in the novel confusions of chronology involving Malcolm X and Charlie Parker involving juxtapositions of their actions, which in fact never took place.

Another gaffe can be found in *Gravity's Rainbow,* a small but, for Thomas Pynchon, a stickler for exactitude and the arcane allusion he so casually drops for his anxious readers, a remarkable one. On page 32 he writes, "it is the exact mischievous Irish grin your Dennis Morgan chap goes about cocking down at the black smoke vomiting from each and every little bucktooth yellow rat he shoots down." As I say, Pynchon, who is pedantically precise about everything, expecting of course that the reader follow suit, should certainly know—or should have checked—that the actor Dennis Morgan was not Irish at all but of *Swedish* descent.[46]

On the other hand, in *Einstein's Beets* Theroux praises Pirate Prentice's banana breakfasts in *Gravity's Rainbow* and quotes the passage

---

46 Theroux spotted this one, not Weisenburger, but since Morgan *played* Irish characters in some films, this is quibbling.

describing them as "an amazing display of culinary imagination."[47] Later in the same book Theroux disagrees with Pynchon's low opinion of British candy, wine-gums in particular (549; see episode 15), and indicates his familiarity with Pynchon's first novel:

> One recollects that among the pals of Benny Profane in Thomas Pynchon's novel, V.—a member of the Whole Sick Crew—is Slab, an artist who cannot seem to paint anything other than cheese danishes. He belongs to the self-titled school of Catatonic Expressionism, "the ultimate in non-communication" and his studio is littered with canvases of cheese danish, symbols he startlingly declares will one day replace the cross in Western Civilization. One can imagine what Audrey Hepburn, who hated cheese danish, as we know, would have thought of Slab, aside from the fact that his only real ambition was to perfect the art of "schlemihlhood." (631)

On 24 November 2006 the *Wall Street Journal* published Theroux's 1,600-word review of Pynchon's 1,085-page novel *Against the Day*, which he told me he read in two days (!). He spends most of the review describing the varied contents of "this wide-ranging, encyclopedic, nonpareil of a novel" and for the first time expresses deep admiration for his contemporary (Pynchon is two years older): he calls him "one of the most original minds in all of American letters"; describes some of Pynchon's comically erudite set-pieces as "spectacular," the "sheer ingenuity" of which "call to mind parts of *Gulliver's Travels* and *Tristram Shandy*—a delightful marriage of satire and scholarship, part serious, part send-up"; and notes that many characters "are named with inventive delight. In this department, no one does it better. Not James Joyce. Not Dr. Seuss. Not Lewis Carroll. Not Vladimir Nabokov. Dare I say, not even Charles Dickens"—high praise indeed from this Dickens fan. "And Mr. Pynchon is a mimic extraordinaire. He do the police in different voices," Theroux adds, quoting his beloved Dickens (a line Eliot used later as the original title of *The Waste Land*). Only near the end does Theroux raise the question of difficulty, which had always hobbled his appreciation for *Gravity's Rainbow*; the final four paragraphs are worth quoting in full (especially since the *Wall Street Journal* hides them behind a firewall, like Brünnhilde at the end of *Die Walküre*):

---

47 *Einstein's Beets: An Examination of Food Phobias* (Seattle: Fantagraphics, 2017), 525–26. Though not published until 2017, Theroux had been compiling this for years.

The novel amasses news on every vagrant ankle-biter, opium fiend and down-and-outer, and it heedlessly digresses. Thomas Ruggles Pynchon Jr. can find words to describe something like no other writer. He has a remarkable ear and eye for everything—ice, anarcho-syndi-calists, cigarette lighters, Eskimo beliefs, ocean liners, time, air, light, anything you wish to name—and a limitless capacity to devote full attention to any subject that swims into his ken.

Therein may lie controversy. To read this book with anything like comprehension, a person has to be, like its polymath author, both in-tellectual and hip, a person mature and profoundly well read and yet something of a true marginal, a word-nerd with the patience of Job. In my charitable estimate that would describe about five out of 500 people that I know.

It may be argued that the novel is darkly, extremely, the author's "Finnegans Wake," so dense, so deeply complex, so long and so re-lentlessly inaccessible in so many places that dissenters may exclaim, as an acquaintance once did to James Joyce of that last complicated book of his: "It is outside of literature, Joyce." (And was he wrong?)

I would make no such assertion. "Against the Day" is a major work of art and, like all creations of surpassing greatness, something to be studied—to cite 2 Peter 3:7 again—"against the day of judgment and perdition of the ungodly men."

Theroux is credited as the first to identify the biblical source of Pyn-chon's title, and while it is gratifying to see Theroux finally come over to Team Pynchon, he wrote this review while putting the finishing touches on his novel *Laura Warholic*, where he shows his contempt for Pyn-chon's third novel by including it as an example of the bad taste Laura's mother has in books: "A large pile of lurid paperbacks and trashy beach-reads . . . filled an old deal bookcase with titles like . . . *Muscle Lover, Tamed Warrioress, Slave Beauty, Glass Dildo, Sheikh of the Desert, Gravity's Rainbow* . . ." (106).

Theroux has written too many other reviews to cover in detail, but here are highlights from some of the others, with the emphasis, again, on what they reveal of Theroux's own aesthetics, for he tends to praise in other writers what he does in his own fiction—though, as I've already shown, he sometimes berates them for the same reason.[48]

48 The dates refer to the publication of the review, usually but not always of the

Susan Hill, *The Bird of Night* (1973); Theroux first professionally published book review appeared in the *National Review*, three years after it published Theroux's essay "The Inarticulate Hero." He's harsh on Hill's seventh novel (which was short-listed for the Booker Prize): "This isn't really a novel. It's a nervous breakdown. It's a confession. [The main character] is totally unrealized, but, rather, thesis-wise, he's shot to us right away in an indescribable shrillness and stays that way. . . ." Given Theroux's fondness for metaphors, it's surprising to hear him say "Irksome is her tendency to constantly speak in metaphors, a self-indulgence that . . . prevents a forward movement in the novel." The review is entitled "A Tale of Madness," so Theroux concludes: "Over this novel, I'm afraid, I still opt for *The Diary of Nijinsky*."

Milan Kundera, *Immortality* (1991): Theroux regards the Czech's "essayistic, characteristically cerebral, sixth novel" more as "a series of witty and insightful lectures . . . not a novel at all, or if a novel, one that quite vividly evokes once again the rubbery flexibility of that genre." He adds: "It is always Kundera's mind that his books are about. When I was in graduate school we always chose courses not by the subject but by the professor, and so it should be with Kundera. He refers to anything at hand. He is a polymath, full of strong opinions and bright observations which, in my opinion, are almost always correct." He concludes: "I think part of the great glory in Kundera's probing novels and short stories is that underneath all the philosophizing and often heavy disquisitions lie those questions that we all, all of us, truly worry and ask about our very selves every day."[49]

Julian Barnes, *Talking It Over* (1991): Theroux describes this as "a novel of adultery, not one French and literary and casual, rather one that is English, obsessive and dangerous"—like his own *An Adultery*—and like Ford Madox Ford's *Good Soldier*, a novel Theroux admired from his early days, which he describes here as a "casebook on love triangles."[50]

---

books themselves; see the bibliography for publication details.

49 In 1991 I invited Theroux to start reviewing for the *Review of Contemporary Fiction*, and this was his first submission. Sometimes I suggested a book, other times Theroux chose his own. After I left the journal in 1996, his reviews dwindled, ceasing in 2001.

50 A 1973 review of his begins: "Ford Madox Ford's masterpiece, *The Good Soldier* (1915), not uncoincidentally links the loss of moral values in the personal lives of his characters . . . with the shabby and deceitful political period in Europe just preceding the German invasion of Belgium on August 4, 1914"— just as Theroux links the lack of Laura Warholic's moral values with the shabby and deceitful U.S.A. of the 1990s. "Might as Well Be Cleveland," *National Review*, 8 June 1973, 645 (a review of fellow-Gambit author Terence de Vere

Though fascinated by "the narrative technique Barnes adopts, a sort of metafictional device where in short monologues, invariably self-defensive, each character comes forward in turn, to have his or her turn 'talking it over,'" he finds the conclusion "insufficient" because the narrative mode denies "any final resolution."[51]

Nicholson Baker, *Vox* (1992): A fan of Baker from his first novel, *The Mezzanine*, even to seeking out his magazine pieces, Theroux praises his fourth as "a remarkable tour-de-force, displaying his characteristic love of detail and almost scientific fascination with the small delicate undersides of thoughts and theories and things commonly come across but rarely seen so well." On the other hand, the principal characters "lose definition" and "there is a repetitiveness here even Nicholson Baker's lubricious fancy and way with words can't vivify or make masterful." "In the end, however," Theroux concludes, "*Vox* for its few hitches is not impaired. It's a delightful novel." He also wrote a review of Baker's *Fermata* (1994), which doesn't appear to have been published. He didn't care for this novel as much as the earlier ones: "For the first time in a Nicholson Baker novel I actually began in places idly flipping pages. The novel is too long and often badly repetitious, always a downside in matters pornographic . . . Not a major point, but I think with novels like this and *Vox* Baker may feel that erotolalia is the quickest way to sell a prurient public his wit—sadly, for his ingenuity is so much vaster."

James McCourt, *Time Remaining* (1993): Theroux admires the erudition in this "campy" novel, and insists "nowhere, except perhaps in Ronald Firbank, can be found writing more arch or wickedly precious. McCourt is a master of observation and obloquy." He concludes, "Language is the real subject, and McCourt is so irrepressible, so charged, that in his excitement his prose tends to crowd itself the way Hart Crane's poetry does, exploding in many directions at once. But if Franz Boas's dictum that 'language is culture' is true, then no better example can be found to prove it than in the unapologetic chant here told in the Queen's Vernacular and told so well."

Milorad Pavić, *The Inner Side of the Wind* (1993): Theroux feels "The narrative technique of using two equal parts for a duple book, bound back to back, was done before, and in my opinion more successfully, in 1973 by Earl Rovit in his novel *Crossings*," and feels the two halves

---

White's *The Distance and the Dark*).

51 This was the first review Theroux wrote for the *Washington Post*, probably the result of the special issue of *RCF* on him that appeared earlier in 1991. Book reviewer editor Michael Dirda saw the issue and soon after invited Theroux to start reviewing for the *Post*.

of "Pavić's surprisingly unsatisfying novel . . . coalesce in only a self-consciously artful, if you will, but contrived way." He admires the book's "bold and insightful gnomic pronunciamenti," and allows "there are wonderfully memorable passages, Felliniesque scenes, a wonderful mind at work, and marvelous sentences, but it doesn't live up to his other books, not by half."

Kathy Acker, *My Mother: Demonology* (1993): A savage dismissal, and evidence of Theroux's hostility toward experimental fiction.[52] He doesn't like anything about the book, beginning with its title, which he says is misleading. "This is neither art nor anything close to it, merely lowbrow, turgid, bottom-feeding backchat, with nothing original to it, not even the transparently crass attempt at simulating narrative cyberpunk and dead-headism. . . . I am familiar with [this] sort of ragged art form, seemingly random notes that achieve self-consciousness and eventually become novels. There's Arno Schmidt's *The Egghead Republic*, *Afternoon of a Faun*, and *Evening Edged in Gold*. Things like Maurice Blanchot's *Writing of the Disaster* epigrams that by accretion produce a world-view. And there is of course Queneau, in his various morphs and manifestations. But there is strength and coherence to these novelists. [¶] Not so with *My Mother*. This is undergraduate writing of the worst sort, open-ended rambling shot through with ersatz poetry and ninety-five cent philosophy. . . . Who is surprised, then, to read on the book-jacket the shameless publisher's claim that this sad excuse for a novel 'pushes at the frontiers of modern fiction'?"

John Updike, *Brazil* (January 1994) and *The Afterlife and Other Stories* (November 1994): Theroux was friends with Updike, and gives a friendly summary of this love story set in Brazil, noting, "There is a wonderful drive to the novel, true lyricism, real drama in the trials and

---

52 See "Theroux Metaphrastes," where he quotes with approval critic Rust Hills's mockery of experimental fiction (21). In conversation, he dismissed Gilbert Sorrentino's *Mulligan Stew* as just "playing around," and in a letter to me dated 27 June 1996 he insisted David Markson's *Reader's Block*, which I had sent him, wasn't a novel at all. After comparing it to his work-in-progress *Anomalies* (see p. 175 below), he wrote: "But Markson's *Reader's Block*, where it touches anomalies, does the same thing. . . . I think to call this a novel, or anything like a framed work, except for the inexplicably added rosary beads, even four pages, listing anti-Semites—the only consistency I can see—is ridiculous. Isn't this 193 pages of literary facts, many of them familiar to any serious reader, or am I missing something? Remarkably, to me, Markson doesn't ever *write* in it. It's a grab-bag of Bartlett, famous names, phony profundities, and completely isolated notes having not the slightest coherence." Like many readers, I disagree: see *My Back Pages*, 520–23.

tribulations the lovers face." A stylist himself, Theroux's most interesting comments are on Updike's style:

> Updike is such a beautifully sensitive writer that nothing fails to flour-
> ish under his gentle hand. Where other novelists have a girl wake
> up, yawn and perfunctorily greet the dawning day, he writes: "When
> she awoke, day declared itself in the blue knives of light suspended
> about her, each with its halo of smoke." Nothing he observes goes
> without tender inspection, a search for an "inscape" he is determined
> to describe. Our virtues are often our vices, however, even if born of
> zeal, and because Updike tends to cherish everything he writes about,
> he overuses adjectives and similes, and style is often polished at the
> expense of story. He also uses vulgar words too often, which detracts
> from his poetry.

Theroux identifies the "ironic, autumnal mood" that suffuses the stories in *The Afterlife*, respectfully summarizes most of them, and near the
end affirms (once against using Hopkins's term for distinctiveness): "No
writer alive is a better observer than Updike. He has an almost uncanny
gift for 'inscape,' for finding the perfect image or evoking the exact words
for a particular smell, a certain thought, fear, an idea, a face . . ."—a gift
that Theroux shares.

William T. Vollmann, *The Rifles* (1994): After summarizing the novel,
Theroux criticizes a tendency he shares with Vollmann: "Being willing to
try to understand everything is one of Vollmann's great traits as a writer
and yet perhaps one of his faults. His fascination for facts, for historical
detail, leaches something in his work from the spontaneity of art, from
entertainment, from his ability to write a novel that beguiles by coziness
and contrivances." In fact he doesn't consider it a novel at all: "I see *The
Rifles* as basically a travel book, nothing like a novel." He complains of
the difficulty of the book and the appendices, but recognizes a writer
after his own heart:

> My criticism here, please, is not an attack on abundance. Vollmann's
> mind is an encyclopedist's, and he should be allowed his pyrotech-
> nics as well as volume. I heartily defend both as virtues in this pres-
> ent godforsaken world of the crimp, undermedicated, and brainless
> novel, where, undaunted, Vollmann, whose conception of the novel
> as a *book*—to be picked up and put down, studied and snooped—is a
> breath of fresh air. I would only plead that such virtues require even

more organization and order to make them accessible.[53]

Gabriel García Márquez, *Strange Pilgrims* (1994): Theroux finds "great sureness" in this short-story collection, and identifies three "classics": "Light Is Like Water," "Miss Forbes's Summer of Happiness," and "The Trail of Your Blood in the Snow."

Jostein Gaarder's *Sophie's World* (1994): "*Sophie's World* is a whimsical and ingenious mystery novel that also happens to be a history of philosophy. I remember fondly looking for such a compendium when I was a bit older than 15-year-old Sophie Amundsen, whose world this is . . . and I remember ultimately settling for the 12 or so paperback volumes of Fr. Copleston, S.J., after becoming doubtful of the work of Will Durant, a disgruntled anti-clerical who, as I recall, breezily dismissed the entire philosophy of the Middle Ages, calling it 'a baffling circuit from faith to reason and then back to faith again.'" Theroux calls the novel "a remarkable but didactic tour de force," though a bit too contrived for his taste. Nevertheless, "What is admirable in the novel is the utter unpretentiousness of the philosophical lessons, the plain and workmanlike prose which manages to deliver Western philosophy in accounts that are crystal clear."

Guy Davenport, *A Table of Green Fields* (1994), *Twelve Stories* (1998), and *Objects on a Table* (1999): Theroux had been an admirer of Davenport since at least 1972; the protagonist of a story he wrote that year, "Herbert Head, Gent.," "reads Davenport's narrative poem 'Christ Preaching at the Henley Regatta' excitedly." That same year Theroux wrote to Davenport, who shortly after ordered a copy of the newly published *Three Wogs*.[54] Davenport was so impressed that he nominated it for the 1973 Pulitzer Prize; in his judges' report, he described *Three Wogs* as "Another wonderful satire, wildly overwritten (but that's one of its comic points), and an understanding and compassionate look at racial prejudice. He seems to me to be better than his brother Paul (we had a collection of his stories in this batch), and to be one of the liveliest satirists to appear recently."[55] Two decades later, Theroux found

53 Intended for the *Philadelphia Inquirer*, but apparently unpublished. Theroux began corresponding with Vollmann, and in *Einstein's Beets* occasionally cites him on food matters (187, 441–42, 586–87).

54 See *Questioning Minds: The Letters of Guy Davenport and Hugh Kenner*, ed. Edward M. Burns (Berkeley: Counterpoint, 2018), 1401, 1402, 1441n64.

55 Heinz-Dietrich Fischer and Erika J. Fischer, *Chronicles of the Pulitzer Prizes for Fiction: Discussions, Decisions and Documents* (Munich: K. G. Saur, 2007), 317. The fiction prize went instead to *The Optimist's Daughter* by Eudora Welty.

many of Davenport's stories in *A Table of Green Fields* too hermetic and inaccessible, "wonderful enigmas but codes too hard to crack, at least for me." Theroux prefers "Davenport the cultural scholar" to the fiction writer. "How refreshing, nevertheless, to find such splendid intelligence in a world of Wallers and Wonks, Angelous and Airheads, Crichtons and Crapola." Theroux likes *Twelve Stories* better (which reprints earlier, less hermetic stories). "To read Davenport, one has to be willing to look up words, ponder phrases, do extramural reading and not be threatened by arcane [a]llusions." After again lambasting popular writers—"Maya Angelou, John Grisham, the dork [Waller] who wrote *The Bridges of Madison County*"—Theroux suggests "Guy Davenport's stories should be read like Cubist essays, for their turns, sides, shapes, and the delectability of their genius." Theroux likes best Davenport's 1998 book on still-lifes, and praises his "Exactitude and his taste for the kind of outré facts which delights Davenportians like myself. . . ."

Harold Bloom, *The Western Canon* (1995): While he shares the Yale professor's "belief in the aesthetic as the sole standard of what we read, and not the ruinously didactic and sectarian indices, so popular today, of social and multi-cultural anti-intellectualism," as well as his disdain for "the parochialists, the pseudo-Marxists, and all the Francophile reductionists who make up what he calls the current 'School of Resentment,'" Theroux finds Bloom "subjective and often loony, weighing in with a lot of wacko pronouncements" on specific writers. Theroux objects in particular to Bloom's antireligious attitude, for "trying to find godlessness in the godly."[56]

William Faulkner, *Novels 1942–1954* (1995): This Library of America edition is "a relative letdown," for not one of the four novels written during this period "measures up to the masterly novels written during that astonishing seven-year-period between 1929 and 1936." Theroux makes intelligent observations on each novel, notes Faulkner's personal problems during those years, and respectfully concludes "if none of these novels can be numbered among Faulkner's successes, it should never be forgotten how brave an experimentalist he was."

Bradford Morrow, *Trinity Fields* (1995): Calling this a "realistic narrative whose splendid evocation of thoughtful adolescence evokes L. P. Hartley's 'The Go-Between' and John Knowles's 'A Separate Peace,'" Theroux gives a detailed plot summary, then concludes: "That Morrow manages to make this string of rather unlikely events completely be-

---

56 It can't have helped that in the appendix, a lengthy list of what Bloom regards as canonical works, there is Paul Theroux's *The Mosquito Coast* but nothing by Alexander.

lievable is one thing. But to make it as rich, as dramatically real and as poignantly felt at almost every point as he has is a remarkable feat." Theroux began contributing to Morrow's superb literary magazine *Conjunctions* in 1993 (and would continue to do so until 2004), which is not to suggest he wouldn't have written as favorable review had he never heard of the magazine.

Will Self, *Grey Area* (1996): Morrow's realistic novel is certainly more to Theroux's taste than this fiction collection, "a jumble sale of oddments that, while often wordily witty, mostly fail to excite." Theroux admires his "antic imagination and technical inventiveness," "his bordering-on-the-hypnotic vocabulary," but concludes: "As far as style and unending cleverness are concerned, Will Self, sentence to sentence, is very much in command. And the ideas for the stories are ingenious. However, they seem curiously uninspired in the telling and are ultimately far less witty than their outlines would suggest."

Patti Smith Complete: Lyrics Reflections & Notes for the Future (1999): Theroux had long admired the rock singer—see "The Tao of Patti Smith" (*CP*, 228)—and took this opportunity to go into fanboy mode: "I love Patti Smith. She believes in herself, hates authority, is strong. She's a tall dark winged angel of confusion, daring, a lot of a kind of genius, womanly courage, and beauty." He quotes favorite lines from her lyrics, declares them "prayers," and concludes: "I'm not trying to baptize the girl. But Patti Smith is a very serious woman."[57]

Patrick French, *The World Is What It Is: The Authorized Biography of V. S. Naipaul* (2008): This *Boston Globe* review is worth noting for an autobiographical anecdote: "I met him once at Wheeler's over dinner, which I shared with him and my brother Paul, in London in 1969. Naipaul questioned me on why in the light of Vietnam I would accept from the US government a Fulbright grant, like some sort of craven, low-brow mendicant. At that time I had no money at all. He, on the other hand, had just received £3,500 from the British Arts Council bursary, taken a grant from the Farfield Foundation to teach at Makerere University, in Uganda, and basically taken every bit of free money he could get. And

---

57 Rock chick Laura Warholic unsurprisingly admires Patti Smith (377, 582, 760) but only for superficial reasons, not for the strengths Theroux enumerates. In *The Grammar of Rock*, Theroux quotes Smith's music-listening criterion— "I don't listen to music by people I don't wanna fuck"—and approves of her movingly ragged duet with Bob Dylan on "Dark Eyes" (Seattle: Fantagraphics, 2013), 119, 232. He quotes her on the importance of vowels in *Estonia: A Ramble Through the Periphery*, and mentions that his wife Sarah once met her (Seattle: Fantagraphics, 2011), 114–15.

did I mention that at that dinner, Paul (who later had a public falling-out with Naipaul) paid the bill?"

Jonathan Lethem, *Chronic City* (2009): Theroux describes this as "an entertaining novel devoted to a kind of loopy urban sociology . . . a prosopographical investigation of New York City by way of a handful of strange, unclassifiable characters (and some remarkable writing)." Theroux reveals his familiarity with Lethem's earlier novels, but isn't impressed with this one: "There is nothing deeply philosophical at stake in any of these pages. It is mostly whimsy, interrupted by splendidly observed if sardonic evaluations. . . . There is no urgency to the plot, however, because there is no plot." Theroux finds superficial similarities to Pynchon in Lethem's love of "crazy names," his reveling "in goofy, puzzling randomness, as well as in the presentation of enthusiastic arcana . . . and the pulse of paranoia."

Gary Dexter, ed., *Poisoned Pens: Literary Invective from Amis to Zola* (2009): This "delightfully malicious compilation of literary invective across the centuries" is right in Theroux's wheelhouse. He cites numerous catty remarks (of the sort he often makes of other writers), and confesses "The effect is oddly pleasurable. Feelings of envy, anger, condescension, contempt and irritation are universal, of course, but writers have a way of expressing such feeling with unusual style and, at times, with astonishing accuracy—when they are not being merely rude, petty and childish." "There are some notable gaps in the collection," Theroux notes, such as Baron Corvo, but he doesn't identify the biggest one: he's not in it.

Bret Easton Ellis, *Imperial Bedrooms* (2010): Clearly no fan of this Brat Pack novelist, Theroux notes that this novel is a sequel to Ellis's 1985 debut, *Less Than Zero*, "a reverse paradigm for everything worthwhile, . . . [that] left no point of shallowness untouched." He calls it "weak in concept and uninspired, mere sequelism"; Theroux admits *American Psycho* "showed some spare and original prose. . . . But there is no originality here. The prose is flat and fizzless."

Tom McCarthy, *C* (2010): Theroux appreciates this "compelling if demanding novel," admiring McCarthy's range of knowledge (he "seems to know everything") and his style: "Mr. McCarthy often employs the historical present, a kind of 'hot news' mode used by Hemingway both successfully ('The Killers') and farcically (*Islands in the Stream*). There is a lot of wordplay, too. Nearly un-get-at-able sentences pop up." And he likes here what he disliked in Barth:

The book is dense with allusions, extravagant and learned. Transi-

tional gaps between the four sections give the narrative an enythme-
mic effect and force a frustrated reader to supply, or imagine, what is
missing. But, one may ask, is that a bad thing?

The formal difficulty of *C* may go back to the postmodern idea
that shifts interest from the "what" to the "how" of art, the game of
problematizing. *C* is a novel of cognition.

He concludes with a salute to McCarthy's austerely aesthetic, noncommercial approach to fiction: "there is an intrepid attitude to Mr. McCarthy's literary sally that has little to do with pleasing publishers or even an
audience. *C* is clever, confident, coy—and cryptic."

Carlos Fuentes, *Destiny and Desire* (2011): Theroux describes this big,
brainy novel in terms that could apply to *Laura Warholic*: "Mr. Fuentes's
novel is allusive, intellectually serious and inclined to wander in all sorts
of directions. At various points we get lavish set-pieces discussing everything from the Pelagian heresy and the history of Mexico City to Errol
Flynn's looks. A cast of secondary characters make their entrances and
exits: an oddball aviator, an intransigent prisoner, a casuistical priest."
Unwittingly describing the experience some readers had with his own
novel, Theroux adds: "for all its appealing richness of theme and character, [*Destiny and Desire*] can be annoyingly difficult to take in. The narrative is often rather cubist, with chronological dislocations, portentous
symbols, biblical allusions and strangely slotted if brilliant asides. . . . A
certain coherence is lost in the collision of literary effects. (I sometimes
wonder whether we have Faulkner to blame for the aimlessness of the
modern novel.)" And like Theroux himself, "Mr. Fuentes has a first-rate,
encyclopedic mind, and ultimately the value of 'Destiny and Desire' may
rest on the author's own rumination and insight, however variously con-
veyed in the novel itself."

Hunter Davies, ed., *The Beatles Lyrics* (2014): In *The Grammar of
Rock*, published a year earlier, Theroux had written, "It was through
their lyrics, examining them, following their bliss, as much as through
the joy of their music, that fans of the Beatles—them more than any
singers I can name—sought the *darshan*, a word that is employed in
India to describe the beneficial glow one feels from a glimpse of greatness" (87). Clearly a fan himself, Theroux here shows his appreciation
for the high quality of the band's "most deathless lyrics," stating for example that those to McCartney's "Eleanor Rigby" "are worthy of a poem
by William Carlos Williams or Edwin Arlington Robinson," and for the
care they took crafting them. As far as I know, this is the last book review
Theroux published.

Books of Curious Facts

I'LL KEEP THIS BRIEF, for it deals with my least-favorite side of Theroux's multifaceted output.

In "Plaid," an essay published in a 1998 issue of the *Yale Review* on the various appearances of the fabric/color/pattern in fiction, fashion, and film, Theroux cites an example from John May's *Curious Facts* (Holt, Rinehart and Winston, 1980). Arranged in alphabetical order by subject, from Acronyms to Zoos, May's book is accurately described on the dustjacket as "An avalanche of the irrelevant, guaranteed to surprise, bewilder, intrigue, and entertain." The book's thesis and raison d'être is summarized in the epigraph to the collection: "Experience has shown, and a true philosophy will always show, that a vast, perhaps the larger, portion of the truth arises from the seemingly irrelevant." I don't know when Theroux acquired this book, but it is a possible inspiration for the largest portion of his oeuvre: *The Primary Colors* (1994), *The Secondary Colors* (1996), *Black* and *White* (written at the same time but unpublished), *The Grammar of Rock* (2013), and the enormous *Einstein's Beets* (2017), as well as shorter pieces like the "Plaid" essay, two chapters in his novel *Laura Warholic* ("Sex Questions" and "What in Love or Sex Is Not Odd?"), and various unpublished writings. These works are evidence of Theroux's extraordinarily wide reading—all the more impressive because most were written before Theroux had access to the Internet—his unbounded interests, his lifelong fascination with paradox and anomaly, and his apparent conviction that trivia is never trivial.

But they are not well-made books. My chief objection to them is aesthetic: they were compiled, not crafted; amassed, not formed, with new material continuously added to them up until the day they were sent to the printer.

His yen for gathering curious facts became apparent with a few of the essays Theroux published in *Art & Antiques* in the late 1980s. "Dabblers and Dabbling" (November 1987) notes that many writers dabbled in art, then provides a couple hundred examples. "Artists Who Kill" (Summer 1988), with an illustration by Edward Gorey, began by enumerating dozens of painters involved in violence of one sort or another; what began in 1988 as a 6,000-word essay grew over the decades as Theroux added further examples of what its original editor called "acts of creative mayhem" until the essay reached nearly 30,000 words (in current manuscript form).[1]

In the April 1990 issue of *Art & Antiques*, Theroux published an essay entitled "Rhapsody in Blue," on the uses of that color in various paintings, which was particularly well received by the magazine's readers. That gave Theroux the idea of doing a book on colors, so "Rhapsody in Blue" became the basis for the first essay in *The Primary Colors* (1994). After beginning with some general observations—"Blue is a mysterious color, hue of illness and nobility, the rarest color in nature"—Theroux opens the floodgates of his vast reservoir of reading and inundates the reader with hundreds of instances of the use of blue in art, literature, language (terms like "blue movie"), and in culture and nature generally, in no discernible order. He wrote two further essays on yellow and red for the 1994 book, avoiding any summary statements about the colors, and in fact arguing that they "evade our knowing," are enigmas that confound us in their many meanings (268). It's a magpie collection of high and low culture, of esoteric and everyday examples, filled with rhetorical questions and curious facts ("Have you ever seen yellow furs? There are yellow bears" [96]). Like May's book, it is "guaranteed to surprise, bewilder, intrigue, and entertain," and leaves one gobsmacked at Theroux's encyclopedic interests. But unlike May's book, it lacks shape or form, avoids thematic groupings, and was assembled haphazardly, as Theroux admitted in a 2011 interview. Speaking of it and its 1996 sequel, *The Secondary Colors*, he said: "in a way they're kind of jazz riffs on the colors, you know? There is no real A to Z or particular chronology to those color things, they're really jazz riffs on the colors, serendipitous at the same time."[2] In the inscribed copy he mailed to me, Theroux even asked, "Do all these circumadjacent facts add up? Doubtful. But neither does life."

---

1 The byline to the original essay states that a collection of Theroux's essays "will be published next spring," and the byline to a December 1988 essay in the same magazine announced the title as *Artists Who Kill and Other Essays*, but it never appeared. Ever the optimist, Theroux often announced forthcoming books in his bylines that he merely hoped to publish quickly.
2 Tom Spurgeon, "CR Interview: Alexander Theroux on Edward Gorey," *Comics Reporter*, posted 22 February 2011.

The result is the literary equivalent of a *Ripley's Believe It or Not!* collection, a book of entertainment rather than a work of art like William H. Gass's *On Being Blue* or the progenitor of both books, the "Whiteness of the Whale" chapter in *Moby-Dick*.[3] Nonetheless—or consequently?—*The Primary Colors* sold well, was reprinted in paperback, published in England, and was later translated into Chinese, German, and Spanish. But Theroux's most successful book quickly became his most notorious.

On 3 March 1995, the *New York Times* reported that a reader had noticed three sentences on pages 16–17 were taken, almost verbatim and without attribution, from a 1954 book on navigation by Guy Murchie entitled *Song of the Sky*, along with some other lines from Murchie's book. The reader contacted the *New York Times Book Review*, which then eventually contacted Alexander Theroux, who told the reporter:

> the copied passages were a result of "stupidity and bad note taking." He said he had read hundreds of books, including "Song of the Sky," while gathering material for "The Primary Colors." But he said his notes from "Song of the Sky" were for a book he was writing on Amelia Earhart and must have got mixed with notes for "The Primary Colors."
>
> Asked why passages appeared verbatim—in one case beginning with the words, "I remember my surprise on first seeing the Yellow Sea"—Mr. Theroux replied that he, too, had seen the Yellow Sea, in the late 1960's. When going over his notes years later, he mistook Mr. Murchie's words for his own, he said.
>
> "I just thought it was my own work," he said. "I can't always remember the source of where I found something."[4]

Theroux then wrote a letter to the *Times*, which was published in its 7 March issue:

---

3 See also the books on colors published in recent years by French professor Michel Pastoureau, which have all the qualities Theroux's books lack.

4 Mary B. W. Tabor, "A Reader Finds That a Current Book Reads Suspiciously Like an Old One," *New York Times*, 3 March 1995, p. 3. The article indicates the first printing of *The Primary Colors* was 12,500 copies. The passage was rewritten for the paperback edition of 1996, in which a half-dozen lines were removed from the "Red" essay as well. In a follow-up piece, Tabor noted two earlier instances when Theroux was accused of using unacknowledged passages from other writers' works ("Book Notes," *New York Times*, 8 March 1995, C20), which inspired sci-fi author Tom Disch to publish a poem entitled "To an Unrepentant Plagiarist" in *Poetry* 171.1 (October–November 1997): 16.

Re "A Reader Finds That a Current Book Reads Suspiciously Like an Old One" (Arts pages, March 3): I truthfully explained to your reporter yesterday that the problem was a nonstory and a matter in editing of dropped quotation marks, several in a book of literary nonfiction with almost a thousand quotations and virtually every one scrupulously attributed. A mistake in our politically correct times is seen as guile. It is Lent. I need the mortification. ALEXANDER THEROUX Coronado, Calif., March 3, 1995

Theroux was in California writing a series of articles for the *San Diego Reader*, and in its 1 June 1995 issue he published a lengthy account of the affair.[5] In addition to giving a credible account of how the unattributed lines made their way into the book from a different project, he convincingly argues that the *New York Times* went out of its way to besmirch his reputation, handling this suspected plagiary case differently than they usually do (which indeed was corroborated for me by David Streitfeld, book reporter for the *Washington Post* at the time). Theroux then begins offering other examples of alleged plagiary, unconscious borrowings, which over time became a separate book of curious facts entitled *Shop Around: An Examination of Plagiarism*, which remains unpublished.

Though rattled by the affair, Theroux's editor, Allen Peacock at Henry Holt and Company, had already signed up a sequel, *The Secondary Colors*, which appeared in the spring of 1996. It has the same pros and cons as its predecessor: an astonishing variety of cultural observations jumbled together helter-skelter, leading to no conclusion other than that orange, purple, and green have been put to endless different uses. Theroux offered Peacock a third book, *Black and White*, but asked for a larger advance and was turned down.[6] He published a few selections from *Black* in 1998 (in *Conjunctions* and *Seneca Review*) and has been adding to it and *White* ever since (now two separate works), hoping to publish them in book form someday.

Theroux's next book of facts wasn't published until 2013, but it too

---

5 "Hateful, Hurtful and Hellish." *San Diego Reader*, 1 June 1995, 30–35. Its original title was "Apologia pro Vita Sua," which he mailed to me in early April.

6 In an email to me (22 October 2018), Peacock explained that Theroux scuttled the deal because of "A roving eye for another editor with the promise of a larger checkbook, and a willful refusal to take honest stock of what sales x royalties would generate in terms of a fair advance." (Peacock offered him $30,000, which Theroux felt was too little.)

has a long history. In 1990 I began assembling the contents of a special issue of the *Review of Contemporary Fiction* devoted to Theroux's work (published in the spring of the following year), and per our format I asked him to send me a literary essay we could include. He sent me a 20-page essay on the grammatical and logical faults in pop/rock song lyrics, which (as a rock fan) I found entertaining but felt was like shooting fish in a barrel: such lyrics are not expected to be written with the same care that goes into serious poetry. At any rate, I told him I wanted something literary instead, and he complied with "The Detours of Art," an autobiographical essay that was intended to form part of the introduction to a forthcoming book of his essays (which never appeared). Five years later, he published a slightly expanded version of the lyrics essay as "The Grammar of Rock and Roll" in the 20 July 1995 issue of the *San Diego Reader*. He kept adding to it over the years (as he does with all of his books, which he works on simultaneously) and in 2013 it was finally published by Fantagraphics under the title *The Grammar of Rock: Art and Artlessness in 20th Century Pop Lyrics*. The emphasis is on "artlessness," cataloguing thousands of examples of dumb lyrics and dumber singers, with occasional mini-essays on singers he admires (like Frank Sinatra). "My book is comic to a degree," he told Paul Maliszewski some six months before it came out, "and frankly in a real sense an autobiography of what I have heard—have been hearing—all my life."[7] Despite the book's title, most examples are taken from the popular song era of 1930–1960 rather than rock music, even though he's well versed in the latter. There's no organization to it; as the reviewer for the *Wall Street Journal* said, "'The Grammar of Rock' reads as if it had been shot at you out of a cannon: no chapters, no table of contents, no organizational structure at all, just a long and entertaining rant about what's wrong (mostly) and right (occasionally) in popular music."[8] It's an encyclopedic display of Theroux's opinionated knowledge of popular music that he displayed earlier in shorter form via Eugene Eyestones's record-collecting habits in *Laura Warholic*.

Eyestones keeps files on unusual aspects of sex to write about in his magazine column, and Theroux had obviously been keeping files for

---

7 "The Back of Beyond: An Interview with Alexander Theroux," *Rain Taxi* Online Edition, Winter 2012/2013. A few years later, Maliszewski assisted with the preparation of Theroux's *Einstein's Beets*.

8 Will Friedwald, "Bad to Verse," *Wall Street Journal*, 13 July 2013, C10. The best, most informed review I've seen is John L. Murphy's "Linguistic Inanities, Sung Howlers, Spoken Clunkers & Verbal Tics: 'The Grammar of Rock,'" *PopMatters*, 21 March 2013.

years on food-related matters, resulting in his latest and biggest book of curious facts, *Einstein's Beets: An Examination of Food Phobias* (2017), which began as an essay in the late 1980s. Like *The Grammar of Rock*, the title is somewhat inaccurate: it's only partly about phobias; the rest is on tangential subjects such as celebrity chefs and food show hosts, food industry outrages, diseases, the Food and Drug Administration, toxic plants, cookbooks, beverages, dietary taboos, crackpot nutritional theories, adversarial relationships between plants (allelopathy), eating habits and table manners, food references in the Bible and literature, PETA, overfishing, and cannibalism, among other things. The announced purpose of the book is to investigate what food preferences and phobias reveal about a person, but that fizzles out into thousands of random food factoids. Throughout the book Theroux makes statements like "So much is said about a person in what he or she—almost always passionately—crucially seeks to avoid in foods or shuns in taste. What could be more informative of a personality?" (131). Following this is a paragraph on various people who disliked beets: Albert Einstein (hence the book's title), Barack and Michelle Obama, Bill Cosby, Faulkner's Joe Christmas (*Light in August*), and food critic Gael Greene. But what does that aversion say about the personalities of such a diverse group of people, or that "the beet was Rasputin the monk's favorite vegetable" (133, quoting Tom Robbins's *Jitterbug Perfume*)? Nothing.[9] I once knew a woman who refused to eat curry because she disapproved of the way women were treated in India; beginning in England in the 1790s, some conscientious people boycotted sugar and rum as the products of slave labor. But most of Theroux's examples are meaningless whims, not meaningful statements, much less psychological clues. And his efforts to make something out of nothing strain too hard for significance: "Disliking a food has its own distinction, offering a definite panache. A negative chic attaches to refusing something outright. The act of *spurning* acquires a kind of power. It gives advantage, dominance. A mysterious side of it solicits guesses as to your motive, for you reveal a sharpness, suggesting, acuity, bravado, judgment" (301, punctuation *sic*). Or it simply means you don't like beets.

Although divided into titled chapters, Theroux frequently departs from their announced subjects, pursues numerous digressions, and merely piles up nearly 800 pages of curious food facts. (By this time

9 Theroux quotes several wildly imaginative flights of fancy on beets from Robbins's hilarious novel, but his reaction is sniffy, maybe jealous. "I gather that his vegetable portraits are meant to be funny"—*meant* to be?!?—and he calls him a "know-it-all," precisely how Theroux comes across in books like this.

Theroux had gained access to the internet, which provided a smorgasbord of material beyond his usual reading and may explain its overstuffed bulk.) Again, the pancultural range of knowledge is astounding—some of it derived from celebrity biographies, for which Theroux has a sweet tooth—and there are many interesting autobiographical tidbits.[10] His animadversions on experimentation in "progressive cuisine" (638–43) informs his dislike of experimental fiction: "Experimentation is often simply an end in itself" (669). But the triviality of so much of it is wearisome—so what if Harry Truman hated onions (613), or Jennifer Aniston drinks Smart Water (*sic*, 323)?—and the book suffers from slack editing/production (smartwater is lowercase and one word, not two) and an incomplete index: Ms. Aniston isn't listed, for example, despite her in-law status,[11] or—more crucial—the foods and beverages mentioned.

Several of Theroux's unpublished manuscripts belong to the same genre, one that he clearly enjoys. I've already mentioned *Black, White,* and *Shop Around,* and the expanded version of "Artists Who Kill." Among his other book manuscripts are *Seacoast in Bohemia; or, The Story of Literary and Cinematic Blunders, Howlers, and Flaps,* which began as an essay written in the 1980s entitled "Bitterns Cheeped," noting a minor factual error in Theroux's own *Three Wogs* before enumerating similar gaffes in the writings of others—currently numbering in the thousands—as in Shakespeare's assumption that Bohemia had a seacoast. He gives two dozen examples of anachronisms, which is ironic in light of those he deliberately committed in *Laura Warholic*.[12] Another is called *Violon d'Ingres: A Study of the Phenomenon of Alternate Vocations,* which informs the reader that (to pluck two random examples) Norman Mailer always wanted to be an engineer, and Jack White of the White Stripes planned to become a priest when younger. He has a 12,000-word essay on "Stutterstepping," his term for redundant statements, as in Senator Joseph Lieberman's 2004 claim "What we need most immediately is a

---

10 Such as "I love John Evelyn" (270), the 17th-century miscellaneous writer, or: "I remember back in college a few friends and I formed a breakfast group called the Runagates Club, named after a John Buchan book, which met very early in the morning, before classes, when in my old '53 Chevy we drove down to the various beaches—this was back in Maine in the early 1960s—where we had cups of coffee and smoked joints, a lovely combination, but on special days, which was most of the time, we drank bottles of white wine" (155).

11 The actress became Alexander's niece-in-in law in 2015 when she married Justin Theroux, the son of his older brother Eugene.

12 Cf. William T. Vollmann's admission in the afterword to his novel *The Lucky Star,* which ends in 2015: "For slatternly narrative purposes I have stirred in anachronisms from 2016 and 2017" (NY: Viking, 2020), 625.

sense of immediacy."

Another accretive project that Theroux began around 1990 is *Anomalies*, now a lengthy manuscript (286,000 words) that he describes on the first page thusly:

> *Anomaly* [sic] is not like any other book. Its range and inclusivity, born, much of it, from my interest in and great pique at the ironies and oddities (and lies) that seem to be everywhere and my discovering, even as—especially as—a young boy, the seemingly endless examples in our culture, proof perhaps of Original Sin, of the guile, bluff, double-dealing, fraud, pretense, treachery chicanery, slyness, and downright duplicity in the hoodwinking of the general public. It covers a diversity of subject matter and reflects the tastes and interests of a busy lifetime.

A noble cause, but here are some random examples of such anomalies: "According to the 1938 edition of Hoyle, according to cartoonist Ben Katchor, creator of *Julius Knipl, Real Estate Photographer*, no rules exist for graciously leaving a game of pinochle to earn a living, to attend religious services, or to answer the call of nature." "Damon Runyon, famous for his big city stories of crime and adventure, was born in Manhattan—Kansas!" Another: "Rudolph Nureyev claimed he danced best when he was tired." One more: "Belgian endive in Belgium is called *chicon* (chicory), and in that country chicory is called *endive*."

In a scene set circa 2008 in Paul Theroux's highly autobiographical novel *Mother Land*, the narrator says of the Alexander character:

> He was embarked on one of his miscellanies, a volume he called *Anomalies*. It was, he said, his big book.
> "Give me an example."
> "George H. W. Bush said, 'Read my lips: No new taxes.' But look closely. He has no lips." (379)

(That's an actual quotation from the manuscript, not a parody.) In published form, it would be around 700 pages long.

Adding all these unpublished books to Theroux's published ones, these miscellanies constitute the largest percentage of his oeuvre; larger than his combined novels and short fiction, larger than his complete poetry, and larger than his uncollected literary essays and reviews. Despite Theroux's high opinion of them, they are essentially books of trivia, which may be the most inconsequential genre there is. I can't think of any other major writer who spent so many years compiling so many books in a trifling genre like this—imagine Nabokov writing more books on chess and butterfly trivia than fiction—especially when Theroux could have been completing his ambitious novel-in-progress *Herbert Head* instead (see appendix). The fact that this multitalented author devoted a large portion of his writing life to compiling these books of curious facts may be the greatest anomaly of all.

The Brothers Theroux

SIBLING NOVELISTS are rare. There are the Brontë sisters and Gon-court brothers, obviously, and less obviously the Russian sci-fi authors Arkady and Boris Strugatsky, who collaborated on two dozen novels dur-ing the Cold War. Thomas Mann has all but eclipsed his older brother Heinrich, whose only claim to literary fame is having written the novel (*Professor Unrat*) on which the film *The Blue Angel* was based. Osbert Sitwell wrote a half-dozen novels, sister Edith wrote one (on Jonathan Swift), but brother Sacheverell stuck with nonfiction. There may be a few others in literary history—add Donald and Frederick Barthelme—but the most prominent in modern American literature are Alexander and Paul Theroux. Unlike all of the above, they not only write novels, they write each other into their novels.

Paul Theroux (b. 1941) was first out of the gate, publishing his de-but novel *Waldo* (1967) when his older brother Alexander (b. 1939) was still in graduate school. By the time Alexander published his first novel, *Three Wogs* (1972), Paul had published four more novels, the most re-cent of which, *The Jungle Lovers* (1971), was set in Malawi, where Paul had lived in the 1960s. This accounts for the chiding reference to him in Alexander's debut novel:

> Then, of some notoriety, was bespectacled Paul the Pseudo-plutarch, American oligosyllabicist, ἀυθρωπάρεοχος, and poet laureate of rural Malawi, who scuttled around in his pants of beaten wool and round cap, waving copies of his own *Velocity: The Key to Writing*, (o.p.) a vade mecum for gerundmongers and the sourcebook of his widely cited, narrowly appreciated, long-held theory that one's literary out-put should cease only when one ran out of possible dedications—and that remained, not a family, but a world away.[1]

1 Alexander Theroux, *Three Wogs* (1972; rpt. Boston: David R. Godine, 1975), 83.

From the beginning, both their styles and motives for writing were completely different. Paul's main motivation for publishing books was financial; when he wrote his first novel, he was already married and expecting his first child, so he needed to write the kinds of books that made money. The ones I've read are more literary than mainstream fiction, and their plots and settings are far more varied than those in Alexander's novels. Paul's characters are more rounded and realistic than the types, approaching caricatures, that Alexander adopted from satiric eighteenth-century writers, nineteenth-century novelists such as Charles Dickens and Herman Melville, and such twentieth-century modernists as Frederick Rolfe, Ronald Firbank, and Samuel Beckett. Paul's novels make no great demands on the reader—they are middlebrow rather than highbrow literature—and though well written, I doubt they contain many sentences like the one above from *Three Wogs*. Nor has Paul ever written a novel on the same order as Alexander's *Darconville's Cat*.

Growing up in a large family in Medford, Massachusetts, the brothers were voracious readers and developed literary ambitions early on. Alexander remembers his "first attempt at fiction. It was a short story, typed on yellow rectangular paper, when I was in the seventh grade. After school my friend Angelo Corrado and I ran over to his house to use the typewriter. My saga, unnamed, was the story, illustrated with cartoons (another early fascination), of a magical breakfast food, and there was in it enough of a pubescently cheeky, if not slightly risqué, even perhaps scatological theme for his mesomorphic older brother, a shadowy oaf who never spoke to me and only to Angelo in Italian, to rip it up one day."[2] Alexander also remembered that "my brother Paul's first tentative attempt at a novel, *The Fat Bird*, had drawings throughout the text."[3] Alexander may have been the first to write a story, but Paul was the first to publish a novel. Admitting to a sense of rivalry in the same 1996 essay, Alexander writes, "I well remember in 1967 when my brother Paul's first novel, *Waldo*, was published, I was a second-year graduate student at the University of Virginia—in literature, no less—and sadly felt one-upped, I have to admit, for there is at best a built-in tension in academic life between creative writers and critics, and, like Paul, I was or wanted to be in the former camp, not one of those scribbling eunuchs

2 "Myself and My Brothers," *San Diego Reader*, 3 October 1996. This autobiographical essay borrows some material from a similar earlier essay, "The Detours of Art," *Review of Contemporary Fiction* 11.1 (Spring 1991): 36–40.

3 "Dabblers and Dabbling," *Arts & Antiques*, November 1987, 107.

who prefer to believe their thin articles and monographs art." He goes on to say that, "in a way, I began to write in order to catch up to him," which is odd because by 1967 he was already writing his *third* novel.

"The first novel was long—amassing pages is a young novelist's delight—originally a play I had written at about the age of 18 called *Edward Jellow*," he recalled decades later, "a comic noir novel (I was a fan of Nathanael West) about a corrupt children's show host."[4] By February 1965 he had already written a second; one of his professors at the University of Virginia, the great Hugh Kenner, who was very impressed by Alexander, wrote to Guy Davenport that month to say: "I have been reading the ms. of his second novel, only academic novel with a student viewpoint, and he threatens me with the third."[5] Theroux later explained that the second novel, entitled *The Butterfinger Years*, featured a protagonist named Paul Margarine, "a composite roughly (and amicably) based on my brother Paul, from whom I believe I even borrowed the name of the college town—we purloined each others' brains freely back then—and a few close friends of mine. . . ."[6] As a doctoral student he developed a taste for the learned wit of Swift, Pope, Fielding, and Sterne, and by the end of the 1960s was under the spell of the novels of Frederick Rolfe: hardly a model for literary success. While writing his dissertation (on Beckett) he also began a third novel entitled *The Lollipop Trollops* (later used for his first book of poetry), in which he aligned himself with a decidedly noncommercial genre:

> The genre to which I am addressing myself is not new, the encyclopedic, or so-called 'learned' novel—a narrative technique that looks nostalgically back to the tradition of the Schoolmen, the humanist pedant, the agitated scholastic. The paradigmatic work in this genre reaches from Montaigne to Baron Corvo (Fr. Rolfe), from Sterne's *Tristram Shandy* to Beckett's *Watt*, from Burton's *Anatomy* to John Aubrey to Jorge Luis Borges, from Rabelais to Joyce.[7]

4 Quoted (from an email dated 6 August 2012) in *Questioning Minds: The Letters of Guy Davenport and Hugh Kenner*, ed. Edward M. Burns (Berkeley: Counterpoint, 2018), 743n40.

5 *Questioning Minds*, 698. Kenner says Theroux's first novel "is (probably) being published by Houghton Mifflin this summer," but Theroux told editor Burns that "Houghton Mifflin was on my mind, simply because it was located in Boston, from where I hale, that and because I had intended to offer it to them" (743n40). Houghton Mifflin became Paul's principal publisher.

6 *Questioning Minds*, 743n40.

7 Quoted in Martin C. Battestin, "Alexander Theroux in Virginia and London, 1964–1973," *Review of Contemporary Fiction* 11.1 (Spring 1991): 81. See "Her-

He set it aside after graduating and, in London during the winter of 1968–69 on a Fulbright Grant, began writing the first novella in *Three Wogs*, originally planning on writing five long stories for the book rather than three.[8] He had trouble finding a publisher for it, and the fact that he had to settle for a small press (Gambit) rather than a big publisher foreshadowed that his road would be different from his brother's. (*Waldo* was published by Houghton Mifflin, and virtually all of Paul's books since then have been published by major publishers.) He resumed work on *The Lollipop Trollops*, as he would in later years before abandoning it, but then fell in love with a student, which resulted in a different novel.

Despite Alexander's dig at Paul in *Three Wogs*, the brothers remained on good terms during the 1970s, when Paul achieved money and fame not from his novels but from his travelogue *The Great Railway Bazaar* (1975). Alexander praised Paul's 1976 novel *The Family Arsenal* in a roundup review of four novels,[9] and his brother did him one better the following year. Asked in 1977 by the *New York Times Book Review* "Who is the living writer you most admire?" Paul generously replied:

> I cannot ignore the fact that for the whole of my life, and especially for the past 20 years, which I have spent learning to speak in prose, the writing (some published, some not) and the brave peregrinations of my brother Alexander Theroux have aroused my keenest admiration.
>
> It has been part of my luck to have been raised in a populous and intelligent family of nine unexampled wits. The first pictures I saw were painted by my mother, the first music I could understand was played on the trombone by my brother Eugene, the first poems and stories I read were written by Alexander who, older than I, showed me how it was done. He is the funniest person I know, a master of the impromptu ghost story, a maniacal stylist who, recently, in the course of an otherwise hilarious letter to me, wrote, "Sorrow is the cause of immortal conceptions."[10]
>
> The experience of several monasteries has left him with Attic

---

bert Head: The Unfinished Novel" below for more on this project.

8 Battestin, 70.

9 "Sun Daze, Bloody Sun Daze," *Boston Magazine*, October 1976, 37–40.

10 Alexander came across this line in *The Confessions of Edward Dahlberg* (1971), and repurposed it as the final sentence in *Darconville's Cat*—the last of many allusions in the novel to Dahlberg's work.

Greek, conversational Latin and a reclusive disposition. Yet he is great
company, a deadly accurate parodist, an expert mimic and a crack
shot. His first book, "Three Wogs," earned him a place in the Ency-
clopedia Britannica, and his next ones, "The Schinocephalic Waif"
and "The Great Wheadle Tragedy"—neither of these wayward mas-
terpieces was reviewed—are presently changing hands at ridiculously
high prices, because of their scarcity value. In a world in which mediocre authors boast of backbreaking jobs they've had (cook, truck-
driver, busboy), Alexander has with quiet brilliance moved from the
priesthood, to a Ph.D., to Harvard. A model scholar; but he has never
ceased to write with dazzling originality, making sentences with the
perfectionism jewelers in oriental courts made filigree.[11]

The following year, Paul published his ninth novel, *Picture Palace*.
In a lengthy and very informative profile entitled "The Theroux Family
Arsenal," also published in 1978, James Atlas noted that some family
members believe Alexander was the model for Orlando in that novel. "If
so," Atlas writes, "it is curiously oblique. Some features of [Alexander's]
temperament are discernible, and a few details are drawn from his life,
but there is none of his defiance, nor the blunt, grandiose intensity and
cultivated outrageousness that distinguish him from Paul."[12] Orlando is
the dead brother of the novel's narrator, an acclaimed elderly photographer named Maude Coffin Pratt, who had an incestuous attraction to
him when alive. Orlando studies poetry at Harvard (where Alexander
was teaching when Paul wrote this novel), and in one scene he silences
a noisy party and begins declaiming the opening lines of Sir Thomas
Wyatt's "They Flee from Me"—the same poem Alexander uses as an epigraph for *Darconville's Cat*, which he finished the same year *Picture
Palace* was published. To be sure, Paul is a well-read man and may have
come across the poem separately, but Orlando's response to a belligerent
partygoer who challenges his literary tastes is pure Alex:

> The boy said, "I loathe the Elizabethans."
> "Wyatt wasn't an Elizabethan," said Orlando. "He was dead before
> Shakespeare was born."[13]

That sort of pedantic comeback can be found in all of Alexander's novels,

11 *New York Times Book Review*, 4 December 1977, 70.
12 James Atlas, "The Theroux Family Arsenal," *New York Times Magazine*, 30
     April 1978, 58.
13 *Picture Palace* (Boston: Houghton Mifflin, 1978), 87.

whose autobiographical protagonists always know more than everyone else around them. When the boy-critic persists and dismisses Wyatt's poem by saying "It sounds very sweet, but it's just artifice, low cunning, a kind of trick—" Orlando "grabbed him by the lapels and flung him across the room" and then knocks him down a second time. Impressed, Maude says, "Orlando's was the best reply I had ever seen, and it taught me everything I needed to know about critics: a critic was someone you wanted to hit" (87–88). That too is pure Alex, though it may be a universal sentiment.

Like Alexander, Orlando Pratt is good at doing imitations, playing charades, and telling scary stories. Virtually everything said about him is positive, which reflects Paul's admiration for his older brother at the time. One episode is worth sticking a pin in: testing the waters, Maude asks, "Did you ever hear of incest?" "Sure I did!" Orlando replies. "Little things, aren't they? With six legs—they climb all over you" (129). About a dozen years later, Alexander would write a poem based on the same incest/insect pun, one that would play a role in the growing antagonism between the brothers. Yet even in 1978, Atlas noticed "a rather pronounced rivalry" between them, and quoted Alexander as saying of his more financially successful brother, "Paul is like all new money. He likes to talk about how much he's made."

Early on in *Picture Palace*, Maud Pratt says "there is no shortage of writers who put themselves into their book—the most notorious example being your modern writer who can't describe anyone else, which makes it pretty easy for biographers but holy hell for anyone else" (43). Paul may have been referring to Alexander's autobiographical *Darconville's Cat*, published in May 1981, where Paul would have found his fourth novel *Girls at Play* (1969) included in Dr. Crucifer's library of misogynist books.[14] Although many reviewers praised Alexander's novel, it received a mediocre review in the influential *New York Times Book Review*, and did not sell as well as the author had hoped, nor was it reprinted in paperback after the customary year or two. In contrast, that fall Paul published his twelfth and most successful novel, *The Mosquito Coast* (in the UK, in the US the following year), the basis for a popular movie. The friendly rivalry between the brothers probably started turning sour at that point.[15] Some have said that Allie Fox, the flamboyant protagonist of Paul's novel, resembles Alexander in some ways, or Paul himself, but

14 *Darconville's Cat* (Garden City, NY: Doubleday, 1981), 449.
15 For an expression of that sourer mood, see Theroux's long poem "Sibling Rivalries" (CP 284–86), though the poem deals with his entire family, not just Paul.

in an interview Paul said "Allie is based on many people I know—and even on Pap, Huck Finn's father."[16]

In 1983, a third Theroux was heard from. Doubleday—which published Alexander's *Darconville's Cat*—brought out *Black Coconuts, Brown Magic* by Joseph Theroux (b. 1953), who had spent time as a Peace Corps volunteer in Western Samoa. I read it when it came out and don't remember any references to his brothers in it (or anything about it, to be honest), and by 1992, when Alexander published his mocking poem "Samoan Brother," they too were clearly at odds with each other.[17]

Alexander published another autobiographical novel in 1987, the grimly elegant *An Adultery*. Protagonist Kit Ford has a brother named Tarquin who can be identified with Paul by way of various incidental details, though Tarquin is not a writer but a lawyer, like their older brother Eugene (b. 1938). He is mentioned in passing a half-dozen times, but nothing substantial is said of him, though the name isn't very flattering: Tarquin is the ravager in Shakespeare's "Rape of Lucrece," and a "recreant knight" in Arthurian romances. The autobiographical elements of *An Adultery* became a Theroux family guessing game. The rare-book dealer Between the Covers once offered a first edition with

> Author's complimentary card laid in. Although not indicated as such in the book, this is the copy of the author's sister Mary. Laid in is an autograph letter Signed to Mary Theroux from her brother, the author Peter Theroux asking her to participate in a game of 'Trivial Adultery' that he and their other brother Paul Theroux are playing, trying to identify the sources for the various adulteries in their brother Alex's novel. In the envelope, Peter has enclosed a typed postcard Signed by Paul Theroux asking Peter to identify four different sources and questions from the book.[18]

Coincidentally, Paul's novels began taking a more overtly autobiographical turn, beginning with *My Secret History* (1989), which purports to be the sexual history of writer Andre Parent. Alexander, whose middle name is Louis, appears a few times as Louie in the novel, a thinly dis-

---

16 "The Perpetual Stranger: Paul Theroux talks about writing and traveling— and the liberation that both provide," *Atlantic Unbound*, 31 March 2004.

17 *The Lollipop Trollops and Other Poems* (Normal, IL: Dalkey Archive Press, 1992), 131; rpt. in *CP*, 516. Since then Joseph has published many essays on Samoan and Hawaiian history, as well as two novels featuring Robert Louis Stevenson as a detective in Hawaii.

18 Accessed from AbeBooks.com in 2018. The asking price was $1,500.00.

guised account of six key sexual episodes in Paul's life, but nothing significant is said of Louie other than he helped his younger brother with Latin once and joined Students for Kennedy during the 1960 election.[19]

The novel was the subject of an amusing letter written six years later by Alexander's then-girlfriend, Laura Markley. Dated 29 July 1995 and addressed to a San Francisco friend named Dan Murtagh, she wrote:

> I'm reading Paul Theroux's *My Secret History* (almost done with it) which I highly recommend. It's a "page-turner," but quite well done & Alex says it's highly autobiographical, though Paul would deny that (on the 1ˢᵗ page Paul says the characters "strolled out of [my] imagination" & even points out that "Andre's spouse is not based on my wife, Anne" when Alex maintains it's completely based on her, & she was furious when the book came out (it details all his love affairs while traveling, and one of hers, when he left her & his small son for 4½ mos. to go to Siberia). The protagonist (if you can call him that), Andre Parent, leads a double life, & feels few pangs of conscience about his secret affairs. He thinks his double life inspires his creativity and sense of independence ("I liked feeling slightly wolfish" he admits at one point). Yet when his wife cheats on him, he goes haywire and concocts an outrageous revenge scheme, which he carries out perfectly. Such hypocrisy! But you can't help liking Andre at the same time, for his sense of humor & interesting observations about the world & people as he travels around and works on various projects.
>
> Last weekend I was sitting in Alex's kitchen drawing a tree outside the sliding glass door, and since it was so hot I was wearing a long (above the knee but close-fitting and transparent) men's white undershirt Alex had given me. Who should walk around the side of the house but Paul Theroux, wearing sunglasses, shorts, & a bemused expression, wondering if Alex was home. I was so embarrassed! Well, I hope he liked what he saw! I got him to sign 4 more books of his I'd bought (Alex insisted he sign them—A. says Paul hates signing books, because he thinks his signature is so valuable, & suspects you'll only sell the book. I don't know who has the bigger ego, Paul or Alex—it's a close race!) Later I realized I'd left the price inside, a pencilled "$1" in each cover, since I'd found these books for nothing at library & yard sales! Faux pas! Of course, Alex was delighted.
>
> The problem with me & Alex is that I think he'd like a woman with a house, a car, an eye for antiques & decorating, a woman who's a gourmet cook & can still dress up like a whore & push him down

19 *My Secret History* (New York: Putnam's, 1989), 35, 98.

on the bed at night.[20] He's that simple. And I'm none of those, except maybe the last, if I'm in the right mood & feel I'm not going to be rejected because it's "too hot" or someone's "too tired." Paul's character Eden (Andre's mistress at the end of *M.S.H.*) is exactly the kind of woman Alex might find it in his heart to love—if he's even capable of that emotion.[21]

As the letter indicates, Alexander and Paul were still on speaking terms in 1995, which suggests that Paul's grotesque caricature of his brother in yet another novel he published the previous year was merely fraternal ribbing. In a story Alexander would write years later entitled "Envenoming Junior," which features a novelist clearly modeled on Paul, the Alexandrian narrator (Jack) claims that the Pauline novelist "had lampooned Jack as a buffoon in several scenes . . . in *The Mad, Mad Magician.*" This is a reference to Paul's magic-realist novel *Millroy the Magician*, in which the title character says of Floyd Fewox, "He's ninety-nine percent buffoon."[22] Millroy is performing at the Barnstable County Fair, where he adopts a neglected fourteen-year-old audience member named Jilly Farina, who becomes his assistant. He warns the girl against Floyd, who drives a Harley motorcycle on The Wall of Death and appears to be a funhouse mirror version of the former Harvard professor and author of the o.p. *Darconville's Cat*:

> "I wrote a book once," Floyd Fewox said, and it sounded like a get-even threat. "I could show you a copy. You'd probably be scared. It's really frank. You don't believe me."
> His spiky graying hair was stuck in little bunches like doll's hair to his scalp, and it was growing in neat scabby rows, as though it had been planted. . . . He had yellowish Italian skin, and his nose was twisted sideways, as though he had tried to straighten it but failed, leaving it looking pinched. He wore high boots, greasy jeans with a silver studded belt, and had a tattoo on his arm that said BORN TO RAISE HELL. His sweaty skin steamed of beer. He was stubbly, he smelled, he wore a filthy T-shirt lettered HARVARD.
> "I used to teach at Harvard," he said. "They said I was trouble. You don't believe me." (27)

20 As in *My Secret History*, 444–45.
21 Letter in my possession. Markley became the model for the title character in Theroux's *Laura Warholic*; Murtagh is mentioned on pp. 427 and 581 of that novel.
22 *Millroy the Magician* (NY: Random House, 1994), 42.

Floyd lusts after the young girl, and a little later Millroy informs her:

> "It's true—this man taught at Harvard. He wrote a book which got respectful reviews. But he was fired for writing threatening letters to his colleagues and for persecuting students. His irrational views were incompatible with those of a great institution. He spent a great deal of time sobbing his heart out in the university infirmary. He was heavily sedated, and finally was discharged." (39)[23]

Millroy then challenges him to and defeats him in a bizarre "psychic duel." Later, Millroy disguises Jilly as a boy and calls her "Alex."

The brothers were clearly drifting apart by 1996 when the older wrote about his relationship to the younger in an essay for the *San Diego Reader* entitled "Myself and My Brothers." Building on the autobiographical portions of "The Detours of Art," Theroux offers a warm, leisurely, and surprisingly modest account of how he and his brothers became writers, and of the influence their father had on his love for literature,[24] before discussing sibling rivalry, in myth, literature, and history as well as in his own family. The revealing essay is mostly about his own literary background and approach to writing, but after noting that "all brothers and sisters are rivals" and that "Tales of competing brothers are the beating heart of fairy tales in every country," he narrows his focus on Paul in a stocktaking passage worth quoting at length:

> I read everybody, including Paul, with a pencil, editing his words, and I have no doubt he does the same. For one thing, as I have mentioned, we have different writing styles, which were as different back in high school when we began turning out poems and stories. I know he thinks my work overfreighted, allusional, and a bit too crabbedly latinate for his tastes. Whereas I have always thought he should take more chances with narrative and dynamize the language in original ways. I am criticized as being hard to read. He is thought to be cynical. I should publish more books, it is said. He publishes too much. We used to read each other's manuscripts and dabble in them, like fingering candies, offering a funnier name for a character, suggesting

23 Alexander left Harvard in 1977 simply because his nonrenewable four-year contract was up.

24 Albert E. Theroux died in May 1995, and later that year his son published a memoir about him: "Decent Life Led by the Ordinary Man," *San Diego Reader*, 9 November 1995, 47–50.

a better ending, criticizing a passage, but no more. Why? It's hard
to say. Young writers need sounding boards. Partners. Foils. I believe
that, in the way families share a particular sense of humor, siblings
in a very real sense write for each other. In a magnanimous moment,
Paul once told me that if he had read my novel *Darconville's Cat* in
high school, he would never have started to write. And in a way, I began to write in order to catch up to him. We have often argued over
words, sentences, endings, reviews, opinions, points of view. Everything. We grew up that way. Even favorite writers. He prefers Conrad
over Melville!

Far more financially successful than I am or will ever be, Paul used
to be impatient with my allusive way of writing, symbolic and often
too rich. He has a much more lucid, accessible style, which is argu-
ably a prose less demanding to write (though I am certain he would
deny it) and one more palatable to the common reader. Many think
my work—I hope no one in my family is numbered among them—pretentious, my sentences too long, my word usage arcane and Brown-
ingesque. God bless the varieties of prose styles! Why should prose
styles be similar in siblings who write? So many variables in so many
personalities inculcate different responses. Why should, how could
anything ever match? As brothers and sisters vary in tastes, so does
their work.

Paul's financial success—and he was earning large advances on
his travel books very early—is well earned. He has written over 30
books, novels, travel books, essays, short stories, Christmas fables, no
end of articles. (He did it all on his own, let me add, without anyone's
help, including V.S. Naipaul, who became friends with Paul when my
brother was first setting out to write but whose assistance constitutes
little more than cheerleading.) Like Anthony Trollope, upon finishing
a book on Tuesday, Paul is at another one the following day. I like to
believe I am no less driven or zealous, but I am told I write not just inaccessible prose but books that publishers, including my own, Henry
Holt & Co., tell me do not fit into easily identifiable genres. As I write,
there are six finished manuscripts sitting in my rooms gathering dust,
with no place to go to and without having been read. A person devoted
to writing popular fiction is not necessarily a sellout—writers all want
to be read—but it seems an odd penalty for someone who doesn't
serve up readily identifiable fare to have his or her manuscripts buried
in a sepulcher.

After this discordant note, Theroux returns to childhood memories and influences, and concludes with this self-evaluation:

> "I don't think anybody has ever felt totally at home in human society,"
> Gore Vidal once wrote. I am inclined to agree. It is my amateur belief
> that in living we, more than anything, contrive to arrange a series of
> refuges, of escapes, of hiding-holes—clubs, travel, our own house-
> holds, hobbies, work can be one, a big one, reading, maybe even eat-
> ing, church, politics, the thousand ways we entertain ourselves—and
> art for me, writing, acts indeed as a very significant refuge. Is it borne
> of disappointment in society? Maybe. Of disappointment of myself
> *in* society? The way society acts on me? More to the point, the way I
> feel about society and my role in it? No doubt, no doubt. Know that
> I never think of it as disdaining the life we are given to live. I see it
> simply as a way of preserving dreams, a way of having vision. I prefer
> to think of myself as having the steadfastness of Keats, looking at his
> bright star.

It's a charming and informative essay, free from the captious tone of
many of his writings. It's a shame that it appeared in a local San Diego periodical and thus went mostly unnoticed, but it's currently available online and is recommended to anyone with an interest in Theroux's
work.[25]

This essay appeared in the *San Diego Reader* in early October 1996,
and its percolating resentment went ballistic the same month when the
mischievous *Boston Magazine* published Alexander's outrageous "review" of Paul's new novel, *My Other Life*, under the title "Blood Feud."
In what the *Spectator* the following January called "the most extraordinary piece of literary criticism published last year,"[26] Alexander not only
trashed the new novel but took the opportunity to fling insults at his
brother and expose his eccentricities. It's a bizarre, anomalous performance.

My Other Life is what Paul calls (in the Author's Note) "the story
of a life I could have lived had things been different." He re-imagines

25 https://www.sandiegoreader.com/news/1996/oct/03/i-am-criticized-being-hard
-read-he-thought-be-cyni/
26 David Sexton, "Strangers and a Brother" [review of Paul's *Collected Stories*],
Spectator, 18 January 1997, 28–29. *TLS* mistakenly predicted, "It's a piece
that'll go down to fame. Henceforth any sisterly rivalry between Margaret
Drabble and A. S. Byatt can only appear consummately genteel by comparison. The secondary literature will be immense, if mostly psychological" (25
October 1996, 16, signed "D.S."). The review received far more attention in
Britain than in the U.S.

eighteen episodes in his life, tweaking them as autobiographical nov-
elists have always done. There are metafictional elements that evoke
Borges—indeed, the novel begins with an epigraph from his "Borges and
I"—and John Barth, who two years earlier published a novel in the form
of a memoir called *Once Upon a Time: A Floating Opera* (which Alexander reviewed). Kerouac's books are mostly memoir novels, and Gore
Vidal once published a book entitled *Two Sisters* that is subtitled "A
Memoir in the Form of a Novel." As the well-read older brother admits,
"The gambit is not new, Nabokov, Borges, and Mailer, to name but three,
have famously and quisquously peopled their own works with their other
selves as fictional characters going under their own names. In *Antaeus*
(Spring 1994), John Updike, confronting his doppelgänger, somewhat
schizoidally confesses to impersonating the 'other' John Updike, author
of all those novels, essays, and poems."[27] He goes on to add, "I myself
love the idea of fictional alter egos, simply because I have learned from
a lifetime not only of reading but also of teaching literature that no figure in a book, whether memoir or biography, novel or autobiography, is
either fully imaginary or completely real, and that only a fool or a silly
naif would insist on such distinctions." Alexander's own novels are highly
autobiographical, yet he complains that it is unclear in *My Other Life*
what is fact and what is fiction. "Shouldn't he simply and manfully tell
us, regarding both the himself who isn't him and the actual characters
he actually names but insists are only fictional, precisely where the real
faces end and the grimaces begin?"

No, he shouldn't, nor would Alexander ask that of any other novelist,
one of many indicators that his complaints are personal, not literary. He
calls it "a novel of contrition, pieced out by way of the contrivance of
a writer at last taking a moment to satirize himself, not subtly, in order
to seek absolution for thirty years of wayward, unfair bitchery and to
come out—even if only for the space of a story—into the sunlight from
the cruel, carious shadows which, like a crab, he has so long chosen to
inhabit." He goes on to dismiss it as "a beach read, a middlebrow brick
just a step above a Judith Krantz or Belva Plain," and then starts making
things up:

> He is ignored by the Academy and smiled down on by the literary
> establishment, for the most part. Nobody I know has written so many
> books (20 novels, 10 travel books) with so little serious critical recogni-
> tion to show for it. None of his books are taught in colleges or have
> cult status or have generated, I believe, a single scholarly essay, and

27 "Blood Feud," *Boston Magazine*, October 1996, 130.

most of them are presently out of print.

I doubt the last clause: a few of Paul's early books may have been o.p. in 1996 but the better-known ones were still available, and this claim is ironic coming from an author whose own books had been o.p. for years. According to the *MLA International Bibliography*, Paul's works had generated about a dozen critical articles by 1996, as well as a book in the Twayne series by Samuel Coale (1987). Paul's *Saint Jack* was taught in a graduate-level course I took at Rutgers in 1986, and I'm sure his other novels have been used in classrooms over the years. Wikipedia notes that the literary establishment, far from smiling down on him, has given Paul numerous awards and honors over the years (a few of which are mentioned on p. 453 of *My Other Life*). With even greater irony, the ferociously satiric Alexander criticizes his brother's tendency to satirize others: "He has ridiculed in print everyone from priests to high school classmates to Cape Codders to fat Samoans to tasteless Americans to tubby Cantonese to lazy Melanesians *to old girlfriends* [italics mine]. . . . He has skewered a former sister-in-law, . . . lampooned his former in-laws, his own children's grandparents, . . . and, never without loud exclamations of denial later, undisguisedly mocked in print even members of his own family. . . ." But then he tells the biggest lie in the review (there's no kinder way to put it):

> Curiously, I am the only member of our family he has, for some inexplicable reason, never dared to satirize. Why? Because I am also a writer? Is it superstition? Cowardice? Amicability? Fear? The taboo of seeming envious? Or churlish? Or graceless? *I* am certain that, with all my faults, there aren't many he could not fail to find, if only he bothered to look.[28]

Alexander then descends into ad hominem personal matters, too petty to repeat here. *Boston Magazine* even allowed him to publish a mocking poem in the middle of the review, "Paul Nosedocks" (reprinted in *CP* 70). In a sentence that applies as much (if not more) to himself as to his brother, Alexander sums him up as "a writer of venomous letters, an inveterate magpie, a rumpled dresser, an egotistical, unsettled eccentric,

28 P. 134. In a postscript to the letter to me enclosing the piece, Theroux wrote, "I only wrote my Paul article because he savaged me. . . ." (22 October 1996, his ellipsis). He admitted it "may have been a pointless & regressive article to write in the first place," and resented *Boston Magazine*'s tacky attempts to publicize it as a "feud."

extremely critical, occasionally funny, a sometime friend and all-time know-it-all." He also says a character in *My Other Life* "baldly plagiariz-es" a line from *Darconville's Cat*: "Paper is patient" (88; *DC* 697)—this from an author who routinely includes unacknowledged quotations in his own work! A simile about a kettle and a pot springs to mind, as does Baudelaire's "*mon semblable, mon frère!*"

A British journalist named Marianne Macdonald, who called the re-view "a magnificently petty piece of work," said "the Paul Theroux side of the family is understood to have perused the article with more hilarity than horror,"[29] but Paul took it seriously. "He's not describing the book," he complained to an American journalist. "He's describing his reaction to me, and the book is kind of the occasion for it. If there's someone who needs to be told what his job is, it's the editor of the magazine. If you were him, would you print seven pages by Alexander Theroux writing about Paul Theroux?"[30] Interviewing him a few months later, however, Macdonald wrote, "Although Theroux initially tried to laugh it off, he admitted that when the review came out last October it made him 'really angry.' He clenched his fist as he said it. But his preferred line is that the review says more about his brother than him, which must be at least partly true. 'He's an excitable guy,' he added rather patronisingly. 'He was used by a magazine editor.'"[31] By the time he was asked about it three years later, Paul had spun it in his favor: "I don't come off badly. When you read things like: 'He's obsessed with his bowels'—I laughed, actu-ally. He also said that I was obsessed with my height and I was enquiring about getting lifts for my shoes! He's a funny guy. We were very close at one time; now we're not at all. He leads his own life."[32]

Paul would return to his brother's insulting review 20 years later in his novel *Mother Land*, where he quotes it at length.

When "Blood Feud" appeared, Paul was presumably finishing his memoir *Sir Vidia's Shadow* (1998), about his relationship to V. S. Nai-paul (1932–2018). Paul's opening remarks in his chapter on the Trinida-dian-British writer's relationship with his younger brother Shiva Naipaul

29 Marianne Macdonald, "Theroux v. Theroux: why a brilliant reputation doesn't always travel." *The Independent*, 25 October 1996.

30 David Streitfeld, "Book Report," *Washington Post Book World*, 27 October 1996.

31 Marianne Macdonald, "Who Is Paul Theroux? *The Independent*, 18 May 1997.

32 Lynn Barber, "Making Waves." *The Observer*, 19 February 2000. Barber adds, "I rang Alexander Theroux in Cape Cod and he sounded eerily like his broth-er, but as soon as I said I was writing about Paul, he referred me to his agent and rang off."

(1945–85) can easily be read as a response to his brother's review:

> Brothers are versions of each other, a suggestion implicit in the word itself, the "other" in "brother." . . . The history of scribbling brothers is full of conflict, which ranges from hurt feelings and petty grumbling ("Why does *he* get all the attention?") to vicious attempts at literary fratricide ("Take that, you bastard!"). One of the brothers is always the other's inferior. Look at the brothers William and Henry James, Oscar and Willie Wilde, James and Stanislaus Joyce, Thomas and Heinrich Mann, Anton and Nikolai Chekhov, Lawrence and Gerald Durrell— there are no intellectual equals here, and, being writers, they are borderline nutcases.
>
> Such brothers are often fratricidal from birth and babyish in their battling, for there are nearly always aspects of lingering infantilism in sibling rivalry. When brothers fight, family secrets are revealed and the shaming revelations often make forgiveness irrelevant—the damage is done. In the literature of sibling rivalry, an enthralling spectator sport but pure hell on the fraternal rivals, the cry is usually "He hit me first!" or "Choose me!" . . . The nicer-seeming brother is not necessarily the better writer, nor even necessarily nicer.[33]

Alexander wasn't through with the nicer-seeming brother. By this time he was composing his next magnum opus, *Laura Warholic*, which alludes to Paul via not one but two characters. The title character's ex-husband is named Minot ("Mickey") Warholic, and though based largely on writer/journalist Alexander Laurence, Theroux gave him some of Paul's alleged faults. "In his egotism," the narrator notes, "Warholic reminded Eugene Eyestones [the protagonist, based on Alexander] of his own brother, Marysas [*sic*]. In his eyes, it was the worst thing he could say of anyone," and later, "In his awfulness, to Eugene, he was Marsyas Eyestones come alive—Eugene often confused his boss with his own brother."[34] Theroux distributes Paul's various shortcomings to both Minot and Marsyas throughout the novel, mostly petty foibles of the sort mentioned in "Blood Freud." The insults are stronger in the original

33 *Sir Vidia's Shadow: A Friendship Across Five Continents* (Boston: Houghton Mifflin, 1998), 250–51.

34 *Laura Warholic*, 43, 477. Marysas is a typo for Marsyas, a Greek mythological figure reviled for his hubris, and once bested in a music competition by Apollo. The name is spelled correctly only twice.

manuscript Alexander finished in 2000; there, for example, the passage
beginning at the top of p. 65 in the published book on "his brother, Marysas, a shifty lawyer," read:

> A Yoruba mask with cowrie-shell eyes hanging over the inside door
> had been the gift from an earlier, more congenial state of affairs of his
> late brother, Marysas, a ham-handed writer, who had a nervous break-
> down—his wife, fed up with his years of philandering, had divorced
> him—with whom, because of the envious things he'd written about
> him, Eugene had had a falling out decades before, and not only with
> him but with his two dependent sons, Loup and Larceny,[35] shallow,
> spoiled, spotty-faced victims (also would-be writers) of that intimidat-
> ing father with whom they had tried to ingratiate themselves all their
> lives, sadly, by spreading further lies about their uncle in print. None
> of them had spoken in twenty years. After fleecing a second wife of
> her estate in an ignoble but all-too-typical affair that became public,
> full trial and exposure, Marysas in a fit of poisonous self-hatred one
> desperate night, unhappy and sitting naked on a pile of his money,
> drank an industrial-size bottle of McIlhenny's Jalapeño Pepper Sauce
> and cacked himself to death. (ms. pp. 85–86)

The revised version of this page is less nasty but just as uncharitable. On
the other hand, the manuscript version of the tirade against Marsyas on
p. 144 was much shorter in the original; the expanded version is more
typical of the changes Theroux made from 2000 until the novel's publication in 2007.

Challenged about his "big-tent prose" in a passage that remained virtually untouched over those years, Eugene/Alexander compares his output to that of Marsyas/Paul:

> "I once knew a brilliant person who wrote an unforgettable book [Eu-
> gene tells his employer], several actually, and his envious brother who
> also wrote—shallow, mediocre things that he cranked out with a mini-
> mum amount of grace or care but that were more acceptable to the
> johnny nitwits out there who buy books as soporifics and not as aids
> to dream or to imagine or to expand their mind—could never quite
> forgive him. Without that one masterpiece, you see, it does not mat-
> ter how much a writer does or what he says. What I'm talking about

---

35 Paul's sons Marcel (b.1968) and Louis (b. 1970). Although this line was cut,
there are a few other demeaning references to them in the published version
of *Laura Warholic*.

is originality, which is rooted in daring and defiance and rage and recklessness and revolution, and not about sucking up to a world of brainless, mouth-breathing inchlings and half-assed dopes and stupid and illiterate mudnuns who read their books aloud and usually line by line with the aid of a running finger." (199)

This is a valuable passage of literary self-assessment, and a preemptive self-defense for any personal shortcomings (Alexander's, that is, not Paul's). He implies that writing a novel like *Darconville's Cat* covers a multitude of sins, and expanded on this notion to biographer Peter Richmond while revising *Laura Warholic*:

> It's the art that matters. That's the temptation among famous people: They don't have to give a shit about anything but the performance. So it doesn't matter how many times you're married, how much of a buffoon you might be. Sinatra is a good example. He was great at what he did. Why did we put up with Wagner's ego? Because he gave us *Tristan and Isolde*. That's what they bank on: that you'll forgive them for what they do. The chaos around them doesn't matter if their art is good. The populace is willing to forgive them if they're good.[36]

Alexander might overlook Paul's faults, he implies, if his brother had written something like *Darconville's Cat*, but he didn't; hence the rancor. And he hopes his readers will do likewise because he did.

The most significant change to the manuscript Alexander made regarding Paul is the scene in chapter XXXI when Eugene and Laura witness a murder at a book signing in Los Angeles. The "tallish, spotty-faced, middle-aged novelist with a British accent [who] was giving a diffident reading from his new book that relied as to both title and theme on Sherlock Holmes" (473) is a stand-in for Paul's oldest son Marcel Theroux, author of *The Confessions of Mycroft Holmes: A Paper Chase* (2001), discussed below. But in the original, Alexander referred to the falling out between Paul and Naipaul:

> One afternoon in a chain-bookstore they both heard a short, balding,

---

36 Peter Richmond, *Fever: The Life and Music of Miss Peggy Lee* (NY: Henry Holt, 2006), 404. Pages 398–405 are devoted to Theroux's friendship with the singer in the early 1990s, and is based on an unpublished memoir of his entitled "Peggy Lee" (2002). Oddly, she is only mentioned incidentally in Theroux's *Grammar of Rock*, not discussed at length, as is Sinatra and some others.

grumpy novelist with an [sic] fake English accent, oily, serviceable shoes, and a youngish woman in tow with whom in spite of his wedding ring (but not hers) he seemed on more than familiar grounds ("Sue, drive the car around front, would you? There's a luv") giving a lecture against the writer, V. S. Naipaul. It was sadly disconcerting to watch that round-as-a-volleyball face, a madman's red eyes cold above his grinning mouth, bearing down with ill-humor, and unctuous self-refulgence upon such a well-known writer, whom in his ceaseless yakking he was clearly calumniating out of nothing more than cantankerous personal envy. . . . A tall scholarly man with beard standing next to Laura leaned over to ask, "Do you, um, know why those two writers hate each other? They're both of them exactly alike: short, bespectacled, parsimonious, mean-spirited, divorced." (ms. pp. 495–96)

Other slurs against Paul/Marsyas occur on pp. 487 and 660, and on pp. 615–16 Alexander castigates his entire family by way of Eugene's colleague R. Bangs Chasuble's animadversions against his family, especially his sisters and their spouses. I'm guessing *Laura Warholic* alienated his entire extended family, at least those who read it.

Compared to Alexander's vicious caricatures, Marcel Theroux's portrait of his eccentric uncle in *The Confessions of Mycroft Holmes* is mild, but Alexander was outraged by it. The protagonist, Damien Marsh, is working in London when he learns that his uncle, novelist Patrick Marsh, has died and left him his house on Cape Cod. Tired of his job, Damien quits and spends a few months living in his uncle's house, where he discovers some unpublished writings, including one about Sherlock Holmes's brother Mycroft (mentioned fleetingly in a few of Conan Doyle's stories). The story is a coded account of Patrick's younger brother, Damien's father, and the novel ends as Damien realizes some dark secrets about his family and paternity.

The main characters are easy to identify: Damien is Marcel, his brother Vivian is Louis, Patrick is Alexander, and his unnamed father is Paul. The description of Patrick's house and contents matches Alexander's: "Patrick had hoarded all sorts of junk: records, books, ice-cream scoops, mechanical banks, marbles, playing cards . . . the confusion, the clutter, the mixture of art and trash reflected him exactly. The house was Patrick."[37] After relating a number of anecdotes about his London-based

37 *The Confessions of Mycroft Holmes: A Paper Chase* (New York: Harcourt,

family's annual visits to "Ionia" (Cape Cod) when younger, Damien concludes: "He was the quintessential eccentric uncle: funny, prone to strange enthusiasms, childless, childish. And he had the capacity to bring out similar qualities in my father, who was two years younger: the same age difference as myself and Vivian" (41).

"Of course, he had a darker side, but he never showed it to us" (41)—meaning him and his brother—but when Damien grew older he learned that Patrick had fallen out with the rest of the family,

> alienating them over the years with stinging letters or cold silences. He suffered from the worst kind of paranoia—the kind that has a firm basis in reality. Of course people talked about him behind his back. Of course people avoided him. Of course people were afraid of him—to have any dealings with him whatsoever was to risk coming into conflict with him. And the most trivial disputes could engender letters so offensive that the insults would be burned onto your consciousness forever. "You have all the attributes of a dog except fidelity," he wrote to an ex-girlfriend. He once told my kindly Aunt Judith she was a two-hundred-pound puff adder.[38] (35)

As Damien goes through his uncle's papers and belongings, he learns less flattering things about him, most of which coincides with what I know of him, and which will sound familiar even to those who only know his work:

> I suppose I was like Patrick, who believed that everyone was tricky and self-seeking. When I got to Ionia, I found a letter in his basement in which he'd written: "Human beings have evolved to be assholes. *Homo simpaticus* is lying at the bottom of Olduvai Gorge with a flint handaxe in his rib cage." (57)

> There were some unspeakable letters to my father; a crazy letter to Nancy Reagan in the White House in which Patrick called her "a one-titted witch. . . ."

2001), 15–16. It was published nearly simultaneously in England simply as *The Paper Chase*—which I suspect is the author's preferred title—with British punctuation and repaginated slightly.

38 In Paul's *Mother Land* (Boston: Houghton Mifflin, 2017), both insults are attributed to the Alexander character (143). In *My Other Life*, Uncle Hal asks the future author: "Paulie, are you one of these people who has all the qualities of a dog except fidelity?" (6).

> Some of them were funny, but too often you felt that Patrick was out of control. It was shocking to feel the force of his hatred, even second-hand. What made them so potent was that the venom was allied with an acute sensitivity to people's weaknesses. He knew where to stick the knife and how to twist it.
>
> Even when his attacks went wide of the mark, there was something so concentrated, so spectacularly ruthless in his efforts to offend, that the effect was unsettling. Everything was thrown at the attackee: crimes, sins, birthmarks, poor grades, big ears, bad debts, flat feet, buck teeth, homely relatives. You sensed Patrick thought somehow that he was always on the side of the angels; somehow he was the one victimized and misunderstood and therefore justified in whatever he flung back at his tormentors. I couldn't face reading more of them. They were an unworthy epitaph: his brilliance, his humour, his erudition, his empathy—all subjugated to the desire to wound. (92)

Realizing later that Patrick was the model for his version of Doyle's Mycroft Holmes—who self-righteously murders a horrible man—Damien returns to the letters:

> Down in the basement, Patrick had saved copies of his rage-filled letters like trophies, like so many scalps that he'd taken from his victims. And to Patrick each of them represented a wrong righted, a humbug exposed, a slight avenged. Mycroft would undoubtedly have approved. He was everything Patrick felt about himself, raised to heroic size: the neglected genius, the avenging angel, the scourge of the powerful, the mould-breaking intellectual. And when Patrick was in a manic, morally indignant frame of mind, he shared Mycroft's confidence that no problem was so complex that it wouldn't benefit from his interference.
>
> And even the more low-key Mycroft recalling his adventures in old age bore similarities to my uncle: the erudition, the reflective melancholy, the obsession with success and failure, the hinted-at burden of guilt. (172–73)

Throughout the novel, Damien notes that he has more in common with Patrick than with his father or brother, and is grateful for the role he played in his younger life:

> My uncle had been indispensable—whatever his faults, his love and curiosity had softened some of the austerity of my childhood. He was a spokesman for the importance of small things, enthusiasms, hobbies,

games, puzzles, jokes, words, hot fudge, cream cakes, fried dough—all
helpful talismans in a cold and draughty world that seemed to belong
on the whole to people like my father. (93)

In the novel's closing pages, Marcel discovers he has more in common
with Patrick than he ever imagined.

Even though *The Confessions of Mycroft Holmes* is a novel, not a
tell-all memoir, and even though Marcel is just as hard on his father
and brother, Alexander felt betrayed by Marcel's portrayal of him (and
perhaps spooked by Patrick's dropping dead at age 63; Alexander was 61
when he read it), and though Uncle Alex wrote a poem about his nephew
and undoubtedly sent a rage-filled letter or two, fiction was his preferred
form of revenge.[39]

He was finishing *Laura Warholic* when he read Marcel's novel, and
inserted this irrelevant sentence into Eugene Eyestones's sex notebook:
"Mr. Fattomale who hated his brother was so driven to equalizing revenge that he forced his easily intimidated older son, Marcel, a spotty,
deceitful little Blifil with a face like a handpuppet and a reptilian need
to please his father, to hate his uncle as well and to write a novel ridiculing him with lies" (ms. 173; Blifil is Tom Jones's hypocritical rival). In
the published version, Marcel is renamed Silvio, and the passage ends
". . . ridiculing him with lies and falsehoods, *and then to pretend he was
his friend!*" (132–33), the redundant "and falsehoods" typical of Alexander's expansion of the shorter original, and the entire passage an example of Patrick Marsh's venomous rhetoric. As noted above, he replaced
Paul with Marcel in the bookstore scene, and after making disparaging
remarks about his appearance and his prose, kills him off via a crazed
woman in the audience. "I suspect it was his angry wife who shot him,"
Eugene tells Laura Warholic, for satirizing her in his novel. "He had
obviously betrayed her—in print, maybe the most craven form of cowardice" (473–74). Again, the pot and the kettle.

But Alexander wasn't through with him. Expanding on the Mr. Fattomale anecdote, Alexander wrote a short story entitled "Envenoming
Junior" in 2001 that begins (in the expanded 2019 version):

Durian Staines, who had always envied and then came fully to hate
his brother Jack, becoming even crustier and more hostile after many

---

39 See "Miniature of a Nephew" (*CP*, 215). *The Paper Chase* is a well-crafted
   novel, as are the others of Marcel's that I've read, especially *The Secret Books*
   (2017). They are more postmodernish than Paul's novels, but less extreme
   than Alexander's.

years, was presently trying to intimidate his older son Blore, now thir-
ty-four, to write something poisonous about his uncle, and as a sop to
the project promised to give him in return his old Jaguar XK120 if he
deigned to do so. "But, as I say, it has to be fiction," soberly warned his
father, making an estimative grimace, which he followed with a wink,
"anything else of course would subject you to libel."

In this highly autobiographical story, Alexander imagines the circumstances in which Marcel was seduced into betraying his uncle in print.
After Durian/Paul senses Blore/Marcel's reluctance to ridicule Jack/Al-
exander, he ups the stakes and offers to give his son one of his houses
as well, which does the trick. In the outer shell of "Envenoming Junior,"
the father pressures the weak son to write a novel, and then coaches him
on how it could be done: "Begin by writing down everything you dislike
about him. Start there," Durian tells Blore.

> His son shook his head slowly. "What, I generally make stuff up?
> What about details? Specifics? Close particulars? You said you would
> help me out, yes, but what about fabricating whole scenes, stories,
> situations?"
> "Easy," replied Durian, his face creasing like an old apple. "There
> are no special rules. You just keep your old guessing machinery well
> oiled. We refer to it as imagination. Throw in some willpower."
> Blore temporized.
> "Have a go."
> "I could pretend I'm Sherlock Holmes," offered Blore, tossing a
> bail of bread to the dog, "and write some rot about his coming across
> a new crime." . . .

And that, Alexander suggests, is how *The Paper Chase* was written.
Within this outer shell of dialogue are pages and pages tabulating all
of Durian Staines's faults, both personal and artistic. (Durian is a film
director, but the names of his films are variants of Paul's novels.) They
include ones first aired in "Blood Feud" and *Laura Warholic*, along with
a slew of others, as if Alexander likewise began by writing everything he
disliked about Paul. And within the catalogue of complaints is a flash-
back to a dialogue Jack once held with a woman while driving home from
visiting Durian. Alexander puts in her mouth the reasons he felt Paul
envied him:

> "It is clear not only that Durian has developed a hatred for you for

being a bolder and more imaginative artist than he himself ever was, but as some kind of detractor he is living in a rival's hell. . . . Worse for him—I honestly hate to be so frank—you are obviously smarter, better educated, much easier to get along with, wittier, stronger, taller, and far and away much better-looking than this poor, scheming, seemingly unhappy, pigeon-toed myope with thick glasses and a round bowling-ball head, which is even now badly balding!"

And the narrator isn't shy about praising Jack:

Jack wrote like an angel, with bold, original prose that cracked like sheet-lightning across a page, and, while Durian got more attention and was by far more widely known and recognized, Jack, to those in the know, those who had taste, had by far the more original mind. Childless, unmarried, something of an *isolato*, Jack also had a wooden leg from a childhood accident and lived in an old Victorian house, painted red. He canoed, traveled, collected books, too many some said, but the fact that he spent more time reading than socializing, cloistered and inaccessible, was apt commentary not only on his immediate family, an uninteresting and selfish and gossiping lot, but on a world that he preferred to shun rather than court. He liked to walk the beach and to garden and to grow vegetables and could be found mostly pottering away at the back of his field—in the world, as he often put it, not *of* it.

But Alexander also notes how much he—that is, Jack and Durian—have in common:

Both brothers shared a dark suspicion that life was a lost cause, that all people were actors, sharpsters kidding themselves in life, which was for the most part an opera buffa if not a pointless odyssey, more buzzing confusion than anything else. A competition in them between creativity and mistrust, suspicion, and disbelief struggled for mastery. It was the tension between two poles—a restless idealism on one hand and a sense of impending doom on the other.

It was deep in the nature of that family to mock, to belittle, and to taunt. Durian often sarcastically referred to Jack as "Legrandin," the rabid but well-read snob in Proust's *La Recherche*. It did not matter to him whatsoever what Jack was like in the essential; Durian simply took the bottle of Jack and poured into it a very different man. Both were given to orating, prating; both were nonconformists, less in open revolt against people than cynical unbelievers in society, unconvinced that much of anything in the waking wistful world was admirable or to be applauded; quite the opposite, they took the ironic view about everything and accepted nothing at face value. They were both masters of—specimens for—that style that Edgar Allan Poe had properly denominated "the awkward left arm of satire—invective."

Durian had a sharp eye not only for a person's weakness but an equally cruel ability to lampoon them. Jack's own extraordinary talent for mimicry and equally amazing eye for detail allowed him to ridicule people *à leur manière*—in their fashion—whenever he chose to as well, whether in the pastiche or to add a finishing touch to some callow portrait in a book. They were both malcontents, movers, ambitious "idea" people, never idle, hyperalert debunkers. Skeptics. Cynics. Neither listened to anyone's advice but plunged straight onto projects with the kind of unquestioned amour-propre that was a family trait. No Staines ever listened, ever, not to anyone. They were both long on memory and short on forgiveness.

The most artful aspect of the story is the dramatization of the origin of the brothers' enmity. Near the beginning, Durian mentions "that poem," and forbids Blore from using it in his novel. At its first mention, the narrator merely says: "It was a poem that Jack had written in good riddance of his brother out of a mood born of the very shock, the disgust, he felt upon learning what, scandalizing him, eventually made any further contact impossible with the guy. It had been published in one of Jack's books of poetry and drew the attention of every member in the family as well, Durian suspected, although it was an instinctive and intuitive policy that nobody ever mentioned it—ever. Nor did he himself." A few more dark references are made to the poem until we finally learn it was about a sexual proposition Durian made to his sister Grace, which "took place during the brief years of his second marriage when, in the company of his wife Priscilla, he felt either bored or deprived or both." The poem is "Insect," which begins with the epigraph, "So awful is the vice of incest that no noun exists for the person who practices it."[40]

I doubt this dramatized revelation would be enough to sustain the interest of the average reader of this captious, unpleasant story. For a fan of either of the Therouxs, however, it is full of fascinating material—allowing for the fabrication that Durian urges on Blore ("Amplify,

---

40 First published in *History Is Made at Night* (Aralia Press, 1992), rpt. in *The Lollipop Trollops and Other Poems* (Normal, IL: Dalkey Archive Press, 1992), 80, and in *CP* 477–78.

inflate, embroider")—especially regarding Alexander's appearances in Paul's novels:

> Durian had lampooned Jack as a buffoon in several scenes not only in *The Mad, Mad Magician* and in *My Divided Life* as well, but in *Anotherland*, barbed, vinegary, and self-indulgent autobiographical films in which comic doofuses appeared that seemed almost to have been conceived as frames to vilify and satirize at points his smarter, more talented brother as a nutty scholar or word-master or eccentric stutterer, all of which fit Jack to some degree. Films lent themselves poorly to identifying portrayals in the strict sense of the word, as such, recognizable lampoons for export, but Durian had no compunction about putting the boot in whenever he could. So Jack appeared as a shrill braggart in *Wright's Tower*, for example, and as a blabby, eccentric mannerbereft in the acrimonious, some say incriminatingly confessional *A Strange Occurrence at Craddock Bridge*, Durian's casually preening cinematic memoir of himself as a virtuous, struggling filmmaker in his twenties.
>
> He characterized Jack as a cursing vulgarian in the crude, semi-pornographic *Skylar Declare*, a ridiculous movie, and coldly assailed him in the weak *Mr. Muckerjee*, an endless, spiteful, nonfictional animadversion—a libelous but characteristic calumny—against a former friend of his in which over the course of several hours Durian artlessly, unrestrainedly, digresses merely to point out that between two or three competing brothers one alone is always to be the more talented, irrationally and haughtily confident in his inartistic stubbornness, vanity, and megalomania that he himself would not only be recognized as such, but by bringing up the subject first, he somehow therefore automatically proved it.
>
> He enjoyed mocking Jack by putting him into other films, another one as a long-winded bore wearing a wig in *The Desai Affair* and a venomous white African loony in *Dengue Fever*, while taking vivid, obvious swipes at his brother in passing not only in the plot-plagiarized, mind-numbingly-dull *Frostjackers*, but in two of his last congested and overlong box-office disasters, *The Last Train to Strango* and *Southern Exposure*, which went straight to video.

I recognize some of these—*The Mad, Mad Magician* is *Millroy the Magician*, *My Divided Life* is *My Other Life*, *Anotherland* is *Mother Land*, *Mr. Muckerjee* is *Sir Vidia's Shadow*, *Dengue Fever* is the title of a story Paul first published in *Playboy* in 1975, *Last Train to Strango* must be his travel book *The Last Train to Zona Verde* (2013)—but I'll leave it to Paul Theroux specialists to identify the others, along with the half-dozen additional films/books mentioned in the story. But who knows whether Paul deliberately modeled these characters on Alexander, or whether only Alexander sees himself in these characters? His nephew Marcel emphasized his paranoiac tendencies.[41]

Alexander sent a version of the story to Paul before he began writing another long, autobiographical novel, *Mother Land* (dated 2015 on the final page, published perversely around Mother's Day 2017).[42] Paul Theroux's previous autobiographical novels were mostly about himself, and partly about his wife and children; *Mother Land* is the first to focus on the family he grew up with. In the concluding paragraph of "The Trouble with Autobiography," published in the January 2011 issue of the *Smithsonian*, Paul writes:

> The more I reflect on my life, the greater the appeal of the autobiographical novel. The immediate family is typically the first subject an American writer contemplates. I never felt that my life was substantial enough to qualify for the anecdotal narrative that enriches autobiography. I had never thought of writing about the sort of big talkative family I grew up in, and very early on I developed the fiction writer's useful habit of taking liberties. I think I would find it impossible to write an autobiography without invoking the traits I seem to deplore in the ones I've described—exaggeration, embroidery, reticence, invention, heroics, mythomania, compulsive revisionism, and all the rest that are so valuable to fiction. Therefore, I suppose my *Copperfield* beckons.[43]

Regarding "taking liberties," interviewer Jim Sullivan wrote: "Theroux

41 When Theroux sent me "Envenoming Junior" in February 2002, he mused: "It's comical, the irony of it, for within a month of writing it last year I had an enjoyable meeting with Paul at a family reunion and we now cordially write to each other. Surprising the effect (every[one] says 'impact' today: why?) of catharsis-by-writing: what you write is what you tend then no longer to feel."

42 At 509 pages, it is a trifle shorter than *My Secret History*, but it was originally longer: Paul told interviewer Jim Sullivan (see n44) that he cut 25,000 words (around 60 pages)—the opposite tendency of his brother, who always adds.

43 Online at https://www.smithsonianmag.com/arts-culture/the-trouble-with-autobiography-75464843/. This passage also appears in *Mother Land* (333), except for the concluding sentence. Earlier in the essay, he states that he doesn't plan to ever write an actual autobiography, and warns he will frustrate any potential biographers.

figures that 60 percent of 'Mother Land' is autobiographical and 40 percent fictional. 'This is a book based, obviously, on my life and elements of my family,' he says. 'Some of it might be stranger than fiction. But, actually, it is a novel. I have to insist that it's fiction. . . . This is what I call a portrait of myself, and that's about as near to autobiography as I will ever get.'"[44] With these caveats in mind, *Mother Land* offers the fullest account of the contentious relationship between the brothers Theroux.

In the guise of one of Durian's movies, the narrator of "Envenoming Junior" describes the novel in a lengthy, typically Therouvian sentence:

> *Anotherland*, his tedious film about his mother—a circuitous meandering through a series of flashbacks from adolescence through middle age to his late years with himself the hero in a family of stick-figure losers—was a truly pitiful, rancorous, self-pitying but inept abortion in which, aggressively and soullessly strip-mining his family in order to ridicule everyone in his family but himself—a shameless two-hour howl of victimization without the feeblest attempt at disguise—he proved only once again that in the artistic realm of reaching into one's own private life for subject matter, the attempt is almost always a confession to the bleak, last desperation of a waning talent.

If *Mother Land* were indeed a film, Alexander would deserve a Best Supporting Actor award for his role as Floyd, narrator JP's older brother. Although the entire Theroux clan is portrayed in the novel, with the narrator's exasperating mother at center stage, Floyd steals every scene he's in, and has all the best lines.

The novel is bookended by the deaths of the clan's father in 1995 and

---

44 Jim Sullivan, "In 'Mother Land,' Paul Theroux Creates a Portrait of Himself," *The ARTery*, 9 May 2017, https://www.wbur.org/artery/2017/05/09/mother-land-paul-theroux. Paul adds: "This is a novel in the mode of, say, Thomas Mann who wrote a book called 'Buddenbrooks' about a family and [Charles] Dickens, who wrote 'David Copperfield,' which is kind of a novel based on his family." Reacting to this remark and to the line "My *Copperfield* beckons" in the *Smithsonian* essay, Dickens lover Alexander added this to "Envenoming Junior": "In interviews a smug and vainglorious Durian, for all of its confessional fantasies, went out of his way to parallel this louche undertaking— a long, tedious, self-regarding, narcissistic calumny against his mother and his siblings—with famous literary autobiographies and in what can only be understood as a huffed-up moment, more blind than vain, even had the effrontery to refer to the thing as 'my *David Copperfield*,' when the fact of the matter was measuring Dickens's masterpiece to this film was like comparing the planet Jupiter to a billiard ball."

mother in 2015 (I assume this aspect is factual: Albert E. Theroux died in May 1995, and Anne Theroux in February 2015, five days before her 104th birthday). Narrator Jay (JP) Justus has returned to Cape Cod, a once-successful author, twice married, now down on his luck and single.[45] As Alexander noted above, there are flashbacks to the family's past, but most of it is set in the two decades between the two deaths. Alexander, saddled again with the plebian name Floyd (cf. Floyd Fewox in *Millroy the Magician*), is featured throughout, beginning with childhood episodes such as his trouble with bedwetting, which Alexander has addressed in several poems ("Fr. Mario," "Sketch of a Sinful Life," "Wound within a Wound"), stories ("Blackrobe," "Genius"), and in *Laura Warholic* (698). This was apparently part of Theroux family lore, for in *The Paper Chase* Marcel refers to the same anecdote that Paul does: one more thing Damien March has in common with his uncle is that they were both bedwetters until puberty. Fortunately, "I grew up in a more enlightened time than Patrick," he writes. "His own uncle, a priest—who like other Catholic priests was considered an authority on children and marriage on account of having no personal experience of either—was delegated to talk to him about it. 'You're killing your mother!' . . . When you're married, are you going to piss on your wife?'" (97–98), which is repeated with a little more detail in *Mother Land*—twice (pp. 24 and 97, the latter probably an editorial lapse). Other details are offered: Floyd was a good high-school basketball player, but a bad trombonist.

Floyd is a poet and a professor of literature at Harvard, but more significantly, "Floyd was a satirist, had been so from childhood. Older than me by two years, he had always loomed large, and was both funnier and more serious than anyone else in the family, marked with the satirist's traits: comedy, severity, cruelty. He was the most tormented, the one with the natural talent. When I wrote well," Jay continues, undoubtedly in the voice of Paul on Alexander, "I was sometimes forced to admit that I was unconsciously mimicking Floyd at his most fluent. He was too good a writer not to be bad influence" (96). He comes off surprisingly well in light of the demeaning things Alexander was writing about Paul during the 1995–2015 period in "Blood Feud," *Laura Warholic*, and "Envenoming Junior," perhaps for the reasons Jay/Paul gives a little later (and which may explain why the Theroux family reportedly reacted to

45 This is the most fictitious aspect of the novel: Paul was financially well-off in 1995, dividing his time between houses in Cape Cod and Hawaii and publishing a half-dozen books between 1993 and 1998, in addition to magazine pieces. His first marriage ending in divorce in 1993, he married his second wife on 18 November 1995.

"Blood Feud" "with more hilarity than horror"):

> Floyd did not flatter me—far from it, he insulted me, but I took that
> as a form of comradeship and was bucked up. He teased me to my
> face, but in the family this sort of teasing was friendly, even flattering,
> sometimes stinging, yet it was strangely companionable in its cruel
> honesty and defiant frankness. . . . [T]easing was a form of discourse
> based on equality. Teasing an inferior was simply cruel and in our
> family amounted to recreational sadism. But teasing an equal was a
> form of sparring: it took nerve, and in the end—if it was calibrated
> so as not to destroy the friendship altogether—made the friendship
> stronger. In our family, teasing someone to their face was unambigu-
> ously friendly. (119–20)

But apparently Alexander's anti-Pauline writings were calibrated so as
to destroy the friendship altogether, for some thirty pages later, two of
Alexander's literary attacks precipitate a major crisis. Floyd coldly abandons Jay after finding out that he has been hiding his relationship with
a woman and talking about him behind his back (mildly, under pressure
from his family). Jay is correcting the proofs for his next novel (which
he also has told no one about), entitled *The Half Life* (i.e., *My Other
Life*), when he receives in the mail a literary magazine that contains "Envenoming Junior," which for Alexander/Floyd is a "characteristic title,
purplish and arcane."[46] Paul/Jay quotes the first page of the story, then
after reading the entire thing gives what most readers would agree is an
accurate critique:

> "Green drinks" and "ferret kennels" were nice touches. Yet I read it
> with my mouth open, hardly believing he could write something so
> ridiculous, and frankly so purple. In his extreme anger, Floyd never
> wished to risk being subtle. . . . Ambiguity was absent from this work,
> and so was Floyd's wild humor; it was all fury and recrimination in
> lurid pastiche. . . . Floyd's elaborately wrought public rejection of me
> had the desired effect. I was troubled by it—by the amount of time it
> must have taken for him to write and publish it. He was not merely
> malicious, he was conscientious in his malice. . . . The attack was so
> concentrated, so vicious in its single-mindedness, it was ultimately
> artless, just a howl of rage and a shallow echo. Its chief aim had been

46 To reiterate, "Envenoming Junior" had not yet been written, much less published at this time. For dramatic reasons, Paul reversed the chronology of it
   and "Blood Feud" (1996).

to make me feel bad. After my initial annoyance, I let go and, like a
good sport, dismissed it. (151–53)

No sooner does he do so than he receives "Blood Feud," which he quotes
over the next few pages (154–56; as the original is nearly impossible to
come by, Paul provides a convenient and accurate précis, bravely quoting
its most insulting passages). Jay is devastated by what he calls "the worst
review of my publishing career," which he claims sinks the novel's sales,
and is especially hurt by the line "The whole family laughs at him." He
turns for support to his indifferent mother and siblings, but they shrug
him off—"He's crazy, you know," one of them says of Floyd—leaving him
with "the sense that all of them believed that I deserved it, that every lie
and wild assertion Floyd had written was essentially true. And so, really,
the whole family *was* laughing at me" (157). It is the most painful episode
in the novel.

The review leaves Jay mired in melancholy for months, unrelieved
by a brief visit from his grown sons Julian and Harry (i.e., Marcel and
Louis). But after a while he sees the silver lining in that sable cloud of
a review:

> Floyd's attack-dog hatred was now so long-standing that it inspired
> fear in the others. There was no way I could think of to make peace
> with Floyd, but as time passed I began to see that I was more for-
> tunate than the others. Because of Floyd's peculiar disposition and
> his demands, it was far more oppressive to be Floyd's friend than his
> enemy. As his enemy, I had long stretches of time to myself, while
> his friends and the rest of the family had to deal with him every day.
> He had done his worst: written his malicious review of my book. But
> though my book had failed, the review was so bizarre, unhinged, and
> incoherent, Floyd had attracted attention by making a fool of himself,
> and unwelcome inquiries and baffled questions began to haunt him.
> (192–93)

Floyd freezes Jay out of his life for seven years, until they find themselves together at their mother's ninetieth birthday, where, as usual,
Floyd teases his brother and everyone else. "This was the Floyd I remembered from happier days, the man who burned up the air in the room
and left people gasping in the vacuum," Jay writes, and he welcomes the
witty ribbing, for "family teasing was the test of friendship, and Floyd
was being friendly. I took his fooling as a peacemaking gesture. Needling
was a form of dialogue" (257, 265). The brothers are reconciled, and

even engage in some childish shenanigans. "We were not close friends now, but we were allies, and in this family being an ally mattered more than being a brother" (359).[47] Jay appreciates the fact that Floyd is the only family member who has read all his books, not to mention a fellow writer, even though he takes a different approach to writing: "Floyd was obsessive, addicted to books, print-hungry, more partial to the glissade of an elaborate metaphor than to its function, because its use was to dazzle, not to advance a narrative. He hated a pithy declarative sentence like this one. . . . I was reminded that he was a kindred soul, sharing my language, a brother in a profound sense" (272). Jay's grown sons visit again, but they are anxious about seeing their uncle, whom Jay describes with the same admiration Paul used in his *New York Times* tribute in 1977: "Uncle Floyd was to them an almost mythical figure, famous for his rages, celebrated for his learning, a well-known poet, a cantankerous Harvard prof, widely published, a man in a black cape who had known Samuel Beckett, and in a sense had been anointed by him, as Joyce had anointed Beckett, extending a literary tradition. Floyd was part of this lineage" (280).[48]

Similar praise for Alexander/Floyd is sprinkled throughout the rest of the novel, remarkable demonstrations of Jay/Paul's forgiving nature, but Alexander was unmoved, and responded with a sonnet entitled "Toad":

> Calumniating his mother by telling lies in print,
> —after she was dead (it fit the author's style)—
> he called his novel fiction but with base intent
> manipulated real facts like any hypocrite vile,
> choosing to indemnify by the further deceit
> of double-dealing falsehoods with half-truth,
> in part to make himself look good yet treat
> disreputable invention as if all solid proof.
> This is the way Iago worked, by base denial,
> mocking innocence by facts he had at hand
> to cripple decency by innuendo, a show trial
> that crucified everybody in his motherland.

47 They discover that their two sisters have been taking financial advantage of their elderly mother for years. For Alexander's reaction to this discovery, see his long poems "Sardines Laced with Anti-Freeze" and "Two Sisters" (*CP*, 263–65, 275–79).

48 For a photograph of Alexander in his black cape, see the previously cited *Review of Contemporary Fiction*, 47. Although he wrote his dissertation on Beckett, he never actually met or corresponded with him.

Motives in cruel Iago remain immune to wit.
Not so in cane toads. Poison's what they spit.[49]

He then added a few hundred more poisonous words to "Envenoming Junior."

Even though the Library of Congress classifies *Mother Land* under "Mothers—Fiction," it is a more significant contribution to the subject of literary brothers, as Paul is well aware, having obviously researched the topic. After Jay reads Floyd's "Blood Feud," he—i.e., Paul, *in propria persona*—provides a brief history lesson (recycled from *Sir Vidia's Shadow*) as well as a psychological evaluation of his relationship with his brother, ending with an elegant evocation of the warring brothers in *Finnegans Wake*:

> In the long history of literary brothers there was no precedent for this attack. Plenty of brothers scribbled and quarreled—in fact, scribbling brothers nearly always quarreled. Thomas Mann had an angry brother, Heinrich. Henry James had William, Chekhov had Nikolai. Wilde had Willie. Joyce had Stanislaus. Lawrence Durrell had Gerald. William Faulkner had John. Hemingway had Leicester, Naipaul had Shiva—all of them rivals, more or less. The nicer-seeming brother is not necessarily the better writer, nor necessarily nicer. All had made belittling remarks, yet none of these men had ever reviewed the other's work, pronouncing the book a failure and the brother a fake. Floyd was the first.
>
> Once, writing about Vidia and Shiva Naipaul, both of whom I'd known, I had mentioned how brothers are versions of each other, a suggestion implicit in the word itself: the "other" in "brother." The unfortunate history of scribbling brothers was full of conflict. There were no intellectual equals in brotherhood, for, being writers, they were borderline nutcases. Literary brothers were often fratricidal from birth and babyish in their battling, because of the lingering infantilism in sibling rivalry. When brothers fought, family secrets were revealed, and the shaming revelations often made forgiveness irrelevant. It is the tale told by Shem and Shaun. (156–57)

Earlier literary brothers quarreled in real life, but rarely within the pages of a novel, as in *Mother Land*. Paul's dramatization of his rivalry with Alexander may become the most historically important aspect of

---

49 Emailed to me on 29 May 2017 after I asked him his opinion of Paul's just-published novel, which he said he had not read.

this novel, as he seemed to sense and predict. Getting no sympathy from his mother, an exasperated Jay tells her (and his readers): "No writer's brother has ever done this, Ma. Hemingway, Henry James, all the rest of them. Like I told you. Their brothers never did this. It's a first. I mean, this would actually be amazingly interesting if it wasn't me, Ma" (165).

AN AFTERTHOUGHT

At first glance, Alexander Theroux's only travel book, *Estonia: A Ramble Through the Periphery* (2011), looks like the sort of book his brother has excelled at; could it be a sibling-rivalrous attempt to match if not best his brother at the genre? Although Paul Theroux's first seven books were fiction, he struck it rich with his first travel book, *The Great Railway Bazaar* (1975), an account of his train trip from England to Japan and back, and since then he has alternated between fiction and travelogues.[50] Alexander may share his brother's mood when traveling, which can be condescending and even misogynistic; at one point he says, "I can hear the charge: you are a truculent traveler, just like your brother Paul, who for the record I benevolently consider nothing less than a realist."[51] But *Estonia* lacks the chronological structure and novelistic qualities of Paul's travel books, and is not organized in any discernible way (except for some historical background upfront). Somewhat like his miscellanies, it is essentially a compilation of facts, anecdotes, observations, and, unfortunately, off-topic digressions. Nonetheless, it is an interesting, appealing book, even if it doesn't rival his brother's travel books, and provides the Theroux fan many insights into his life and opinions.

Alexander had written a few travel pieces in the past. In March 1991 he went to Santa Fé to write about its art scene for *Art & Antiques* (published the following year), and devoted many column inches to describing the scenery within a seventy-mile radius of the city during various side-trips. There's a long digression on the Penitentes, an order of religious fanatics (much of it cut for the published version), and with novelistic flair he describes his attendance at a highly dramatic *morada*, "the Penitente rites [that] commemorated the flight of the Apostles and the death of Christ." In 1996 he published an essay on Tijuana, and the fol-

---

50 For Paul's approach to travel writing, see his introduction in *To the Ends of the Earth: The Selected Travels of Paul Theroux* (NY: Random House, 1991).

51 *Estonia: A Ramble Through the Periphery* (Seattle: Fantagraphics Books, 2011), 220. Like many others (Hans Christian Andersen, Jane Austen, Julio Cortázar, Stephen King, Thomas Pynchon, David Foster Wallace), Paul is not included in the book's patchy index.

lowing year one about the California desert (both published in the *San Diego Reader*). Aside from those, the only other travel writing he had done was a number of poems recording his responses to foreign locales, such as South Africa, Sri Lanka, and Thailand.

In 2007, Sarah Son-Theroux was awarded a Fulbright Grant, in affiliation with the Estonian Academy of Art, for a residency in Estonia to paint landscapes. She left for the country in late November—her husband commemorated the sad occasion with a poem (*CP* 383–84)—but they missed each other so much that Alexander flew there to join her in February 2008. He had been working on a novel, he says, but abandoned it and spent the rest of the winter and spring sizing up the country for a book.[52] He left a month or so before she returned to America in June 2008. Less than a year later he completed a 200-page, double-spaced typescript (emailed to me on 27 February 2009), then added another 40 pages while trying to find a publisher that year (expanded version emailed on 12 December). Following his usual modus operandi, he continued adding material over the next year and a half (including 130 endnotes), doubling the length of the original manuscript by the time it was published by Fantagraphics in November 2011.

In the first paragraph of his "Overture," Theroux names 15 famous travel writers, and two pages later adds 15 more; Paul's name is conspicuous in its absence. If nothing else, he demonstrates his familiarity with the classics in that genre, and for the first 50 pages or so he stays on track. But then he starts making off-road excursions into topics unrelated to Estonia (Israeli politics, the Bush administration's use of torture, decoding, Greta Garbo, the Klingon language, his religious beliefs, the vanity of actors, the plight of the serious writer, bad American eating habits, etc.), most of which were added to the shorter, more focused original manuscript (shades of *Laura Warholic*). An unfortunate ploy of his is to mention someone or something *not* present in Estonia, and then to spend half a page or more discoursing on the topic. Such digressions can be interpreted favorably as Theroux's generous desire to share what he knows, "enjoyably esoteric information that tells us little about Estonia but a lot about Mr. Theroux's magpie mind," as one reviewer put it.[53] Another favorably inclined reviewer had to admit, "Yet the divagations into marginalia and wide-spread panic (the amount of annual U.S.

---

52 There are references to the novel on pp. 10 and 61. This would be *Herbert Head: Biography of a Poet*.

53 Andrew Stuttaford, "Stranger in a Strange Land," *Wall Street Journal*, 15 December 2011, A21.

aid to Israel) both crystallize and corrode this 'travel' book."[54] But as a less-charitable reviewer complains, "he has failed to restrain himself from leaping onto innumerable hobby horses that carry him from merely opinionated to outright tendentious and just plain offensive. So a book that should have been a fun ride ends up resembling being trapped in a cramped airline seat for the longest flight on the planet, subjected to a champion talker's endless obsessions and prejudices."[55]

The most negative, if best qualified, review came from Toomas Hendrik Ilves, president of Estonia while Theroux was there. Asked in 2012 if he had read Theroux's book, he answered:

> Yes, I read it too, but then I am probably the only person in Estonia who also read his *Darconville's Cat* in 1981, and *Three Wogs* as well. I'd say it's typical Alexander Theroux, one of the most misanthropic writers there are. I mean, if you remember, in *Darconville's Cat* he has a thirty-page chapter called "Magnificarum," which is just a collection of curses in Latin, most of them obscene, and then the English translation. So this guy comes to Estonia, he is here for the dreariest months, he hates everything he sees—but okay, it's just one view and it's fine. . . . Basically the book struck me as the kind of book someone would write if he'd only been in one other country his entire life. I have found that when people move out of their native country for the first time, all they do is look at the differences and complain.[56]

Similar sentiments can be found in the Amazon.com reviews of the book. This is a shame because, as some of the same reviewers noted, there are many wonderful passages in the book and colorful writing throughout (even in the diatribes and digressions). If a "best of" compilation of Theroux's writings is ever assembled, it would have to include the chapter Pynchonesquely titled "The Whole Squalid Crew," which describes Sarah's fellow Fulbright scholars in hilarious comic detail. (Benny Profane from *V.* is mentioned on page 210.) In a bravura five-

54 Greg Gerke, "Living Letters: On Gass's *Life Sentences* and Theroux's *Estonia*," *The Millions*, 19 April 2012.

55 Martin Rubin, *Washington Times*, 24 February 2012.

56 Ieva Lesinka, "The Proud Estonian: An Interview with Toomas Hendrik Ilves," *Eurozine*, 18 June 2012. The former president obviously didn't read the book closely, for Theroux mentions the many other countries he has visited in his lifetime. His "Magnificarum" reference confuses and conflates chapter LXXXIX ("Malediction!") with LXXXII ("The Unholy Litany"), neither of which is in Latin.

page analysis of the reluctance of Estonians to smile or display cheeriness (195–200), Theroux keeps his magpie tendency under control as he compares their nondemonstrative greetings with other nationalities, then is reminded of a line from the movie *A Thousand Clowns*, the sole reference to smiling in Dante's *Inferno* by way of Etienne Gilson, laughter in Proust, churlish behavior in Austen's *Northanger Abbey*, smiles in other countries and contexts, Simone Weil ("I am extrapolating Weil to explain Estonians," he needlessly explains), Judy Garland's song "Lose That Long Face," a list of dour characters in happy films, the nude in Western painting by way of John Berger, Spiro Agnew on America's greatness, then concludes his free-association spree with a quotation from Swiss writer Robert Walser justifying his own angry response to Estonian brusqueness: "I am not here to write, but to be mad," most of which was in the original manuscript. There are some slack sentences and redundancies here and there (and hair-pulling misuse of punctuation throughout), but in general Theroux's maximalist style, capacious vocabulary, boundless imagination, eye for the absurd, and astounding erudition are in full force.

An unconventional writer, it should not surprise anyone that Theroux wrote an unconventional travel book. But there's a difference between unconventional and undisciplined, self-indulgent writing. In his poem "Neglected," Theroux implies that he exerted discipline in his early writings, but after years of neglect has come to "like it over here in the shade and write for myself." *Estonia*, like all of his later books, shows no sign of self- or professional editing, which is the way Theroux seems to like it. The material is there, the talent is there; if only *Estonia* had been properly edited, or published in its original form, it might have rivaled one of his brother Paul's travel books.

APPENDIX

An Interview with Alexander Theroux

STEVEN MOORE: Did your years as a religious prepare you in any way for the literary life? What parallels are there in the devotion inherent in both callings? Is the artist indeed, as Stephen Dedalus has it, a priest of life?

ALEXANDER THEROUX: Both are vocations, certainly. I was always a dreamer, an "introspective voyager," as Wallace Stevens put it. I never supposed divine things might not look divine. The Church sedulously encourages the Imagination. I was the world which I walked on. I believe that writing continues the work of the Evangelists. The Church gave me an interest in miracle, mystery, and ritual, and imprinted its visions on me. It also shaped my nightmares. I believe in grace. And I share Dedalus's interest in taxonomies. Catholic children, at least years ago, used to have to memorize many lists.

SM: Your first publications were in poetry and drama, but since then you've devoted yourself to prose. Did those earlier genres simply lose their appeal for you?

AT: I had brilliant friends at the University of Virginia, many who were actors. The plays I wrote were for the most part vehicles for them, many one-act plays for workshops and then two staged productions, *The Viceroy* and *The Secretive World of Miss Ball*. I began writing poetry in the Trappist monastery, deep and meaningful things of the confessional sort—I always tended to be among the Pale and Interesting group—one of which began, "Swift, swift, yea, they come / Fresh pluck'd from the bowers of never ending thought . . ." [*pause*] I must have been reading too much Francis Thompson.

SM: Was that your very first work?

AT: My first effort was writing and illustrating a novel in the seventh

grade at a neighborhood chum's house, an Italian boy, using his ma-
chine to type the text on the backs of yellow recipe cards. His older
brother later got angry with him about something and tore it up.

SM: When writing *Three Wogs*, were you conscious of working in any
particular literary tradition, or in the manner of any specific writer?
"The Wife of God," for example, is highly reminiscent of Firbank.

AT: Well, I had read Firbank by then. I've always admired stylists. I put
the writers of bumphable, ready-to-wear prose, calculated to sell,
guaranteed not to shock, in the same category as artists who can't
draw. There is a lack of bravery and a lot of fraud in them. I have tried
never to write a book that didn't attempt something new in the way
of narrative technique. Writing is an assault on cliché. I find little to
admire in writers who make no attempt at originality. (I remember,
among other things, effortfully working to make the perambulations
in London of Roland McGuffey recapitulate the lines of the Union
Jack.) It's death commercially, of course, but I knew from the beginning that I was too opinionated, literate, and unconventional to enjoy
a widespread reputation. It doesn't bother me in the least. I've always
been too busy to make money. I'm among the freest people I know.

SM: You mean that?

AT: In the sense of not needing fame, yes. A psychiatrist once told me,
"You're always trying to get out of the world." So? We all have to man-
age that one day. Maybe I'm only practicing my technique.

SM: Something Darconville shares.

AT: And Marina, in *An Adultery*. There is a method, a deliberateness in
a way of writing that has its parallel in the way of living. I'm talking
about being loyal to your own vision, not living by borrowed apocalypse or polluting your dreams, in life or art, just for success. It's interesting, fashion is the enemy. True style means more than anything
a refusal to compromise.

SM: You mean to be true to yourself?

AT: Basically. Write the books you should, be the person you are. I wanted to write a *roman d'analyse*, for example, with *An Adultery*. A new
genre. Plot didn't interest me in the least. Character is plot, anyway.
Start delineating a figure—merely describe a person—and he or she
will begin to act, do things, go in a particular direction. I set the
novel up as a syllogism and purposely wrote balancing rhythmic and
arhythmic sentences. I think its rewards come only if you're willing to
think, to come to terms with what I set out to question, sort through,
analyze. [*pause*] Nothing there for the Leon Uris crowd—beach readers, military minds, people who flip pages to pass time. I wanted the

book to be what it was, no self-promotion, no hook for a publishing scheme. There's a mystical passivity in refusing the entrepreneurial.

SM: Marina does show that.

AT: Yes.

SM: A simple girl.

AT: Simplicity has its own unique beauty. It was her unawareness that made her simple. But that unawareness bled into not being conscious of Christian. She was unaware of even the depth and love she stirred in him. Farol was the opposite, a passenger, a lamprey, an incomplete and basically sexless woman like a weak diode, who didn't really cast light, but sort of emitted it. Why can so many see a fire and not see a faker? I think it was my brother Peter in his book *Sandstorms* who pointed out—was he speaking of the Israelis?—that though they possessed nothing but chaos, they put it to use by trapping other people in it. Farol was like that. Hideous. She was cold in her shadow. But Marina fought for nothing. Her goodness asked for nothing. Desire implies lack. Too much "possibility" leads to the madhouse. "Kill the Buddha." Even attachment to him may get in the way of ultimate perception.

SM: That's not futility?

AT: Fatality, maybe.

SM: You admire Marina's self-negation?

AT: I share it. Strangely, I've become something of a pathological recluse. It's not only that we're manipulated in the everyday process of living like Third World chickens. I've begun to find art more real than life. I really mean that. Music, books, museums, even my dreams have come to replace, well, "living" I guess would be Norman Vincent Peale's word. As time went by, after writing *An Adultery*, I found the need to be alone, went into a sort of self-imposed exile. Everybody's at his own movie, anyway. I became more and more disillusioned with friendship, which I sometimes see as having no spiritual significance, as the negative of the irremediable solitude to which every human being is condemned, but which somehow the artist knows how to put into account. I don't know, his task, so to speak, in this brief life. [*pause*] Have you ever read Villiers de l'Isle Adam's play *Axel*? "Let our servants live for us."

SM: Oh, but many people speak of you as being gregarious, a mimic, great company?

AT: Will the Blakean war explain it? I suppose, if not, it's either a question of psychological arm-wrestling, or schizophrenia. My friends all suffer from each as they suffer from both. A woman friend of mine in

New York once wrote me a trenchant little poem about it:

> I've cooked a roux
> Read billets doux
> And met a Sioux.
> Not really noux
> To say Theroux.
> I thought I knoux
> And now I doux
> There are twoux
> (At least) of youx,
> Theroux!

SM: *An Adultery* shows a different style than *Darconville's Cat*. A more sinuous line, an almost measured, sometimes hypnotic pace, less joy.

AT: Well, it's told in the first person, and it's an adulterer's voice. There are of course many puppets in a writer's box. But I also wrote most of that novel tired, dangerously underweight—thin as a hop pole. I was teaching at MIT at the time. Whereas I undertook the task of initially deliberating whether Christian only wanted Farol's body, merely clothing his desire in an elaborate structure of moral validation, delaying his gratification while reviling her for seeking her own at everybody's expense, I eventually came to see that I had to dismantle four personalities to know, just as four personalities were dismantled. There are real Farols. They're neither bright nor perceptive, and denial allows them anything, but I frankly believe that one day they do come to see themselves for what they really are. [*pause*] I wonder if Hallmark makes a card for an occasion like that.

SM: Tell us about the composition of *Darconville's Cat*. Did it begin as a shorter novel of revenge before burgeoning into a Burtonian anatomy of misogyny, replete with catalogs and an anthology of narrative forms, or did you contemplate a "big, bold, pumpkinified compendium" from the beginning?

AT: Revenge, one of my theories, is the main theme of the greatest works of Western literature. Epics, novels, poems, etc. Have you read my essay on revenge? But it had little to do with the book, though I did conceive the idea for it in a low state of mind in the fall of 1973, on a plane, pondering the binaries of love and hate. I was amazed that one could feel both simultaneously. The two chapters "Love" and "Hate" were to be bookends. I always had a grand scheme in mind in writing it, because what I closed in on, its subject, like the girl I loved, often receded. That is one of the main challenges of writing. Epistemology is always involved in writing good fiction. Before being happened on by people, an object exists not without interpretation but with infinite interpretation. When you limit your description of it to what you see, feel, hear, and alone connect it with, exclusive of what of the world's knowledge you can acquire and so apply to it, you fail to capture the object itself. The narrower your description, the more clichéd and uncommunicative, the more of the object you leave behind. Art is simply being able to communicate an object in its entirety, and it is just beyond the realm of human capability. The proponents of the encyclopedic novel, the so-called novel of learning, Sterne, Rabelais, Cervantes—and Burton in his book—have nevertheless had great fun trying to refute this.

SM: They're not average books.

AT: *Tristram Shandy* made Sterne famous virtually overnight, in fact. But ours is a different age. The visual is slowly replacing the verbal.

SM: *Darconville's Cat* was nominated for the National Book Award as the best novel of 1981, critic Anthony Burgess called it one of the greatest books of the century, yet it failed to make the *New York Times Book Review list* of the hundred or so notable novels of the year.[1] Did you anticipate such disparity of response?

AT: It was reviewed by a tiny aging intellectually egg-bald mediocrity from Amherst College named Benjamin DeMott, an envious professor whose own books add verifiable proof to the theory that the average human head needs something removed from it rather than have something inserted.

SM: So the book didn't sell?

AT: He strangled the baby in its crib. It sold 15,000 copies or something like that, thanks to him, nothing much, roughly the population of a mile of houses in North Medford. No, the fiduciary slant on my work regarding this interview won't boggle any minds, I'm afraid.

SM: Some people found the book hard to read.

AT: That, to make an understatement, is an overstatement. I was particularly surprised so many people missed so many points. It's supposed to be often funny. Nobody seemed to see that "Why Don't You— ?" was a chapter about verbs, "The Unholy Litany" about nouns. Someone said there are only 2400 people in the world worth writing for, anyway. I wonder if that's true. But readers are so lazy. The several books I've written have won me no fame. I do not complain of this,

1 [I wrote a letter to the editor complaining of the omission, which was not published.]

any more than I boast of it. I feel the same distaste for the "popular author" genre as for that of the "neglected poet." I marvel at writers who write a book a year, approaching mass production. I apologize for not being terribly impressed.

SM: Marvel at their speed?

AT: Their shamelessness.

SM: No aspect of your work has attracted more attention (or more abuse) than your astonishing vocabulary. Knowing full well that even an editor of the OED would be unfamiliar with hundreds of your words, were you at all concerned that your lexical precision would be lost on most readers, or did you expect them to look up every unknown word as they went along? Are you saying you write to learn? That reading is studying?

AT: All is never said. Knowledge is involved everywhere. You have to shape the truth. "Everyone applauded, and I'm glad he did," is ugly, but grammatically correct, while "I don't think anybody knows what they are" is the opposite. I'm only saying that we have to try to contest what we want to come to terms with, whether readers or writers. It depends on how much intensity a person has, how curious he is, and whether he or she wants to live a life of meaning. I have always tried to tell my students, especially those who every June apply to law school or business school in such a perfunctory way, as if, you know, those were the only alternatives—a condition abetted in the Ivy League by the army of secular and soulless mechano-moronic professors and deans who view education solely as a means of entering the labor force—that the point of living is trying to figure it out. My ideal reader burns with what Walter Pater described as a "hard gem-like flame." [*pause*] In any case, Tolstoy somewhere speaks of the psychological law which compels a man who commits actions under the greatest compulsion to supply in his imagination a whole series of retrospective reflections to prove his freedom to himself. It sounds a bit didactic, but it explains one aspect of writing.

SM: You've written that of the writers who have "taught me some of the ruses of the trade" the most influential are Homer, the Cicero of the *Letters to Atticus*, Rabelais, Shakespeare, Milton, Aubrey, Trollope, Proust, Dostoyevsky, Dickens, Rolfe, Joyce, Saki, Borges, and your acknowledged mentor, Juvenal. Have they also informed your style?

AT: Possibly, in the subtle and mysterious way influences work. But of course the sources of a person's style are everywhere, his face, where he lives, the amount of sunlight through his windows. I also learned a lot from early radio, old animated Disney movies, the stories my father passionately read to us in bed. *The Arabian Nights!* Magic! "During the reign of the Caliph Harun al-Rashid. . . ." My compulsion to overwrite, for circumlocution, I can probably attribute to the ponies I read in the early grades, the lead-heavy prose I turned into even more tortured English in my Latin and Greek classes.

SM: I notice no Americans are on your list. But certainly there are some American writers you feel akin to? Stylistically, for example, Melville, or possibly the Djuna Barnes of *Nightwood*?

AT: Both, definitely. And of course Thoreau, Henry James. Did I mention Wallace Stevens?

SM: You've also taught at Harvard, MIT, Yale. Has the world of pedagogy, or scholarship, made a difference of any kind in your writing life?

AT: I enjoy the classroom. Good students, whom I've always had the good luck to teach, have blessed my life. It's the faculties I've come to loathe. [*pause*] Yale was an awful place, a school of social counterfeits, slope-headed he-women, aggrieved blacks, frightened department heads, cowardly deans, and no end to whistling pendants trying to gussy up the status of their books by giving them the pseudo-Hellenistic label of "hermeneutics." [*pause*] Professors there worked hard to seem polite. All were grave, none serious. Most were knife-throwers. Eunuchs. Like most academics.

SM: Why is that?

AT: I have no idea. The emperor Nero habitually peered through an emerald to watch lions eating the Christians. Was this a covert need to temper his cruelty? Or just cowardice? [*pause*] Anyway, college allows you libraries. But the time spent teaching to earn money in order to write books prevents you from ultimately having the chance to do so.

SM: Does one always write the same book? You've written two books about lost love.

AT: So people say. I've always thought *An Adultery* was about the pollution of language, and *Darconville's Cat* about the redemption of the imagination. We get back to paradise that way. Yeats has written some wonderful poems along these lines. If I may quote myself, "Art is the Eden where Adam and Eve eat the serpent," or words to that effect.[2] [*pause*] There is without a doubt a shared theme in both books of romantic disappointment. The without-hope-ness of not being in love, whether a person be young or old, single or married, is the worst thing on earth—in my opinion, the main reason for crime. I also recall reading somewhere that the majority of people in mental institutions have been disappointed in love. The essence of loneliness

2 [*Darconville's Cat*, 688.]

is that one both remembers and hopes, though in vain, in the midst of one's dissolution. Plain nothingness compared to it is a comfort, a kind of hibernation, a tundra of arctic whiteness that negates feeling and want. Loneliness, not hatred, is the antithesis of love. No, I won't deny it, the subject, its conflicts, its drama, fully fascinates me. "On the day on which I am no longer in love," Puccini said, "you can hold my funeral." How wonderful it is to be able to care for someone who depends on you and to hope for the same from her. At the same time, I am reminded that we are largely the architects of our own romances. It's a revealing paradox, I suppose, that Puccini's wife was so destructive. [*pause*] I am half-Italian, remember, and share his Tuscan sadness. "*La mestizia toscana.*"

SM: You're pessimistic about love?

AT: No, only what comes in to replace it. But I am not at all surprised that the line that follows the seemingly hopeful "When the moon comes over the mountain" is "I'll be alone with my dreams."

SM: Going back for a moment, you mention paradox. It's everywhere in your books. It's a figure of speech that seems to intrigue you.

AT: I love paradox. Keats's subjects are usually auditory. Milton rarely mentions birds. Rembrandt loved to put dogs in his paintings. My love is paradox. Not the mere play of words Chesterton bored us with, those tired anti-symmetries. It's related to irony, the way people should be. Did you know Flaubert knew a prostitute named "Crucifix"? The Athanasian Creed sparkles with paradox. It's everywhere in my writing. "Opposites are one." Freud's darkest truth.

SM: The self that emerges from your writings is, in many ways, an anachronistic one, even a reactionary one: devoutly Catholic, decidedly misogynistic if not misanthropic, elitist if not aristocratic, and highly opinionated. Would you say this is a fair deduction?

AT: I would agree with Dr. Crucifer, without embracing anything else, that "no man ever rose to any degree of perfection but through obstinacy and an inveterate resolution against the stream of mankind."[3]

3 Conducted by mail in 1990, published in *Review of Contemporary Fiction*, Spring 1991, pp. 29–35.

Herbert Head

The Unfinished Novel

AFTER HE FINISHED writing *Three Wogs* in 1971, Theroux returned to a far more ambitious novel that he had been working on for years, eventually called *Herbert Head: Biography of a Poet*. According to University of Virginia professor Martin Battestin, with whom he studied 18th-century British literature in the late 1960s, it was originally entitled *The Lollipop Trollops*, and under that name Theroux submitted a proposal to the Guggenheim Foundation in the fall of 1971 for a grant, which was rejected. (He would get a Guggenheim five years later for a related project, *Darconville's Cat*.) Battestin included the proposal as an appendix to his engaging memoir "Alexander Theroux in Virginia and London, 1964–1973" (*Review of Contemporary Fiction* 11.1 [Spring 1991]: 81–83), which reads as follows:

> The Proustian equation, Beckett insists, is never simple. Thus it is, with both a sense of methodic futility and an obvious sense of limitation here, that I formally propose my creative project, the writing of a novel, the working title of which is *The Lollipop Trollops*. I have been gathering data for this for four years. Broadly, my subject deals with the theme of forgery as a comic treatment of the church in general, and, specifically, with a psychic portrait of a wildly intransigent Catholic, haunted into his intellectual impasse by history, by logic, by our times. The genre to which I am addressing myself is not new, the encyclopedic, or so called 'learned' novel—a narrative technique that looks nostalgically back to the tradition of the Schoolmen, the humanist pedant, the agitated scholastic. The paradigmatic work in this genre reaches from Montaigne to Baron Corvo (Fr. Rolfe), from Sterne's *Tristram Shandy* to Beckett's *Watt*, from Burton's *Anatomy*

of Melancholy to John Aubrey to Jorge Luis Borges, from Rabelais to Joyce.

My novel is to be constructed as a nest of Chinese boxes, a story within a story. In a localized way, it is the story of the odyssey and growth of an Oxford scholar, confessionally (and comically) related by that central character himself, Herbert Head—polymath, bibliobsessive fanatic, and Catholic eccentric—whose ultramontane journey has led him into, through, and beyond the secularist vicissitudes of the world and eventually to the Monastery of Our Lady of Sotto Voce, a philosophically ambiguous resolution, I'll try to show, to the problems raised in getting there. Narratively, however, I hope to construct this novel between 'bookends,' i.e., further reading will confirm that Head's Confessions (apologiae poured forth from the soul of the novice Frater Morov, quondam Herbert Head) are, as they have been all along, in manuscript form, which manuscript is being glossed and annotated by a certain Abbot Sacrapanti, an aged monk there whose penitential work (the bibliographic scholarship) is predicated upon a former life, a nasty former life, which is, in turn, remarkable, we will see, for its curious connectives—in time, place, and coincidence— with the life of an Oxford don and poet named Smegma, a homosexual who surrounds himself with nothing but the color red (ashtrays, clothes, food). This Smegma, about whom Fr. Sacrapanti seems morbidly silent, has an even greater monomania: a consuming love for Herbert Head. The great battles of the sacred and the profane—a sort of prose mystery play set in Oxford, England—become only small bits of smalto in the greater mosaic of intellectual and theological forgery that takes place (slowly) in the almost microscopic area between manuscript and gloss, i.e., in the scriptorium of the monastery between the dead author and the living annotator.

Herbert Head is dead, for this is a murder story, as well. The reason Herbert Head has been shot—a gruesome scene which takes place during the Mandatum of Holy Week (and recorded, i.e., glossed, on the following day)—is revealed in the manuscript itself through intellectual revelations having nothing whatsoever to do with the factual, literal murder. But it is not coincidence, and not paradoxically he finishes the manuscript as he is finished. Once finished with the reading of the manuscript, however, the reader sees that Head has epiphanized his one powerful monomania: the attempt to prove as heretical, foolish, false, and superfluous every major religion down through history to the present, excluding—and, of course, this is the substantific marrow of the book—Roman Catholicism. In that attempt, Herbert has become all head, gathering to himself in his pre-monastic life an armoury of bibliothecal rarities, a range of collectibles, simply to cripple any attempt, real or imaginary, to refute him in his unbudging, if maniacal, conclusion. I envisage a battle of the books *extraordinaire* (at once a plot device, a satire on the very genre I am employing, and a comic compendium of very real literature). All of the written disjecta of the Catholic World from its inception to now Herbert Head will marshal to his side to sustain his bias, refute his enemies, find his niche, follow his star, praise his God, and save his soul, for the last matter becomes his increasingly triumphant preoccupation, borne in on him with nose-thumbing logic and with no possibility of alternative. He will try, as I hope to show in the novel, to piece together (as I have already tried to do) a *summa* of non-contradictory and age-old Catholic matter, which, of course—as all such edifices must—becomes a massive forgery of out-of-print tracts, incunabula, and yellowing manifestos: an ore of comedy, for our purposes, rarely touched now-a-days.

I intend to write, along with the novel, an essay on bibliomania, the linchpin of 'learned' comedy. And to that end, I have planned many materials for Herbert Head in the form of rubber-covered books (used at bath); books with perforated leaves (to be jettisoned); books to be eaten (with *papier de guimauve*, a marshmallow paper for the bibliophage); rare minims, to be tucked into secret places; wordless books allegorizing the opposition of virtue to vice strictly in colors; cutisbound books; gigantic head-tall books in which one may stand; soft but huge books to be slept upon; and so forth. A self-conscious, sarcastic, bitter, and often paranoid language must be used, and then, quickly, that language must give way to a soft, pleading, then convinced, even aureate writing to make certain that the novel remains a very funny, highly polemical tour de force, showing, at the same time, the great bifurcations and connections, automatically raised as points of issue and without which the novel would be incomplete, between Art and Life, Man and God, the Mortal and the Immortal, the Religious and the Secular, the Ideal and the Real, the Head and the Heart, the Soul and the Body, and, certainly, between Fiction and Fact.

My first novel flirts with many of these ideas. Now, I am ready to write them and write them well. I lack only the time and the support.

When *Three Wogs* was published in January 1972, Theroux boiled down the above for Longwood College's school newspaper as a novel about "the irreducibility of the Catholic Church. Oddly enough, it's a murder mystery, the plot of which has its point of departure in the absurdity of all heretical religions."[1] In August of that year, he submitted a story entitled "Herbert Head, Gent." to Gordon Lish at *Esquire*, who turned it down. This 15,000-word comedy provides a glimpse of what the proposed novel looked like at that early stage. Theroux's amplified prose style is turned up to eleven in this highfalutin hoot about the lengths the nerdy Herbert Head goes to research his book (entitled *Grimoires*) "on the insufficiency of *every* non-Catholic religion."

A more ludicrous champion of Catholicism is hard to imagine than this short, fat, near-sighted, unpopular, beret-wearing "bibliobsessive phanatique": "Herbert Head, Esq., *aet.* twenty-six, exilarch, stavrophon, bibliolater, was a genius. Simply that. He had a most uncommon IQ, thrice fifty plus, into which, confectioning, he rummaged, as if for chocolates, all to sweeten and re-sweeten that crucial, not always gentle apologetics which His Church, in those times, so desperately needed." He is a grad student at Chryses College in Swinford, Massachusetts, when in "a freakily catch-all underground tabloid" he spots an announcement for a revivalist sermon to be preached at the Wyanoid Baptist Church in Albuminuria, Virginia, on 10 October 1972. Deciding that would provide valuable material for his book, he hops a bus and arrives on the afternoon of the 9th, spends the night in a tourist home like the one described in Theroux's early story "The American Tourist Home," attends the sermon the next day, then boards the same bus to head back north, satisfied that he now has enough material for his chapter entitled "The Codpiece of Protestantism." There is an amusing subplot concerning the proprietress of the tourist home, an evangelical named Mrs. Whitlatch, who Herbert fears has designs on him but who turns out to be the mistress of the pastor who delivers the hectoring sermon. It is an obstreperous contribution to the tradition of learned wit.

When Theroux wrote this story, he was in love with one of his students, was dumped by her the following year, and in revenge dumped *Herbert Head* to begin a new novel, originally entitled *Linda van der Lubbe* (her married name). By then he was at Harvard, and he published two selections from it in the *Harvard Advocate*, announcing in a headnote that the complete novel would be published in 1974. Had that happened, it probably would not have been much longer than *Three Wogs*. But at that point he decided to adapt some of the material from *Herbert Head* and over the next six years converted his new project into

---

1 "Dr. Alexander Theroux Publishes First Novel," *The Rotunda* 51.15 (23 February 1972), 4.

the learned, encyclopedic novel of his Guggenheim proposal, transforming *Linda van der Lubbe* into *Darconville's Cat*. After repurposing the sermon episode in "Herbert Head, Gent." as a humorous essay—which Lish also rejected[2]—Theroux revised it for chapter XLVI of the published novel. He also transferred many of the ludicrous protagonist's qualities to the learned Abel Crucifer: like Head, Crucifer is a "polymath, bibliobsessive fanatic, and eccentric Catholic," but instead of a "battle of the books" on Catholic writings, Theroux assembled a bibliographic chapter on the literature of misogyny. The language of *Darconville* resembles that he envisioned for *Herbert Head*: "A self-conscious, sarcastic, bitter, and often paranoid language must be used, and then, quickly, that language must give way to a soft, pleading, then convinced, even aureate writing to make certain that the novel remains a very funny, highly polemical tour de force. . . ."

It could be argued that the girl who jilted him saved Theroux's writing life. Had they married, as he planned, and had he finished *Herbert Head* along the lines of the Guggenheim proposal, the result might have been a bizarre, forbiddingly erudite theological novel that would have repulsed most publishers. As dazzling as "Herbert Head, Gent." is, 700 pages in that mode would appeal to a very small audience. (Me and a couple hundred other "bibliobsessive fanatics"?) And had they remained married, there presumably would be no *An Adultery* or *Laura Warholic*.

Decades later, after *Laura Warholic* was published, Theroux decided to resume work on *Herbert Head*. In early 2008, he told an interviewer that he was working on both it and the nonfiction book on Amelia Earhart he had abandoned in the 1990s.[3] This is the novel Theroux says he was writing when he left for Estonia later in 2008.[4] More intriguingly, in March 2009 Theroux told an audience at Texas State University that he was still working on *Herbert Head*, which had taken on new features:

> It's kind of based upon my years of life—it's the ultimate book, birth to death—I'm using photographs in it from houses and pictures I've taken over the years. I wrote the poetry for it. I'm halfway through

2 It was eventually published as "The Evangelist" in the January 1982 issue of *Harper's*.

3 Sean P. Carroll, "An Interview with Alexander Theroux," *Bookslut*, March 2008. Entitled *Becoming Amelia*, much of the Earhart biography was researched at the Schlesinger Library at Radcliffe. Theroux resumed work on it in the fall of 2019.

4 *Estonia: A Ramble Through the Periphery* (Seattle: Fantagraphics Books, 2011), 10, 61.

the book. It's almost as if you're reading the biography of a person named Herbert Head, but it's fiction. It's a person that I've given a lot of my life to, but he's a kind of eccentric—dies in the Middle East in a desert on a kind of monastic retreat. But it's a fun novel to write, not very difficult to read, since you're just traveling through chapters of his experiences.[5]

But at that point he abandoned the novel for good, writing his book on Estonia instead and seeing other books through the press. When I asked him about the novel years later, he replied, "With the concatenation of my marriage (2005), the economic downturn of 2008, the birth and care of two children in 2014, and writing books—what, three or four of them—for which I was never given any advances to speak of, I never had the free time or financial freedom to work on *Herbert Head* or my Amelia Earhart book" (email 4 April 2019).

In June 2019 I discovered "Herbert Head, Gent.," among Lish's manuscripts at Indiana University's Lilly Library;[6] when I notified Theroux of this, he had no recollection of the story, "part of a book I am still mentally living with, wanting only for time (the children have made a big dent in my writing operations, as you know)" (email 21 June 2019). I obtained and sent him a copy, encouraging him to add it to his *Collected Stories* manuscript, to which he reluctantly agreed, calling it "a self-conscience ramble that reminds me of John Kennedy Toole and Charles Portis— although not as good" (email 28 July 2019). I told him I disagreed.

I don't imagine any more of the ambitious novel will be published. Literary history is haunted by the ghosts of unfinished novels by Sterne, Sade, Austen, Flaubert, Dickens, Kafka, Proust, Musil, Nabokov, Ellison, and many others. One occasionally sees features such as Bess Lovejoy's "10 Famous Authors and Their Unfinished Manuscripts,"[7] or reads of fictional places like the Graveyard of Unwritten Books in Nedim Gürsel's *The Last Tram* (1991). Sadly, *Herbert Head: Biography of a Poet* belongs in their gloomy company.

---

5 See video recorded 5 March 2009 at Texas State University around the 42:30 mark.

6 The Lish collection contains many other manuscripts Theroux sent him— seven were published in *Esquire* between 1973 and 1976, the rest elsewhere— many with Lish's editorial marks and suggestions.

7 http://mentalfloss.com/article/67424/10-famous-authors-and-their-unfinished-manuscripts.

Checklist of Publications

A. BOOKS & PAMPHLETS

A1 *Three Wogs*
   a. Boston: Gambit, January 1972. Note: The dust-jacket of the first issue
   prints the author's photo on the rear flap in reddish-brown as opposed to black in the second issue, and, in the text below the photo,
   "a Trappist monastery" is followed by "in Kentucky," which was
   deleted from the second issue jacket (because the monastery was in
   Massachusetts).
   b. London: Chatto & Windus, 1973
   c. London: Wildwood House, 1973 (paper)
   d. Boston: David Godine, 1975 (paper; "Theroux Metaphrastes" [A2]
   added as an appendix)
   e. New York: Holt/Owl, 1997 (paper)

A2 *Theroux Metaphrastes*
   a. Boston: David Godine, 1975 (pamphlet)

A3 *The Schinocephalic Waif* (illustrated by Stan Washburn)
   a. Boston: David Godine, 1975

A4 *The Great Wheadle Tragedy* (illustrated by Stan Washburn)
   a. Boston: David Godine, 1975

A5 *Master Snickup's Cloak* (illustrated by Brian Froud)
   a. Limpsfield, Surrey: Paper Tiger Books, 1979
   b. New York: Harper & Row, 1979 (rpt. in A6, 140–44)

A6 *Darconville's Cat*

  a1. Garden City, NY: Doubleday, May 1981 [p. 483 printed as dot matrix]
  a2. limited reprint with p. 483 as solid black rectangle, per author's
   insistence
  b. London: Hamish Hamilton, 1983
  c. New York: Holt/Owl, 1996 (paper), with revisions in lighter type

A7 *A Christmas Fable*
  a. Privately printed pamphlet of 50 copies, December 1983

A8 *An Adultery*
  a. New York: Simon & Schuster, October 1987
  b. London: Hamish Hamilton, 1988 (offset from US edition, i.e., 396
   pp.)
  c. New York: Collier Books, 1988 (paper)
  d. London: Paladin/Grafton Books, 1990 (paper; reset with British punctuation; 496 pp.)
  e. New York: Holt/Owl, 1997 (paper)

A9 *A Christmas Prayer*
  a. Privately printed card, December 1987

A10 *History Is Made at Night*
  a. West Chester, PA: Aralia Press, March 1992 (ltd. to 150 copies; rpt. in
   A11 and A20)

A11 *The Lollipop Trollops and Other Poems*
  a. Normal, IL: Dalkey Archive Press, August 1992 (paper; rpt. in A20)
  b. Ibid., cloth edition
  c. Ibid., signed ltd. ed. (100 cc; half for sale, half *hors de commerce*)

A12 *Watergraphs*
  a. Boston: Base Canard, August 1994 (trade ed., 100 copies, many left
   unbound)
  b. Ibid., deluxe ed. (15 copies)

A13 *The Primary Colors*
  a. New York: Henry Holt, August 1994
  b. New York: Quality Paperback Book Club, 1994
  c. London: Picador, 1995 (paper)
  d. New York: Holt/Owl, 1996 (paper, with some excisions)

A14 *The Secondary Colors*
  a. New York: Henry Holt, April 1996
  b. New York: Holt/Owl, 1997 (paper)

A15 *The Enigma of Al Capp*
  a. Seattle: Fantagraphics Books, January 1999

A16 *The Strange Case of Edward Gorey*
  a. Seattle: Fantagraphics Books, August 2000
  b. Revised ed., Fantagraphics, May 2002
  c. Expanded cloth edition, Fantagraphics, January 2011

A17 *Laura Warholic, or The Sexual Intellectual*
  a. Seattle: Fantagraphics, December 2007

A18 *Estonia: A Ramble Through the Periphery*
  a. Seattle: Fantagraphics, November 2011

A19 *The Grammar of Rock: Art and Artlessness in 20th Century Pop Lyrics*
  a. Seattle: Fantagraphics, February 2013

A20 *Collected Poems*
  a. Seattle: Fantagraphics, May 2015

A21 *Einstein's Beets: An Examination of Food Phobias*
  a. Seattle: Fantagraphics, May 2017

B. CONTRIBUTIONS TO BOOKS & PAMPHLETS

B1 *Five Poets*. Edited by Nana Lampton
  a. Charlottesville, VA: privately printed, 1966
  Contains: "Erkomai" and "Reveries of Children Dying" (11–14); the latter rpt. in A11 and A20 (as are virtually all poems listed hereafter)

B2 *London Magazine Stories 5*. Edited by Alan Ross
  a. London: London Magazine Editions, 1970
  Contains: "Mrs Proby Gets Hers" (14–45), rpt. from *London Magazine* (1969)

B3 *Mom, the Flag, and Apple Pie*. Edited by the editors of *Esquire*
  a. Garden City: Doubleday, 1976

Contains: "The Psychiatrist" (198–210), rpt. of "The Shrink" (1975)

B4 *The Pushcart Prize, First Edition 1976–77*. Edited by Bill Henderson
   a: Yonkers: Pushcart Press, 1976
   b. New York: Avon Equinox, 1976 (paper)
   Contains: "Lynda van Cats" (139–43), rpt. from *Antaeus* (1975)

B5 *Self-Portrait: Book People Picture Themselves*. Edited by Burt Britton
   a. New York: Random House, 1976 (cloth and paper)
   Contains: AT's cartoon self-portrait (38)

B6 *Ariel: The Book of Fantasy*, vol. 4. Edited by Thomas Durwood
   a. Kansas City, MO: Ariel Books/Ballantine, 1978
   Contains: "The Night of the Niffelheim Dwarves" (66)

B7 *Fritz Eichenberg: The Artist and the Book*
   a. New Haven, CT: Yale University Library, 1979 (pamphlet)
   Contains: "Fritz Eichenberg" (9–15).

B8 *Junk Food*. Edited by Charles J. Rubin, David Rollert, et al.
   a. New York: Dial, 1980
   b. New York: Delta, 1980 (paper)
   Contains: "The Chinese Restaurant" (133–35)

B9 *The Best of Modern Humor*. Edited by Mordecai Richler
   a. New York: Alfred A. Knopf, 1983
   b. London: Allan Lane, 1984
   c. London: Penguin, 1984 (paper)
   Contains: part 1 of "Mrs. Proby Gets Hers" (453–66), from A1

B10 *Reading Adrienne Rich: Reviews and Re-visions, 1951–1981*. Edited by
Jane Roberta Cooper
   a. Ann Arbor: University of Michigan Press, 1984
   Contains: "Reading the Poverty of Rich" (304–8), rpt. from *Boston
      Magazine* (1976)

B11 *Vice & Virtue in Everyday Life: Introductory Readings in Ethics*. Edited by Christina Hoff Sommers
   a. New York: Harcourt Brace Jovanovich, 1985
   Contains: "Revenge" (280–91), rpt. from *Harper's* (1982)

B12 *Remembering Fritz Eichenberg: Friendship Celebrated.* Edited by
Antonie Eichenberg
   a. New York: Donnell Memorial Library, 1991. Limited edition of 250
      copies.
   Contains: brief memoir on the artist (cf. B7)

B13 *The Pushcart Prize XVII: Best of the Small Presses 1992–1993.* Edited
by Bill Henderson
   a. Wainscott, NY: Pushcart Press, 1992
   Contains: "A Note on the Type" (268–70), rpt. from *Review of Contem-
      porary Fiction* (1991)

B14 *The March of Literature,* by Ford Madox Ford
   a. Normal, IL: Dalkey Archive Press, 1994
   Contains: "Introduction" (ix–xviii)

B15 *The Return of the Native,* by Thomas Hardy
   a. New York: Modern Library, 1994 (cloth)
   b. New York: Modern Library, 2001 (paper)
   Contains: "Introduction" (xi–xv)

B16 *The Penguin Book of Infidelities.* Edited by Stephen Brook
   a: London: Viking, 1994
   b. London & New York: Penguin, 1995 (paper)
   Contains: untitled excerpt from *An Adultery,* 196–200 (29–32)

B17 *The Art of the Essay: The Best of 1999.* Edited by Phillip Lopate.
   a: New York: Anchor Books, 1999.
   Contains: "Black" (311–25), rpt. from *Conjunctions* (1998)

B18 *The Pushcart Prize XXIV: Best of the Small Presses 2000.* Edited by
Bill Henderson.
   a. Wainscott: Pushcart Press, 1999.
   Contains: "Odd Collections" (334–44), rpt. from *Yale Review* (1998).

B19 *Chick for a Day: What Would You Do If You Were One?* Edited by
Fiona Giles
   a: New York: Simon & Schuster, 2000
   Contains: "Spelunking" (69–79).

B20 *Hadrian the Seventh,* by Fr. Rolfe (Baron Corvo)

a. New York: New York Review Books, 2001
Contains: "Introduction" (ix–xv)

B21 *Take My Advice: Letters to the Next Generation from People Who Know a Thing or Two.* Edited by James L. Harmon.
a. New York: Simon & Schuster, April 2002.
Contains: brief, untitled passage and a photo of AT (92)

B22 *Ted Williams: The Pursuit of Perfection.* Edited by Jim Prime and Bill Nowlin
a. Champaign, IL: Sports Publishing, Inc., July 2002
Contains: "Ted Williams' Edge" (249–50) (First broadcast on radio? note reads: Courtesy of National Public Radio's *Morning Edition*)

B23 *The Pushcart Prize XXVII: Best of the Small Presses,* 2003. Edited by Bill Henderson
a: Wainscott, NY: Pushcart Press, January 2003
Contains: "Camp Cedar Crest" (125–32), rpt. from *Conjunctions* (2001)

B24 *The Next American Essay.* Edited by John D'Agata
a. St. Paul: Graywolf, January 2003.
Contains: "Black" (319–31), rpt. from *Conjunctions* (1998)

B25 *The Comics Journal* 301. Edited by Gary Groth
a. Seattle: Fantagraphics, February 2011
Contains: "Crumb Goes to Church" (123–35)

B26 *The Comics Journal* 302. Edited by Gary Groth
a. Seattle: Fantagraphics, 2013
Contains: "Mr. Grumpy in Kiddlebookland or a Textbook Case of the Anti-Self" (110–25; on Maurice Sendak)

B27 *Feelings: Soft Art.* Edited by Loren Olson
a. New York: Skira Rizzoli Publications, November 2015
Contains: "Soft Balm, Soft Menace" (6–8: introduction)

B28 *We Told You So: Comics as Art.* Edited by Tom Spurgeon with Michael Dean
a. Seattle: Fantagraphics, December 2016
Contains: untitled tribute to Fantagraphics Books (585)

B29 Charles M. Schulz. *Peanuts Every Sunday*, vol. 5: 1971–1975. Edited by Gary Groth

a. Seattle: Fantagraphics, November 2017
Contains: "Peanuts: The Sagacity of Common Sense" (5–7)

C. CONTRIBUTIONS TO PERIODICALS

[BR=book review; D=drama; E=essay; F=fiction; P=poetry]

"Over Edom Will I Cast Out My Shoe." *Canticle* [St. Francis College, Biddeford, ME] 8.1 (1964): 9–17. [F]

"The Stride: A Gnoem." *Canticle* 8.1 (1964): 21–22. [P]

"Must Thou Char the Wood . . . ?" *Canticle* 8.1 (1964): 34–37. [BR: James Baldwin's *The Fire Next Time*]

"The Invisible Man." *Canticle* 8.2 (1964): 8–11. [E]

"The Unaffiliated and the Lack of Affiliation: An Approach to Estrangement in Modern Man." *Canticle* 8.2 (1964): 19–34. [E]

"The Tin Drum." *Canticle* 8.2 (1964): 58–67. [BR of Günter Grass's novel]

"Christmas Eve at the Gordon Crumms." *Rapier* [University of Virginia] 1.2 (January 1967): 14–15, 31, 33, 36–37. [D]

"The Sweethearts and Chagrin of Roland Maguffy." *Rapier* 1.3 (April 1967): 29–31, 37–38. [D: the basis for "Childe Roland" in *Three Wogs*]

"The Meeting of the Heads" and "In the Children's Parks Is Fun." *Poetry Bag* 1.4 (Summer1967): 32–33. [P; both rpt. in A11 and A20, as are most poems that follow]

"Over Edom Will I Cast Out My Shoe." *Plume & Sword* [University of Virginia] 7.4 (Summer 1967): 2–8. [F: rpt.]

"Part of Loving's Leaving." *Plume & Sword* 7.4 (Summer 1967): 16. [P]

"The Rape of the Carnival Woman One Hot Funless Night by the Muffin Boy, the Jobbing Tailor, and Myself." *Plume & Sword* 7.4 (Summer 1967): 17. [P]

"The Confessions of Mrs. Motherwell." *Rapier* 2.1 (November 1967): 26–29, 35–36. [D]

"Admissions." *Transatlantic Review* 27 (Winter 1967–68): 73. [P]

"By the Waters Now of Doom I Sit" and "The Gesture of Vanni Fucci." *Latitudes* 2.2 (1968): 45. [P]

"The Water Babies." *Christian Science Monitor*. [E: untraced; in letter dated 5 May 1969, AT says he just finished a three-part article on Russia for *CSM*]

"Mrs Proby Gets Hers." *London Magazine* 9.6 (September 1969): 5–36. [F: rpt. in A1 and B2]

"Part of Loving's Leaving." *Georgia Review* 23.4 (Winter 1969): 530. [P]

"The Inarticulate Hero." *National Review*, 24 February 1970, 199–201. [E]

"Free Enterprise." *The Rotunda*, 11 October 1972, 2, 6. [letter to editor of Longwood University's school newspaper]

"Beware the Cheshire Cheese, Home of the Mad Train Maven." *New York Times*, 11 February 1973, "Travel and Resorts," 1, 13. [F]

"A Tale of Madness." *National Review*, 27 April 1973, 479. [BR: Susan Hill, *The Bird of Night*]

"The American Tourist Home: In the World, but Not of It." *New York Times*, 20 May 1973, "Travel and Resorts," 1, 51. [F]

"Might as Well Be Cleveland." *National Review*, 8 June 1973, 645. [BR: Terence de Vere White, *The Distance and the Dark*]

"Fark Pooks." *London Magazine* 13.2 (June/July 1973): 48–56 [F]

"Fark Pooks." *Esquire*, August 1973, 104, 126–27. [F: simultaneous with above]

"Berliner Ensemble." *National Review*, 31 August 1973, 955–56. [BR: Vladimir Nabokov, *A Russian Beauty and Other Stories*]

"Mrs. Marwood's Spunkies." *Antaeus* 11 (Autumn 1973): 90–96. [F]

"A Wordstress in Williamsburg." *Antaeus* 13/14 (Spring/Summer 1974): 346–51. [F: partly subsumed into A6]

"The Incredible Revenge of Edward Gorey." *Esquire*, June 1974, 110–11, 144, 146, 148. [E]

"Scugnizzo's Pasta Co." *Encounter* 43.3 (September 1974): 3–7. [F]

"From *Linda van der Lubbe*." *Harvard Advocate* 107.1 (Fall 1974): 17–19. [F: rpt. in A6, 29–40]

"Divvy Up Dollars and Eat More." *Atlantic Monthly*, April 1975, 94–96. [E: an abridged version of A2]

"Good Old with Everything." *Esquire*, April 1975, 79, 148, 150, 152, 156, 158, 160. [E: Samuel Eliot Morison]

"'Want Me? It'll Cost You!'" *Esquire*, July 1975, 112–15, 136–38. [E: on lobsters]

"Auden's Face." *Harvard Advocate* (Special Auden Issue) 108.2–3 (September 1975): 17. [P]

"The Sissy." *Esquire*, October 1975, 198–201, 218, 220. [E]

"The Caliph Omar Confounded: Delights of Book Collecting." *Harvard Magazine*, November 1975, 58–60. [E]

"Lynda van Cats." *Antaeus* 19 (Autumn 1975): 47–51. [F; rpt. in B4, revised for A5 and A6]

"The Shrink." *Esquire*, December 1975, 166–68, 185–86. [E; rpt. in B3]

"Silent Nights, Holy Daze: A Seasonal Meditation." *Boston Phoenix*, 9 December 1975, 20, 22. [E]

"Three Grown-up Fantasies." *Esquire*, April 1976, 73. [E]

"The Cape of Good Hope?" *Boston Magazine*, June 1976, 140, 125–26. [E]

"No News Is Agnew's." *Boston Magazine*, July 1976, 49–51. [BR: Spiro Agnew's *The Canfield Decision*]

"No Lady, Madonna." *Boston Magazine*, August 1976, 39–42. [BR: James Carroll's *Madonna Red*]

"Finocchio, or the Tale of a Man with a Long Nose." *Massachusetts Review* 17 (Summer 1976): 234–42. [F]

"The Class Menagerie." *Esquire*, September 1976, 61–65. [E: a satire on five university types; the last, "The Old Scholar," reappears as Prof. McGentsroom in A6, 406–8]

"Shelling Hard-boiled Higgins." *Boston Magazine*, September 1976, 58–60. [BR: Jack Higgins's *Judgment of Deke Hunter*]

"Sun Daze, Bloody Sun Daze." *Boston Magazine*, October 1976, 37–40. [BR: Geoffrey Wolff's *Black Sun: The Brief Transit and Violent Eclipse of Harry Crosby*; on p. 40 are brief comments by AT on four "Recommended" titles: Martin Green's *Children of the Sun*, Everett S. Allen's *A Wind to Shake the World*, Cornelius S. Hurlbut Jr.'s *The Planet We Live On*, and Paul Theroux's *The Family Arsenal*]

"The Poverty of Rich." *Boston Magazine*, November 1976, 46–48. [BR: Adrienne Rich's *Of Woman Born*. Rpt. in B10]

"The Flesh Made Word." *Boston Magazine*, December 1976[?], 26, 28, 30–31. [BR: Richard Selzer's *Mortal Lessons*; on p. 31 are three "Recommended" titles: Charles Higham's *Adventures of Conan Doyle*, Joseph Frank's *Dostoevsky: The Seeds of Revolt*, and Meta Carpenter's *A Loving Gentleman*]

"'Speak for Yourself, John'—A Line Never Uttered?" *New York Times*, 16 November 1977, "Living," C8. [E]

"Southern Manners." *Canto* 2.2 (Summer 1978): 153–60. [E; revised for A6, chap. 7]

"A Polish Joke." *Paris Review* 20 (no. 74)(Fall/Winter 1978): 90–100. [F]

"St. Winifred's Bells." *Boston Monthly* 1.2 (June/July 1979). [F]

"Matters of Taste." *Harper's*, August 1979, 94, 96–97. [E: on candy]

"Captain Birdseye's Expedition." *Hard Scuffle*, Folio/79 (1979): 48–49. [F]

"Captain Birdseye's Expedition." *Iowa Review* 11.2/3 (Spring/Summer 1980): 35–38. [F; rpt. of above]

"Cape Cod's Elegant Primitive." *Boston Magazine*, November 1980, 91–92, 95–96. [E: on Ralph Cahoon]

"The Home of 'Jingle Bells.'" *New York Times*, 27 December 1981, "Travel," 19. [E: Christmas memories of Medford]

"The Evangelist." *Harper's*, January 1982, 73–77 [E: an essay version of A6, chap. 46]

"Dedicated Followers of Fashion." *Sportscape: The Boston Sports Journal,* Spring 1982, 29–30. [E]

"The Falmouth to Provincetown Canvas." *New York Times,* 13 June 1982, "Travel," 45. [E]

"The Court of Kings." *Sportscape* 2.5 (October 1982): 22–24, 27. [E]

"Revenge." *Harper's,* October 1982, 26–31. [E]

"Pick of the Prep Schools." *Travel & Leisure,* November 1982[?]. [E]

"Thanksgiving and Thoreau." *New York Times,* 24 November 1982, 17, 20. [E]

"How Curious the Camel." *Reader's Digest,* February 1983, 90–92. [E]

"The Doom Sellers." *Boston Globe Magazine,* 27 February 1983, 8–9, 40–41, 44–45. [E]

"I Sing the Parrot!" *Reader's Digest,* May 1983, 103–6. [E]

"Alex at Andover." *Andover Bulletin* 76.4 (Spring 1983): 12–13. [E]

"Watergraphs." *Boston Globe Magazine,* 9 October 1983, 10–11, 16, 22, 24, 28, 30, 34. [F: rpt. in A12]

"Fear and Loathing on the Ski Trail." *Sportscape* 3.9 (November 1983): 25–26. [E]

"Twinkle, Twinkle, Little Bat." *Reader's Digest,* January 1984, 161–62, 164. [E]

"The Word from New England: The Light at the End of a Long, Cold Tunnel." *Vanity Fair,* April 1984, 92. [E]

"The Name of the Nose." *New Age Journal,* September 1984, 104. [E; originally entitled "Odor of Sanctity"]

"Dwindling Days, Widening Vistas: Off Season on the Cape." *Boston Globe,* 28 October 1984, "Travel," 26–27, 32, 38–39. [E]

"A Woman with Sauce." *Boston Globe Magazine,* 13 January 1985, 10–11, 18, 20, 22, 24, 26, 28, 30, 32, 41–42. [F]

"New England Brigadoon: The Discreet Charms of Oak Bluffs." *New England Monthly* 2.8 (August 1985): 41–44. [E]

"John Fowles Poses Another Literary Riddle." *Boston Sunday Globe,* 18 August 1985, A9, A12. [BR: Fowles's *A Maggot*]

"The Cape Complaint." *Boston Globe Magazine,* 6 July 1986, 18–24. [E]

"Nerd University." *New England Monthly* 3.10 (October 1986): 60–65. [E: on MIT students]

"Chasing Mermaids." *Art & Antiques,* November 1986, 86–90, 116, 118. [E: on Ralph and Martha Cahoon]

"The Wragby Cars." *Mississippi Review* 15.3 (no. 45)(Spring/Summer 1987): 101–3. [F]

"The Perfect Scoop." *Art & Antiques,* May 1987, 95–96, 113. [E: on ice-cream scoopers, including AT's own collection]

"Caution: Geniuses at Work." *Reader's Digest*, October 1987, 215–20. [E: abridged version of "Nerd University"]

"Silent, Solitary: The Cape in Winter." *New York Times Magazine*, Part 2: "The Sophisticated Traveler," 4 October 1987, 10, 82. [E]

"Dabblers and Dabbling." *Art & Antiques*, November 1987, 107–8, 110, 113–16. [E; AT's self-portrait from B5 is reproduced on p. 109 among other "dabblers"]

"Do Not Print This Letter." *Harper's*, January 1988, 70–73. [E]

"Mortal Goddess." *Art & Antiques*, March 1988, 84–89, 116–18, 120, 122. [E: on Botticelli's model Simonetta Vespucci]

"Artists Who Kill." *Art & Antiques*, Summer 1988, 95–104. [E]

"The Sphinx of Delft." *Art & Antiques*, December 1988, 84–89, 120, 122, 124. [E: on Vermeer and Proust]

"Only Collect." *Art & Antiques*, March 1989, 112–18, 120, 122, 124, 126. [E]

"Yin and Yanks." *Boston Globe Magazine*, 2 July 1989, 1, 22–25, 28, 31, 34–41. [E]

"People Looking for Things to Need." *Boston Globe*, 23 July 1989, "Focus," 65, 67–68. [E]

"Edward Hopper's Cape Cod." *Art & Antiques*, January 1990, 56–67, 97–98. [E]

"What's the Word for . . . ?" *Harper's*, February 1990, 45–51. [A forum where several writers suggest and define neologisms; AT contributes six items]

"Rhapsody in Blue." *Art & Antiques*, April 1990, 70–77. [E: expanded as "Blue" in A13]

"Henry James's Boston." *Iowa Review* 20.2 (Spring/Summer 1990): 158–65. [E]

"Raphael's Lost Madonna." *Art & Antiques*, December 1990, 82–87, 122, 124. [E]

"The Detours of Art." *Review of Contemporary Fiction* 11.1 (Spring 1991): 36–40. [E]

"A Note on the Type." *Review of Contemporary Fiction* 11.1 (Spring 1991): 41–42. [F; rpt. in A12 and B11]

"The Lollipop Trollops." *Review of Contemporary Fiction* 11.1 (Spring 1991): 83. [P; rpt. as "Mother Gideon" in A11 and A20]

"Comfort Food." *Lear's*, February 1991, 82–87. [E]

[Letter to the editor]. *New York Times Book Review*, 26 May 1991, 4. [re: a review of George Howe Colt's *The Enigma of Suicide*]

[BR of Milan Kundera's *Immortality*.] *Review of Contemporary Fiction* 11.3 (Fall 1991): 265–67.

"Was It Something They Said?" *Washington Post Book World*, 13 October 1991, 5. [BR: Julian Barnes's *Talking It Over*]

"Santa Fé Trails." *Art & Antiques*, February 1992, 40–51, 84–87. [E]

"Dial F for Fantasy." *Washington Post Book World*, 9 February 1992, 3, 7. [BR: Nicholson Baker's *Vox*]

"Wittgenstein's Proposal" and "Vinyl Junkie." *Poetry East* 33 (Spring 1992): 150, 151. [P]

"Eye of the Beholder." *Washington Post*, 10 September 1992, "Style," C2. [BR: Siri Hustvedt's *The Blindfold*]

"Sweetly Singing." *Washington Post Book World*, 6 December 1992, 9. [BR: Sayers and O'Brien's *Sinatra: The Man and His Music*]

[BR of Camille Paglia's *Sex, Art and American Culture*.] *Review of Contemporary Fiction* 13.1 (Spring 1993): 289–92.

"The Stendhal Syndrome." *Art & Antiques*, April 1993, 72–77. [E: on overwhelming responses to art]

[Letter to the editor.] *New York Times Book Review*, 4 April 1993, 34. [Protests D. M. Thomas's "vile remark" in his review of Philip Roth's *Operation Shylock* and the bigotry of all involved]

"Six Poems." *Conjunctions* 20 (May 1993): 127–29. [P: Jesus and the Cat; Jonah Considers His Right Hand from His Left Hand; What Mr. Ambidextrine Was Told at Confession at the 31st St. Shrine; Consolation of Philosophy; Lucifer Is Haunted by the Echo of His Last Goodbye; Willow Tree]

"Portrait of Laure: Life and Hard Times of a Novel's Narrator." *Philadelphia Inquirer*, 5 September 1993. [BR: Kathy Acker's *My Mother: Demonology*]

[BR of James McCourt's *Time Remaining*.] *Review of Contemporary Fiction* 13.3 (Fall 1993): 207–8.

[BR of Milorad Pavić's *The Inner Side of the Wind*.] *Review of Contemporary Fiction* 13.3 (Fall 1993): 216–17.

[BR of Gabriel García Márquez's *Strange Pilgrims*.] *Review of Contemporary Fiction* 14.1 (Spring 1994): 211.

"The Paradoxial Poet." *Chicago Tribune*, 23 January 1994, 9 [BR: Peter Levi's *Tennyson*]

"The Tropics of Updike." *Chicago Tribune*, 30 January 1994, "Books," 1, 9. [BR: John Updike's *Brazil*]

"A Taste for the Difficult Place: Expatriate Paul Bowles' Lifetime of Letters." *Chicago Tribune*, 13 February 1994, "Books," R3. [BR]

[BR of William T. Vollmann's *The Rifles*.] *Philadelphia Inquirer*, March? 1994 [possibly unpublished].

"Yellow in Spectrum: A Jaundiced Etymology." *Harper's*, March 1994,

68–75. [E: expanded as "Yellow" in A13]

"America's Poetic Heritage." *Chicago Tribune*, 20 March 1994, "Books," 6.
[BR: Library of America's *American Poetry: The Nineteenth Century*]

"Drifting around the Island of Self." *Chicago Tribune*, 29 May 1994,
"Books," 6–7. [BR: John Barth's *Once upon a Time*]

[BR of Frances Karttunen's *Between Worlds*.] *Boston Globe*, Summer 1994
(untraced).

"The Novel of Learning: Endangered Species." *Review of Contemporary
Fiction* 14.2 (Summer 1994): 192–98. [E: recycles parts of A2]

[BR of Guy Davenport's *Table of Green Fields*.] *Review of Contemporary
Fiction* 14.2 (Summer 1994): 201.

"Order from Anguish." *Chicago Tribune*, 24 July 1994, "Books," 5. [BR: T.
S. Eliot's *Varieties of Metaphysical Poetry*]

"Tolstoys in Torment." *Chicago Tribune*, 31 July 1994, "Books," 1, 6. [BR:
Shirer's *Love and Hatred: The Stormy Marriage of Leo and Sonya
Tolstoy*]

"The Many and the One." *Cups: A Café Journal*, September 1994, 10. [P]

"Witches a la Rice: Rich in Sorcery and Soap Opera, Serves at Least
600,000." *Chicago Tribune*, 9 October 1994, "Books," 5, 8. [BR: Anne
Rice's *Taltos*]

"The World as She Found It." *Washington Post Book World*, 23 October
1994, 7. [BR: Jostein Gaarder's *Sophie's World*]

"A Friendship Most Puzzling." *Chicago Tribune*, 30 October 1994, "Books,"
4. [BR: Richard Holmes's *Dr. Johnson and Mr. Savage*]

"Observations at Sunset." *Chicago Tribune*, 20 November 1994, "Books," 3.
[BR: John Updike's *The Afterlife*]

"Everyday Evil." *Chicago Tribune*, 15 January 1995, "Books," 3. [BR: William Trevor's *Felicia's Journey*]

"How to Read a Mug: I Would Vote for Lauren Bacall as Having the Perfect Mouth." *San Diego Reader*, 19 January 1995, 42–46. [E: on mouths]

"Canon Law." *National Review*, 23 January 1995, 65–66. [BR: Harold
Bloom's *The Western Canon*]

[BR of Philippe Sollers's *Watteau in Venice*.] *Review of Contemporary Fiction* 15.1 (Spring 1995): 163.

"Faulkner the Preacher." *Chicago Tribune*, 29 January 1995, "Books," 6–7.
[BR: *Novels: 1942–1954*]

"What Paul West Has Learned from a Lifetime Study of Pain." *Chicago
Tribune*, 19 February 1995, "Books," 13. [BR: West's *A Stroke of Genius*]

"'Primary Colors' Error Was Case of Punctuation." *New York Times*, 7
March 1995, A10. [letter to editor responding to charges in 3 March edition of plagiary in *The Primary Colors*]

"Nuclear Triangle." *Chicago Tribune*, 26 March 1995, "Books," 5. [BR: Bradford Morrow's *Trinity Fields*; excerpts rpt. *Chicago Tribune*, 7 April 1996, "Books," 8.]

"Out of North Park: Ted Williams's Climb to Greatness." *San Diego Reader*, 11 May 1995, 46–50. [E]

"Hateful, Hurtful and Hellish." *San Diego Reader*, 1 June 1995, 30–35. [E: on plagiary charges in *New York Times*]

"Bits from a Beat." *Chicago Tribune*, 11 June 1995, "Books," 5. [BR: Allen Ginsberg's *Journals Mid-Fifties*] Rpt. in *Contemporary Literary Criticism Yearbook*, vol. 109 (Gale, 1998).

"Californians Are an Idle, Thriftless People." *San Diego Reader*, 6 July 1995, 38–40. [E: on Richard Henry Dana's (*Two Years before the Mast*) opinions of San Diego]

"Birth of the Pill." *Chicago Tribune*, 9 July 1995, "Books," 1, 11. [BR: Bernard Asbell's *The Pill*]

"Anthony Burgess on the Kit Marlowe Case." *Chicago Tribune*, 16 July 1995, "Books," 3, 11. [BR: Burgess's *A Dead Man in Deptford*]

"The Grammar of Rock and Roll." *San Diego Reader*, 20 July 1995, 22–35. [E: the basis for A19]

"On Walden Pond." *Chicago Tribune*, 20 August 1995, "Books," 1–2. [BR: Thoreau's *Walden: An Annotated Edition*]

"O.J.'s Trial Part of Civil Rights Struggle?" *San Diego Reader*, 5 October 1995. [E]

"Red." *Manchester Guardian Weekend*, 28 October 1995, 14–22. [Rpt. from A13]

"Decent Life Led by the Ordinary Man." *San Diego Reader*, 9 November 1995, 47–50. [E: on AT's father]

"A Fellini Self-Portrait." *Chicago Tribune*, 17 December 1995, "Books," 6–7. [BR: Charlotte Chandler's *I, Fellini*]

"Every Time I Go Out among Men, I Come Back Less a Man." *San Diego Reader*, 21 December 1995, 1, 24–26, 28, 30, 32–34. [E: on Trappists]

"When Songs Were Golden." *Chicago Tribune*, 24 December 1995, "Books," 1, 6. [BR of several books on Gershwin, Hammerstein, Lerner, and Sinatra]

"Food and Thought." *Chicago Tribune*, 31 December 1995, "Books," 3. [BR: M. F. K. Fisher's *Last House*]

"Avenida Revolucion: Big Curio Store, Long Bar, Hotel Nelson, Foreign Club, Sara's, Maxim's, Caesar's Hotel, Jai Alai." *San Diego Reader*, 1 February 1996. [E; on Tijuana]

"The Nature of Ansel Adams." *Chicago Tribune*, 11 February 1996, "Books," 4. [BR: Jonathan Spaulding's *Ansel Adams and the American Land-*

scape]

"Shorty Gets Even." *Boston Magazine*, March 1996, 83, 137. [BR: William Bulger's *While the Music Lasts: My Life in Politics*]

"The Epic Journey of Capt. Lewis." *Chicago Tribune*, 3 March 1996, "Books," 1, 11. [BR: Stephen Ambrose's *Undaunted Courage*]

"Oh, You Leonardo!" *Los Angeles Times Book Review*, 10 March 1996. [BR: Jack Dann's *The Memory Cathedral: A Secret History of Leonardo da Vinci*]

"Adrift in Edisto." *Chicago Tribune*, 31 March 1996, "Books," 9. [BR: Padgett Powell's *Edisto Revisited*]

"Orange." *Yale Review* 84.2 (April 1996): 43–60. [E: abridged from A14]

"An Uneven 'jumble sale of oddments' from Comic Writer Will Self." *Chicago Tribune*, 7 April 1996, "Books," 6–7. [BR: Self's *Grey Area*]

"The Din of Dining Out." *Cosmopolitan*, June 1996, 36. [E]

"Last Eden." *San Diego Reader*, 13 June 1996, 1, 16–20, 22, 24, 26, 28–31. [E: on San Diego's nudist Black's Beach]

"Quick to Buy, Easy to Hold, Cheap and Delicious." *San Diego Reader*, 3 July 1996, 1, 18–20, 22, 24, 26, 28, 30, 32, 34. [E: on hamburgers]

"An Ex-priest Lays His Unhappiness at the Feet of God, Family and War." *Chicago Tribune*, 14 July 1996, "Books," 3, 11. [BR: James Carroll's *An American Requiem*]

"The Little Scamp." *Chicago Tribune*, 21 July 1996, "Books," 1, 9. [BR: Joyce Milton's *Tramp: The Life of Charlie Chaplin*]

"Poems." *Exquisite Corpse* 58 (July 1996): 35. [P: Gertrude on Top; Chapultepec Crunch; Everything Smells Like Something Else]

"Myself and My Brothers." *San Diego Reader*, 3 October 1996, 24–26, 28, 30, 32, 34, 36, 38. [E: on his writing brothers; recycles some material from "The Detours of Art" (1991)]

"Blood Feud." *Boston Magazine*, October 1996, 130–36. [BR: Paul Theroux's *My Other Life*; includes first appearance of AT's poem "Paul Nosedocks" (134). The review is quoted at length in Paul's novel *Mother Land* (Houghton Mifflin, 2017), 154–56]

"Evocative Absences." *Modern Literature Collection* [Washington University, St. Louis] 2.1 (Fall 1996): 6. [Contribution to forum on lost works]

"Mendicancy Chic." *Boston Mercury* 3.1 (February 1997): 8–9. [E: against fund drives]

"A Wanderer in the Wasteland." *San Diego Reader*, 13 February 1997, 1, 16–18, 20, 22, 24, 26, 28, 30, 32. [E: on the Californian desert]

"Desert Hermits" and "The Ames Bros." *Yale Review* 85.2 (April 1997): 108, 109. [P]

[BR of Jonathan Cott's *A Journey into the Number 13*.] *Los Angeles Times*

Book Review, 13 April 1997, F.

"Ceylon's Isle" and "African Reflections." *Denver Quarterly* 31.3 (Winter 1997): 73, 74. [P]

"Garbo's Voice" and "Meadow Glen Drive-In." *Michigan Quarterly Review* 36.2 (Spring 1997): 267, 268–69. [P]

"Rev. Elks in His Midden." *Urbanus*, Summer 1997, 45. [P]

"Shattered." *Los Angeles Times Book Review*, 27 July 1997, 6. [BR: Gary Indiana's *Resentment*]

"Taking Stock." *Los Angeles Times Book Review*, 3 August 1997, 9. [BR: John Ashbery's *The Mooring of Starting Out*]

"A Moral Responsibility?" *Los Angeles Times Book Review*, 24 August 1997, 10. [Letters to the editor from Ashbery and AT on previous review]

[BR of David Gelertner's *Drawing Life: Surviving the Unabomber.*] *Boston Mercury*, November 1997.

"Odd Collections." *Yale Review* 86.1 (January 1998): 1–12. [E] Rpt. in B18.

"When Vilma Banky Married Rod LaRoque." *Antioch Review* 56.1 (Winter 1998): 47. [P]

"Shiloh" and "Italian Girl." *Poetry* 171.4 (February 1998): 264, 265. [P]

"Punk with a Red Mohawk" and "Kiowa Buffalo." *Edge City Review* 8 (February 1998): 9. [P]

"The Restless Realist." *Wall Street Journal*, 6 February 1998, A13. [BR: Linda Davis's *Badge of Courage: The Life of Stephen Crane*]

"Black." *Conjunctions* 30 (Spring 1998): 115–26. [E] Rpt. in B17.

"Dropping Fleas into a Glass of Water" and "To Mickey Hood Who Travels the World and Visits Monasteries on His Motorcycle." *Gargoyle* 41 (June 1998): 173, 174–75. [P]

[BR of Guy Davenport's *Twelve Stories.*] *Review of Contemporary Fiction* 18.2 (Summer 1998): 224–25.

"Plaid." *Yale Review* 86.3 (July 1998): 33–48. [E]

"Imagine Black," "Ped Xing," and "Culver City, 1930." *Paris Review* 147 (Summer 1998): 186–88. [P]

"Sex and Blackness." *Seneca Review* 27.2 (Fall 1998): 65–76. [E: from *Black*]

"Weighing Words' Worth." *Wall Street Journal*, 27 November 1998. [BR: Reynolds Price's *Learning a Trade*, Anne Fadiman's *Ex Libris*, Anna Quindlen's *How Reading Changed My Life*, and Frederick Busch's *A Dangerous Profession*]

"Bumps in the Night." *Wall Street Journal*, 4 December 1998, W17. [E: on radio host Art Bell]

"Everything Smells Like Something Else." *Image: A Journal of the Arts & Religion* 21 (Fall 1998): 93–94. [P]

"The Many and the One." *Prairie Schooner* 72.4 (Winter 1998): 183. [P; rpt. from *Cups* (1994)]

"The Olympic Sham." *Wall Street Journal*, 13 January 1999, A22. [E]

"A Daring Plunge into Oceans of Verse." *Wall Street Journal*, 2 April 1999, W6. [BR: Edward Hirsch's *How to Read a Poem* and several current books of poetry]

"Cape Cod's World of Summer Delights." *Los Angeles Times Magazine*, 25 April 1999, 42–44, 60–61. [E: drastically edited from AT's original]

"The Real Menace." *Wall Street Journal*, 14 May 1999, W15. [E: on the *Star Wars* phenomenon]

"The Real Menace." *The Responsive Community: Rights and Responsibilities* 9.3 (Summer 1999): 82–85. [E; rpt. of previous entry]

[BR of Guy Davenport's *Objects on a Table*.] *Review of Contemporary Fiction* 19.2 (Summer 1999): 126.

[BR of *Patti Smith Complete: Lyrics, Reflections & Notes for the Future*.] *Review of Contemporary Fiction* 19.2 (Summer 1999): 129–30.

"Readings from the Library of His Mind." *Wall Street Journal*, 17 August 1999, A18, A20. [BR: Jorge Luis Borges' *Selected Non-fictions*]

"Mother Cochin." *Anomaly* 4 (1999): 8. [P]

"Tolstoy Need Not Apply." *Wall Street Journal*, 22 October 1999, W1. [E: on creative writing programs]

"James Joyce: A Reverie and a Reverdie." *The Recorder: The Journal of the American Irish Historical Society* 12.2 (Fall 1999): 31–35. [E]

"Helen Silencieux." *Fence* (Fall/Winter 1999–2000): 18. [P]

"Laura Warholic." *Conjunctions* 34 (June 2000): 107–19. [F: first appearance of a selection from A17]

"Krackles for a Girl." *Prairie Schooner* 74.3 (Fall 2000): 156. [P]

"Edward Gorey, 1925–2000." *The Recorder: The Journal of the American Irish Historical Society* 13.2 (Fall 2000): 32–38. [E: abridged version of A16]

"Three Poems." *The Recorder* 13.2 (Fall 2000): 39–42. [On a Photograph of Mia Farrow in a Stone Garden; I See Only the Roses of Shadows; The Dreadful Reality of Being Oneself Eventually Becomes a Comfort]

"Five Poems" [Polonnaruwa; Why Mow?; Jack and His Jungle Jacket; Tulips in Green Paper; Sipapu]. *Cahiers Charles V* 29 (December 2000): 54–58. [A special issue entitled "États-Unis: Formes récentes de l'imagination littéraire," guest-edited by Marc Chénetier, who provides a note on AT (p. 53).]

"When Vilma Banky Married Rod LaRoque." *Antioch Review* 59.2 (Spring 2001): 383–84. [Rpt. from Winter 1998 issue for this Anniversary Issue of *Antioch Review*]

"Queen Gloriana's Revenge." *Conjunctions* 36 (June 2001): 221–25. [F: a fable later included in A17]

[BR of *Pynchon and "Mason & Dixon,"* ed. Horvath and Malin.] *Review of Contemporary Fiction* 21.2 (Summer 2001): 176.

[BR of Carter's *Marcel Proust.*] *Review of Contemporary Fiction* 21.2 (Summer 2001): 177–78.

"Nantucket from the Air." *Nantucket Magazine*, Summer 2001, 119. [P]

"Camp Cedar Crest." *Conjunctions* 37 (Fall 2001): 374–80. [E: memoir on summer camp]

"Thelma Ritter." *Michigan Quarterly Review* 41.1 (Winter 2002): 59–60. [P]

"A Quaker on Nantucket Visits a Store in 1859." *Yale Review* 90.4 (October 2002): 82–83. [P]

"Black-and-White or Color, Does It Really Matter?" *Newsday*, 20 October 2002, A–34. [E on Dürer's *St. Jerome in His Study*]

"Louise Brooks and Greta Garbo Spend a Night Together." *Gobshite Quarterly* 1 (February 2003): 74. [P; AT listed on masthead as member of Advisory Board]

"Mutrux's Confession; or, He Who Gets Slapped." *Gargoyle* 47 (September 2003): 258–76. [F: from A17]

"Louise Brooks and Greta Garbo Spend a Night Together." *Gobshite Quarterly* 4/5 (Nov. 2003/Feb. 2004): 49. [Corrected version of earlier publication]

"Chico Marx Floruit." *Italian Americana* (Winter 2004): 45. [E on Italian-American stereotypes]

"Chris Ware: Portrait of the Artist as Thinker." *Comics Journal* 4, Special Edition (Winter 2004): 63–66. [E; on the graphic novelist]

"Two Poems" [Winged Monkeys; Franchot Tone]. *Conjunctions* 42 (May 2004): 44–46.

"In Tunis I Walked Through Halfaween." *Italian Americana* (Summer 2004): 165. [P]

"Ben Katchor." *BOMB* 88 (Summer 2004): 30–35. [Interview with the graphic artist]

"Norma Shearer" / "Sunlight, Shadowlight" / "A Poule at Pavillon." *BOMB* 91 (Spring 2005): 88–89. [P]

"The Maroon of My Copper Beech" / "Chocolate Hills" / "Sarah Son Painting at Scorton Creek." *Provincetown Arts* 20 (Summer 2005): 136–37. [P]

[BR of Sue Grafton's *S Is for Silence.*] *Wall Street Journal*, 3–4 December 2005, 15.

"Thai Silk." *Poetry* 187.4 (January 2006): 296. [P]

"Fantastic Journey." *Wall Street Journal*, 24 November 2006. [BR of

Thomas Pynchon's *Against the Day.*]

"In Defense of the Non Non-Fat Diet." *Wall Street Journal*, 20–21 January 2007. [BR of Barry Glassner's *Gospel of Food.*]

"Jugaya's Dream." *Italian Americana* (Summer 2007): 180. [P]

"Apocalypse." *Green Mountains Review* 20.1–2 (2007): 127. [P]

"A Man Who Knew Everyone." *Wall Street Journal*, 4 October 2008. [BR of *The Selected Letters of Thornton Wilder*]

"Inventing Vidia." *Boston Globe*, 23 November 2008. [BR of Patrick French's *The World Is What It Is: The Authorized Biography of V. S. Naipaul*]

"On the Cape, Vows Rewritten." *Boston Globe*, 25 January 2009. [BR of Reuel K. Wilson's *To the Life of the Silver Harbor: Edmund Wilson and Mary McCarthy on Cape Cod*]

"A More Literary Amour." *Wall Street Journal*, 13 February 2009, A11. [BR of Diana Secker Tesdell's *Love Stories* and Charlotte Higgins's *Latin Love Lessons.*]

"Sipapu" and "A Woman Who Wore Panties the Color of a Glacier." *Foto8: The Photography Biannual*, no. 28 (Spring 2009): 89. [P]

"Bad Memories, Hard Feelings." *Wall Street Journal*, 25 April 2009, W9. [BR of Joe Queenan's *Closing Time*]

"The Master Takes a Tour." *Wall Street Journal*, 28 May 2009, A13. [BR of *The Complete Letters of Henry James, Vol. 1*]

[BR of Anne Conover Heller's Ayn Rand biography in *Boston Globe*, untraced, possibly unpublished]

"Urban Ardor, Urban Angst." *Wall Street Journal*, 14 October 2009, A21. [BR of Jonathan Lethem's *Chronic City*]

"India's Melting Pot of Paradoxes." *Boston Globe*, 20 October, 2009. [BR of Aravind Adiga's *Between the Assassinations*]

"In the Cards, a Last Hand." *Wall Street Journal*, 20 November 2009, W15. [BR of Vladimir Nabokov's *The Original of Laura*]

"A Nasty Way with Words." *Wall Street Journal*, 27 November 2009, W242. [BR of *Poisoned Pens*, ed. Gary Dexter]

"The Misfit and Her Muses." *Wall Street Journal*, 7 December 2009. [BR of Joan Schenkar's *The Talented Miss Highsmith*]

"Painted into a Corner." *Wall Street Journal*, 14 January 2010, A17. [BR of Elizabeth Kostova's *The Swan Thieves*]

"Back from the Beyond." *Wall Street Journal*, 15 May 2010. [BR of James L. Haley's *Wolf: The Lives of Jack London*]

"Zero Progress." *Wall Street Journal*, 17 June 2010, A19. [BR of Bret Easton Ellis's *Imperial Bedrooms*]

"On the Surly Bonds of Marriage." *Wall Street Journal*, 26 June 2010. [BR of Adam Ross's *Mr. Peanut*]

"Down and Out in Gotham." *Wall Street Journal*, 29 July 2010, A11. [BR of Gary Shteyngart's *Super Sad True Love Story*]

"The Fear of a Failure to Communicate." *Wall Street Journal*, 10 September 2010, W4. [BR of Tom McCarthy's *C*]

"Intellectual Intrigue in Mexico City." *Wall Street Journal*, 8 January 2011, C7. [BR of Carlos Fuentes's *Destiny and Desire*]

"The Trouble with Ardor." *Wall Street Journal*, 4 May 2011, A15. [BR of Lila Azam Zanganeh's *The Enchanter: Nabokov and Happiness*]

"And Then Came Savagery." *Wall Street Journal*, 15 October 2011. [BR of Ha Jin's *Nanjing Requiem*]

"Still Searching." *Wall Street Journal*, 24 March 2012. [BR of Louis Begley's *Schmidt Steps Back*]

"A Victim, or a Villain?" *Wall Street Journal*, 22 August 2012. [BR of John Follain's *A Death in Italy: The Definitive Account of the Amanda Knox Case*]

[Untitled essay on semicolons.] *Apology* 1 (Winter [February] 2013): 129–33.

"Take a Song, and Make It Better." *Wall Street Journal*, 21 November 2014. [BR of Hunter Davies's *The Beatles Lyrics*]

"Godfather Drosselmeier's Tears." *Conjunctions* Online, 13 August 2019, http://www.conjunctions.com/online/article/alexander-theroux-08-13-2019-2 [P: expanded version of poem in A20, in commemoration of Theroux's eightieth birthday]

[Eight poems on Henry David Thoreau.] *The Rupture* 109 (June 2020), www.therupturemagazine.com.

D. TRANSLATIONS

三原色: 藍黃紅. Trans. Leng Bumei. Taiwan: Linking Publishing Co., 1997. [Trans. of *The Primary Colors*]

Blau: Anleitungen eine Farbe zu lesen. Trans. Michael Bischoff. Hamburg: Europäische Verlagsanstalt, 1998. [Trans. of "Blue" from A13.]

Gelb: Anleitungen eine Farbe zu lesen. Trans. Michael Bischoff. Hamburg: Europäische Verlagsanstalt, 1998. [Trans. of "Yellow" from A13.]

Rot: Anleitungen eine Farbe zu lesen. Trans. Michael Bischoff. Hamburg: Europäische Verlagsanstalt, 1998. [Trans. of "Red" from A13.]

Orange: Anleitungen eine Farbe zu lesen. Trans. Sebastian Wohlfeil. Hamburg: Europäische Verlagsanstalt, 1999. [Trans. of "Orange" from A14.]

Purpurn: Anleitungen eine Farbe zu lesen. Trans. Sebastian Wohlfeil. Hamburg: Europäische Verlagsanstalt, 2000. [Trans. of "Purple" from A14.]

Grün: Anleitungen eine Farbe zu lesen. Trans. Michael Schmidt. Hamburg: Europäische Verlagsanstalt, 2000. [Trans. of "Green" from A14.]

Trois métèques: Contes drolatiques du racisme ordinaire. Trans. Marc Chénetier. Paris: Éditions Phébus, 2002. [Trans. of A1]

Los Colores primarios: tres ensayos. Trans. Ariel Dilon. La Bestia Equilátera, 2013. [Trans. of A13]

Los Colores secundarios. Trans. Ariel Dilon. La Bestia Equilátera, 2015. [Trans. of A14]

E. INTERVIEWS

Carroll, Sean P. "An Interview with Alexander Theroux." *Bookslut*, March 2008, http://www.bookslut.com/features/2008_03_012503.php.

Filbin, Thomas. "Pilgrim of the Absolute: An Interview with Alexander Theroux." In *The VP Annual 2016*. Edited by G. N. Forester and M. J. Nicholls. Singapore: Verbivoracious Press, 2016, 144–48.

Laurence, Alexander. "An Interview with Alexander Theroux." *Cups: A Café Journal*, February 1995, 16–17, http://portable-infinite.blogspot.com/2014/05/alexander-theroux-interview.html

Madera, John. "*Bookforum* Talks to Alexander Theroux." *Bookforum*, 23 December 2011, https://www.bookforum.com/interviews/-8796

Maliszewski, Paul. "The Back of Beyond: An Interview with Alexander Theroux," *Rain Taxi* Online Edition, Winter 2012/2013, https://www.raintaxi.com/the-back-of-beyond/

Marshall, Colin. "Committing Savage Satire, Respecting Readers and Finding the Odd in Sex: Colin Marshall Talks to Alexander Theroux, Author of *Laura Warholic: or, The Sexual Intellectual*." *3 Quarks Daily*, 24 May 2010, https://www.3quarksdaily.com/3quarksdaily/2010/05/committing-savage-satire-respecting-readers-and-finding-the-odd-in-sex-colin-marshall-talks-to-alexa.html

Moore, Steven. "An Interview with Alexander Theroux." *Review of Contemporary Fiction* 11.1 (Spring 1991): 29–35. Rpt. above, 217–24.

Silverblatt, Michael. *Bookworm*, 21 September 1992, https://www.kcrw.com/culture/shows/bookworm/alexander-theroux

Spurgeon, Tom. "CR Interview: Alexander Theroux on Edward Gorey," *Comics Reporter*, 22 February 2011, http://www.comicsreporter.com/index.php/cr_interview_alexander_theroux_on_edward_gorey/

Index

academic novel genre, 50n21
Acker, Kathy, 149, 154, 162
Adam and Eve, 24, 30, 45n13
Adams, Ansel, 149n33
Adiga, Aravind, 149
adultery in fiction, 31–35, 52–53, 146, 160
Agnew, Spiro, 214
Alexandrianism, 29
Allen, Woody, 109
Allik, William, 66
Anasi, Robert, 63
anatomy genre, 26, 220
Andreas Capellanus, 152
Angelou, Maya, 165
Aniston, Jennifer, 175
Anstey, F., 20
anti-Semitism, 76, 108, 118, 119, 120, 146
Arabian Nights, The, 223
Art & Antiques, 31, 60, 169–70, 211
Ashbery, John, 105, 149, 155, 156
Athanasian Creed, 224
Atkins, Dale, 59, 115n20
Atlas, James, 35, 37 40n4, 41, 43, 47, 148, 182, 183
Aubrey, John, 137, 180, 226
Auden, W. H., 118
Austen, Jane, 74, 151, 211n51, 214, 230

Bacon, Francis, 43n10, 66
Baker, Nicholson, 10, 144, 149, 161
Baldwin, James, 132
Balzac, Honoré de, 120

Barber, Lynn, 192n32
Barbey d'Aurevilly, Jules, 45
Barnard, Megan, 8n1
Barnes, Djuna, 10, 14, 35, 38, 45, 136n11, 223
Barnes, Julian, 149, 160–61
Barth, John, 10, 14, 39, 47, 133, 149, 154–55, 167, 190
Barthelme, Donald, 10, 178
Barthelme, Frederick, 178
Barthes, Roland, 27–28, 30, 133
Battestin, Martin, 13, 133n2, 147, 225
Baudelaire, Charles, 45, 118, 192
Beahrs, Andrew, 101
Beatles, the, 149n33, 168
Beats, 105, 114
Becanus, Johannes Goropius, 30
Beckett, Samuel, 38, 132–34, 137, 138n16, 143, 179, 180, 209, 225
Begley, Louis, 149
Bellow, Saul, 14
Beowulf, 39, 137
Berger, John, 214
Berlin, Irving, 110
Berryman, John, 105n5
Best American Poetry 2018, 108, 110, 114
Bible, 16, 114, 118, 159, 174
bigotry. See prejudice
Blake, William, 107, 219
Blanchot, Maurice, 162
Bloom, Harold, 149, 165
Blount, Thomas, 19n10
Boas, Franz, 161

Borges, Jorge Luis, 149, 155–56, 180, 190, 226
Bosch, Hieronymus, 81
Boston Globe, 31, 142, 149
Boston Magazine, 149, 151, 155, 189, 191–92
Botticelli, Sandro, 152
Bourdain, Anthony, 120
Bowles, Paul, 149
Brackenridge, Hugh Henry, 38
Bradham, Jo Allen, 28n22, 50
Braverman, Kate, 136n11
Breughel, Pieter, 118
Brokeback Mountain (film), 78
Brontë sisters, 178
Brooke-Rose, Christine, 136n11
Brophy, Brigid, 136n11
Brown, Frederick, 78
Browne, Thomas, 112
Browning, Robert, 17–18, 20–22, 144, 188
Buchan, John, 175n10
Bucher, Matt, 8n1
Buckingham, George Villiers, Duke of, 46, 47
Budgen, Frank, 143
Bukowski, Charles, 120
Bulger, William, 149n33
Burgess, Anthony, 28, 38, 79, 136, 149, 154, 221
Burstein, Mark, 78–79
Burton, Gabrielle, 136n11
Burton, Linda Ann, 43n10, 59, 138, 228–29
Burton, Robert, 26, 27n18, 38, 49, 81, 118, 135, 180, 220–21, 225–26
Bush, George H. W., 176
Bush, George W., 78, 212
Butler, Samuel, 30n24
Byron, George Gordon, Lord, 32

Cabell, James Branch, 38
Caesar, Julius, 70
Capp, Al, 8, 10
Carlyle, Thomas, 38
Carrigan, Henry L., Jr., 80
Carroll, James, 149
Carroll, Lewis, 38, 158

Carroll, Sean P., 65n22
Carter, William, 141n19
Catullus, Gaius Valerius, 26
Céline, Louis-Ferdinand, 55
Cellini, Benvenuto, 110
Cervantes, Miguel de, 38, 57, 118, 137, 151, 221
Chandler, Raymond, 120
Chaplin, Charles, 121, 149n33
Chekhov, Anton, 193, 210
Chekhov, Nikolai, 193, 210
Cheney, Dick and Lynne, 78
Chesterton, G. K., 224
Chicago Tribune, 80n41, 149, 154
Chopin, Frédéric, 107
Cibber, Colley, 104
Cicero, Marcus Tullius, 137
Cloud, Maurice, 113
Coale, Samuel, 191
Coleridge, Samuel Taylor, 107n7
Conjunctions, 9, 64n17, 67, 98–99, 100, 119n24, 166, 173
Conolly, Jeff, 62, 84
Conrad, Joseph, 151, 188
Contemporary Literature, 9
Cooper, Jane Roberta, 151
Coover, Robert, 10
Copleston, Frederick, 164
Cornford, Frances Crofts, 16n5
Corot, Jean-Baptiste-Camille, 120
Corrado, Angelo, 179
Cortázar, Julio, 211n51
Corvo, Baron. *See* Rolfe, Frederick
Cosby, Bill, 174
Coulton, G. G., 98
Crane, Hart, 161
Crane, Stephen, 149
creative-writing programs, 143–44
Crichton, Michael, 165
Crosby, Harry, 149
Crumb, R., 121
Cups, 60, 61n9, 83

Dahlberg, Edward, 27, 49n19, 181n10
Dalkey Archive Press, 7, 8–9, 69, 97, 98, 104n3, 111, 144, 154
Dante Alighieri, 214; in Theroux's poetry, 125

d'Arch Smith, Timothy, 154n42
Davenport, Guy, 10, 39, 149, 164–65, 180
Davidson, Gustave, 43
Davies, Hunter, 168
Davies, Robertson, 106
decadence, 29
Demosthenes, 40
DeMott, Benjamin, 221
Denver Quarterly, 9
Dershowitz, Alan, 109
Dery, Mark, 68n28
Desani, G. V., 20
DeWitt, Helen, 136n11
Dexter, Gary, 167
Dickens, Charles, 110, 137, 158, 179, 204, 205n44, 230
Dickey, James, 95
Dickinson, Emily, 104, 107
Dirda, Michael, 161n51
Disch, Tom, 171n4
Dixon, Richard Watson, 98
Dolger, Jonathan, 36
Dostoevsky, Fyodor, 137, 149, 151
Doyle, Arthur Conan, 149, 196, 198
Driggs, Ilse, 71, 76n37
Ducornet, Rikki, 136n11
Durant, Will, 164
Durrell, Gerald, 193, 210
Durrell, Lawrence, 38, 193, 210
Dushku, Eliza, 120n26
Dylan, Bob, 166n57

Earhart, Amelia, 60, 171, 229
Ebo von Michelsberg, 40
Eichman, Erich, 150n34
Einstein, Albert, 174
Eliot, T. S., 114, 149, 158
Elizabeth I, 43–44
Elkin, Stanley, 10, 49n20
Ellis, Bret Easton, 167
Ellison, Ralph, 230
Emerson, Ralph Waldo, 50n21, 122
encyclopedic fiction, 25, 57, 63, 70, 76, 158, 163, 168, 180, 221, 225–29. *See also* learned wit
Endrigkeit, Sam, 27n18, 29n22
Engel, Monroe, 11

Erasmus, Desiderius, 38
Esquire, 94, 95, 228, 230n6
Essex, Robert Devereux, Earl of, 44
Evelyn, John, 175n10
Exley, Frederick, 7
experimental fiction, 133, 162, 165, 175

Fairbanks, Lauren, 154n42
Faliero, Marino, 32
Fantagraphics Books, 68–72, 93, 123, 212
Faulkner, William, 149, 151, 165, 174, 210
Fellini, Federico, 149n33, 162
Fielding, Henry, 122, 180, 199
Filbin, Thomas, 35
Firbank, Ronald, 10, 14, 22–23, 35, 161, 179, 218
Fisher, M. F. K., 149n33
Flaubert, Gustave, 31, 40, 78, 224, 230
Fonda, Peter, 134n7
Ford, Ford Madox, 144–46, 160
Fowles, John, 149
French, Patrick, 166
Freud, Sigmund, 224
Friedwald, Will, 173
Froud, Brian, 97, 98
Fuentes, Carlos, 149, 168

Gaarder, Jostein, 149, 164
Gaddis, William, 10, 29, 38–39, 41, 57, 138n14
Garbo, Greta, 212
García Márquez, Gabriel, 149, 164
Gargoyle, 67
Garland, Judy, 214
Gass, William H., 10, 24, 171
Gauer, Jim, 93, 120
Genet, Jean, 118
Gerke, Greg, 212–13
Gilman, Greer, 136n11
Gilson, Etienne, 214
Ginsberg, Allen, 105, 118, 143n23, 149
Glassner, Barry, 149n33
Godine (David R. Godine, Publisher), 97, 134
Goethe, Johann Wolfgang von, 32, 56, 122

Goncourt brothers, 178
Gorey, Edward, 8, 68n28, 97, 111, 119n24, 170
Gosse, Edmund, 35
Gould, Eric, 9
Grafton, Sue, 149
Grass, Günter, 132
Grayson, Richard, 102
Greene, Gael, 174
Grimes, Tom, 143
Grisham, John, 165
Groth, Gary, 68–69, 79, 93–94, 121
Guggenheim Foundation, 92, 225
Gürsel, Nedim, 230

Hagee, John, 95
Halpern, Daniel, 96
Handel, George Frideric, 56
Hardy, Thomas, 146
Harry Ransom Center, 8, 97, 98
Hartley, L. P., 165
Harvard University, 14, 144, 182, 186–87, 220, 223, 228
Hatch, Robert, 118
Hawthorne, Nathaniel, 26
Heller, Steven, 98
Hemingway, Ernest, 151, 167, 210–11
Henry Holt and Company, 28n21, 172, 188
Hepburn, Audrey, 158
Higgins, Jack, 149
Highsmith, Patricia, 149
Hill, Susan, 160
Hills, Rust, 162n52
Hoffmann, E. T. A., 32, 119
Homer, 39, 137
homophobia, 76
Hopkins, Gerard Manley, 106, 163
Horace, 19
Houghton Mifflin, 180n5, 181
Housman, A. E., 114
Howard, Gerald, 67
Hustvedt, Siri, 149
Huysmans, Joris-Karl, 45

Ilves, Toomas Hendrik, 213
Indiana, Gary, 149
intertextuality, 154–55

invective, 29, 81, 107, 167; Poe on, 202
Iowa Writers' Workshop, 143–44
Irving, Washington, 38, 43

Jackson, Melanie, 67, 156
James, Henry, 14, 31, 149, 151, 193, 210–11, 223
James, William, 193, 210
Jefferson, D. W., 38, 48, 49–50
Jesus, 75, 109, 120; in Theroux's poetry, 127
Johnson, Diane, 40n3, 135
Johnson, Lionel, 23n13
Johnson, Samuel, 45n14
Joyce, James, 10, 36, 38, 81, 118, 136–37, 138, 143, 144, 145, 148, 158, 180, 193, 209, 226; *Finnegans Wake*, 42, 159, 210; *A Portrait of the Artist as a Young Man*, 43, 112, 217; *Ulysses*, 40, 136
Joyce, Stanislaus, 193, 210
Judd, Alan, 144–45
Juvenal, 45, 107, 137

Kafka, Franz, 120, 230
Katchor, Ben, 176
Keaton, Buster, 121
Keats, John, 43, 47, 104, 189, 224
Keightley, Thomas, 96
Kenner, Hugh, 105, 180
Kerouac, Jack, 66, 190
King, Stephen, 211n51
Kirk, Russ, 78
Knowles, John, 165
Knox, Amanda, 149n33
Kostava, Elizabeth, 149
Krantz, Judith, 190
Krauthammer, Charles, 66
Kuchar, Mike, 62n12
Kuehl, John, 29n22
Kundera, Milan, 149, 160

Lamb, Charles, 24n15
Lannan Foundation, 8–9
Larkin, Philip, 104
Laurel and Hardy, 144
Laurence, Alexander, 9, 60–65, 193
Lawrence, D. H., 10

Lear, Edward, 47
learned wit (and learned novel
    genre), 23, 29, 38–51, 76, 142, 180,
    221, 225–29
LeClair, Tom, 75
Lee, Karen An-hwei, 136n11
Lee, Michael, 80
Lee, Peggy, 195n36
Leonardo da Vinci, 149n33
Lethem, Jonathan, 149, 167
Lewis, Merriwether, 149n33
Lieberman, Joseph, 175
Lish, Gordon, 36, 94, 228–29, 230
London, Jack, 149
Los Angeles Times Book Review, 105,
    149–50, 155
Lovejoy, Bess, 230
Lucian, 38
Luke, Peter, 147
Lyly, John, 134n5
Lyres, the, 62, 84

Macdonald, Marianne, 192
Mailer, Norman, 10, 175, 190
Maliszewski, Paul, 67, 156, 173
Mann, Heinrich, 178, 193, 210
Mann Thomas, 43n9, 178, 193,
    205n44, 210
Mano, D. Keith, , 16
Markley, Laura, 59–65, 73, 77, 82–83,
    115–16, 154, 185–86
Markson, David, 13n1, 39, 108n8,
    162n52
Marlowe, Christopher, 136n10, 154
Marryat, Frederick, 145
Marshall, Colin, 29n22
Marston, John, 27
Martial, 14n3
Maso, Carole, 136n11
Mathews, Harry, 10, 39
maximalism, 29, 57, 75, 134–38, 140,
    147, 214
May, John, 169, 170
McCaffery, Larry, 29n22, 63
McCarthy, Tom, 149, 167–68
McCourt, James, 149, 161
McElroy, Joseph, 10
Mead, Clifford S., 7

Melville, Herman, 38, 63n15, 81, 171,
    179, 188, 223
Menippean satire, 76
Messalina, 28
Michelangelo, 79
Mickey and Sylvia, 76
Middleton, Thomas, 48n18, 104
Miernik, Mirosław Aleksander,
    147n28
Miller, Anthony, 69
Milton, John, 30, 39, 43, 104, 137, 224
minimalism, 29, 145
misandry, 151
misanthropy, 76, 118, 146, 213
misogyny, 23, 28, 45, 49–50, 76, 78,
    146, 152, 183, 220, 229
MIT (Massachusetts Institute of
    Technology), 14, 144, 220, 223
Mitchner, Stuart, 80n41
Monroe, Marilyn, 10, 73, 75
Montaigne, Michel de, 135, 180, 225
Morgan, Dennis, 157
Morrow, Bradford, 67, 149, 165–66.
    See also Conjunctions
Moulin, Pierre du, 49
Mozart, Wolfgang Amadeus, 55
Murchie, Guy, 171
Murphy, John L., 173n8
Murtagh, Dan, 185, 186n21
Musil, Robert, 230

Nabokov, Dmitri, 150
Nabokov, Véra, 151
Nabokov, Vladimir, 10, 39, 144, 149,
    156, 158, 177, 190; *Ada*, 150, 156;
    Lolita, 17n7, 150; *Look at the
    Harlequins!*, 154; *The Original of
    Laura*, 59, 150, 230; *Pale Fire*, 150;
    A Russian Beauty, 150
Naipaul, Shiva, 192–93, 210
Naipaul, V. S., 149, 166–67, 188,
    192–93, 195–96, 210
National Review, 149–50, 160
Nero, 223
Nesbit, Evelyn, 79
Newman, Frances, 136n11
New York Times, 28, 171–72, 183
Night Porter, The (film), 72

Nijinsky, Vaslav, 160
Nixon, Richard M., 120
Nokes, George Augustus, 95
Noor Al-Hussein, 77
Nureyev, Rudolph, 176

Obama, Barack and Michelle, 174
obscurantism, 105–6, 156, 158–59, 165
Oloixarac, Pola, 136n11
Olson, Charles, 105
Ossian (James Macpherson), 122
Otter (Laura Campbell), 62, 84

Paglia, Camille, 115, 152–54
paradox, 224; in *An Adultery*, 31
Pastoreau, Michel, 171n3
Pater, Walter, 222
Pavić, Milorad, 149, 161–62
Pavlov, Ivan, 157
Peacher, Georgiana, 136n11
Peacock, Allen, 71n33, 172
Peacock, Thomas Love, 147
Peale, Norman Vincent, 219
Petronius, Gaius, 38
Phillips Academy, 120
Pietsch, Michael, 67
Pigge, Albert, 40
Pinker, Michael, 29n22, 34
Plain, Belva, 190
Poe, Edgar Allan, 34, 107, 118, 155, 202
Pope, Alexander, 38, 104, 116, 122, 133, 137, 180; *The Dunciad*, 81, 133n2, 142
Portis, Charles, 230
postmodernism, 49n20, 57, 80, 168
Pound, Ezra, 105, 114
Poussaint, Alvin, 141–42, 142n21
Powell, Padget, 149
prejudice (bigotry, racism), 76, 109, 142; in *Three Wogs*, 14–23, 164
Proust, Marcel, 26, 31, 34, 42–43, 46, 52, 73, 137, 138–41, 143, 145, 149, 151, 201, 214, 225
Publishers Weekly, 13, 36–37
Puccini, Giacomo, 101, 224
Pynchon, Thomas, 10, 39, 41, 138, 149, 156–59, 167, 211n51; *Against the Day*, 158–59; *Gravity's Rainbow*,
14, 29, 57, 67n27, 156–59; *Mason & Dixon*, 156; *V.*, 158, 213

Quarles, Francis, 24, 45n13
Quelvée, François, 54
Queneau, Raymond, 162
Quinn, Paul, 80
Quintilian, 30

Rabelais, François, 26, 36, 38, 39, 81, 118, 135, 137, 180, 221, 226
racism. *See* prejudice
Rand, Ayn, 149
Rasputin, Grigori, 174
Reagan, Nancy, 197
Reid, Calvin, 69
Rembrandt van Rijn, 224
revenge theme, 6, 41–42, 45, 59n2, 101, 137–38, 140, 153, 185, 220
Review of Contemporary Fiction, 132, 142, 145, 149, 153, 156, 160n49; Theroux/West issue of, 7–9, 13n2, 69, 141, 173
Rice, Anne, 149
Rice, Condoleezza, 77
Rich, Adrienne, 151–52, 154
Richmond, Peter, 195
Richter, Jean Paul, 145
Rilke, Rainer Maria, 111
Robbins, Tom, 174
Robinson, Edwin Arlington, 114, 168
Rohmer, Sax, 14–15
Rolfe, Frederick, 10, 14, 29, 35, 38, 40, 43n9, 137, 143, 146–48, 167, 179, 180, 225; *The Desire and Pursuit of the Whole*, 14, 147n27; "Dux Amor," 31n26; *Hadrian the Seventh*, 146–47; *Nicholas Crabbe*, 14n3, 147n27; *The Weird of the Wanderer*, 147n27
Ross, Adam, 149
Rovit, Earl, 161
Rubin, Martin, 213
Runyon, Damon, 176
Ruskin, John, 140
Russell, Ray, 102

Sade, Marquis de, 45, 230

Saki (H. H. Munro), 137
Saltus, Edgar, 10, 38
San Diego Reader, 60, 61n9, 63, 172, 173, 187–89, 212
Sanger, Margaret, 80
Sapienza, Marie, 120
Sarduy, Severo, 27
Scaramelli, Richard, 7, 32n28
Schiele, Egon, 116
Schmidt, Arno, 162
scholasticism, 29, 49, 225
Scoppa, Patricia, 31, 96, 98
Self, Will, 149, 166
Selzer, Richard, 149n33
September 11 attacks, 78, 115
Seuss, Dr., 110, 158
Shakespeare, William, 27, 39, 46, 81, 104, 114, 134n5, 136n10, 137–38, 144, 175, 184, 210
Shteyngart, Gary, 149
Simmons, Richard, 108
Simon & Schuster, 53, 72n33, 92
Sinatra, Frank, 149n33, 173, 195
Sitwell family, 178
Smart, Elizabeth, 136n11
Smith, Patti, 149n33, 166
Smith, Zadie, 136n11
Socrates, 47
Sollers, Philippe, 149
Son of Sam (David Berkowitz), 100
Son-Theroux, Sarah, 70n32, 100, 114, 118, 166n57, 212, 213, 230
Sorrentino, Gilbert, 10, 14, 39, 49n20, 162n52
Southey, Robert, 30n23
Spackman, W. M., 34
Squishy (Sarah Davison), 62, 84
Stein, Gertrude, 105
Stendhal, 65
Stern, Richard, 80n41
Sterne, Laurence, 10, 30n23, 38, 39, 47, 51, 57, 81, 118, 137, 144, 158, 221, 225, 230
Stevens, Wallace, 56, 104, 106, 112, 114n17, 217, 223
Strachey, Lytton, 23, 44
Straus, Roger, Jr., 36
Streitfeld, David, 172, 192

Strugatsky, Arkady and Boris, 178
Stuttaford, Andrew, 212
Sullivan, Jim, 204
Swift, Jonathan, 36, 38, 39, 46, 104, 158, 178
Symeon Metaphrastes, 135

Tabor, Mary B. W., 171n4
Teasdale, Sarah, 114
Tertullian, 49
Theroux, Albert E., 181, 187n24, 206, 222–23
Theroux, Alexander: early life of, 101, 141, 175n10, 179–82, 187–88, 217–18, 223; plagiary charges against, 71n33, 171–72; pronunciation of surname, 220; racism and, 108, 141–42; religion and, 40, 41, 118, 120, 217; scholarship on, 28n22; sexual misconduct charge against, 120; teaching career of, 41, 43, 120, 141, 144, 145, 182, 186–87, 190, 220, 222, 223; travels of, 20n11, 95, 143, 166, 171, 181, 211–14
WRITINGS
ART CRITICISM: 31, 60, 118, 169–73; "Dabblers and Dabbling," 169–70; "Mortal Goddess," 152; "Rhapsody in Blue," 170; "The Sphinx of Delft," 26; "The Stendhal Syndrome," 152–53
BOOK REVIEWS: 132, 149–68
ESSAYS: "Artists Who Kill," 170, 175; "Blood Feud," 189–93, 200, 206–8, 210; "The Detours of Art," 141, 173, 187; "The Evangelist," 228–29; "Hateful, Hurtful and Hellish," 172; "The Inarticulate Hero," 134n7, 149, 160; "Myself and My Brothers," 179, 187–89; "The Novel of Learning," 50n21, 142–43; "James Joyce," 143; "Plaid," 143n23, 169; "Revenge," 59n2, 138n12, 220; "Stutterstepping," 175; "Theroux Metaphrastes," 24, 39–40, 41, 75, 103–4, 117, 134–38, 142–43, 148, 162n52; "Tolstoy Need Not Apply," 143–44

FABLES: 40, 97–100; *The Great Wheadle Tragedy*, 97, 182; "Julia de Chateauroux," 98, 142; *Master Snickup's Cloak*, 13, 48, 97; *The Schinocephalic Waif*, 97, 182

NONFICTION BOOKS: *Einstein's Beets*, 157–58, 158n47, 164n53, 169, 173n7, 174–75; *The Enigma of Al Capp*, 8, 10, 68; *Estonia*, 166n57, 211–14, 229–30; *The Grammar of Rock*, 141, 166n57, 168, 169, 172–73; *The Primary Colors*, 60, 71n33, 136n11, 156, 169, 170–72; *The Secondary Colors*, 60, 156, 169, 170, 172; *The Strange Case of Edward Gorey*, 8, 68n28

NOVELS: *An Adultery*, 8, 9, 14, 16, 31–35, 52–56, 58, 59–60, 61, 71n33, 96, 115n20, 146, 149n33, 160, 184, 218–20, 223, 229; *Darconville's Cat*, 7–9, 13, 14, 16, 17n7, 23, 25–31, 35–37, 39–51, 52–53, 57–58, 59, 66, 97, 112, 137–38, 140, 142, 179, 182, 183, 186–87, 188, 192, 195, 213, 218, 220–24, 228–29; *Laura Warholic*, 7, 9, 58, 59–91, 98–99, 101, 115–16, 138, 152, 154, 156, 159, 160n50, 166n57, 168, 169, 173, 175, 186n21, 193–96, 199, 206, 212, 229; *Three Wogs*, 13, 14–23, 27, 35, 39, 41, 43, 52, 134, 135, 140n18, 142, 147, 164, 175, 178–79, 181, 182, 213, 218, 227

PLAYS: 21n12, 180, 217

POETRY: 60, 61, 103–31, 202, 206, 209–10, 212, 214; *Collected Poems*, 61n10, 103, 107–19; *History Is Made at Night*, 104; *The Lollipop Trollops*, 7, 69, 100, 103, 104, 106, 110, 111, 115, 141–42, 147n27, 153, 225

SHORT STORIES: 16, 24–25, 92–102, 137; "The American Tourist Home," 95, 228; "Blackrobe," 100, 206; "Envenoming Junior," 65, 93, 100–101, 186, 199–204, 205, 207–8, 210; "Fark Pooks," 24–25, 95, 96; "Finocchio," 25, 96; "Genius,"

102, 206; "Grasso Sovrapesso and the Bent Nail," 93, 101, 120n27; "An Interview with the Poet Cora Wheatears," 102, 114n17; "Mrs. Marwood's Spunkies," 25, 96; "Over Edom Will I Cast Out My Shoe," 94, 95; "Scugnizzo's Pasta Co.," 25, 96; "Summer Bellerophon," 100, 115n20, 120n27; "Watergraphs," 9, 31, 66, 96; "A Woman with Sauce," 31, 96; "A Wordstress in Williamsburg," 25, 96

THESES: 132–34, 138n16, 142, 180, 209n48

UNFINISHED BOOKS: *Becoming Amelia*, 60, 171, 229n3, 230; *Herbert Head*, 35, 62n12, 94, 147n27, 164, 177, 180–81, 212n52, 225–30

UNPUBLISHED BOOKS: *Anomalies*, 156, 162n52, 176; *Artists Who Kill and Other Essays*, 170n1; *Black*, 60n3, 156, 169, 172–73; *The Butterfinger Years*, 180; *Collected Stories*, 92–102, 230; *Edward Jellow*, 180; *Godfather Drosselmeier's Tears and Other Poems*, 103, 111n12, 119–20; *Seacoast in Bohemia*, 156–57, 175; *Shop Around*, 172; *Truisms*, 103, 109n9, 120–22; *Violon d'Ingres*, 175; *White*, 60n3, 156, 169, 172–73

Theroux, Anne, 181, 206
Theroux, Ann Marie and Mary, 184, 209n47; poems about, 130
Theroux, Eugene, 41, 175n11, 181, 184
Theroux, Joseph, 13, 184
Theroux, Justin, 175n11
Theroux, Louis, 73, 194n35, 196, 208
Theroux, Marcel, 73, 101, 148, 194n35, 195, 196–204, 206, 208
Theroux, Paul, 13, 39n2, 65, 73, 120, 149, 155, 164, 166–67, 178–211, 212, 214; *Girls at Play*, 39n2, 183; *The Great Railway Bazaar*, 181, 211; *The Family Arsenal*, 181; *The Jungle Lovers*, 178; *The Last Train to Zona Verde*, 203–4; *Millroy the*

Magician, 186–87, 203, 206; *The
Mosquito Coast*, 39n2, 165n56,
183–84; *Mother Land*, 101, 115,
176, 192, 197n38, 203, 204–11;
My Other Life, 189–92, 197n38,
203, 207; *My Secret History*, 154,
184–86; *Picture Palace*, 39n2,
182–83; *Saint Jack*, 191; *Sir Vidia's
Shadow*, 192–93, 203, 210; *Waldo*,
178, 179, 181
Theroux, Peter, 13, 41, 184, 219
Theroux, Shiloh and Shenandoah,
114, 120, 230
Thompson, Francis, 217
Thoreau, Henry David, 119n22, 120,
122, 149, 223
Tikhomirov, Rodion, 66
Tintoretto, Jacopo, 79
Tolstoy, Leo, 31, 145, 149, 151, 222
Toole, John Kennedy, 230
Tourneur, Cyril, 48, 104
Treadwell, Tom, 48
Trevor, William, 149
Trollope, Anthony, 188
Truman, Harry S., 175
Twain, Mark, 101, 184

Updike, John, 10, 14, 149, 162–63, 190
Uris, Leon, 109, 218

Valenti, Kristy, 71, 76n37
VanderMeer, Jeff, 80
Vermeer, Jan, 26, 138–40
Vidal, Gore, 189, 190
Villiers de l'Isle-Adam, Auguste, 45,
46n15, 219
Virgil, 39
Vollmann, William T., 83, 149, 163–64,
175n12
Voltaire, 141

Wagner, Richard, 64n18, 195
Wallace, David Foster, 8n1, 138,
211n51

Waller, Robert James, 165
Wall Street Journal, 143, 150, 155, 158
Walser, Robert, 214
Warhol, Andy, 65n19
Washburn, Stan, 97
Washington Post, 80, 149, 161n51
Webster, John, 104
Weeks, Cathy, 115n20
Weeks, Donald, 43n9
Weil, Simone, 214
Weisenburger, Steven, 157
West, Mae, 110
West, Nathanael, 180
West, Paul, 8–9, 141, 149
Wharton, Edith, 100
White, Jack, 175
White, Terence de Vere, 160n50
Whitman, Walt, 46
Wilde, Oscar, 35, 193, 210
Wilde, Willie, 193, 210
Wilder, Thornton, 149
Williams, Ted, 10
Williams, Tennessee, 90
Williams, William Carlos, 168
Wilson, Scott Bryan, 80
Wodehouse, P. G., 19, 81
Wolfe, Tom, 80
Wordsworth, William, 115
Wouk, Herman, 109
Wronoski, John, 66, 73
Wyatt, Thomas, 182–83
Wylie, Elinor, 114

Yale University, 14, 108, 119, 142, 144,
145, 150, 223
Yeats, William Butler, 104, 106, 223
Young, Marguerite, 136n11
Yourcenar, Marguerite, 118

Zanganeh, Lila Azam, 150–51
Zisblatt, Irene Weisberg, 99
Zukofsky, Louis, 105